# BARTER AND SOCIAL REGENERATION
## IN THE ARGENTINEAN ANDES

# Barter and Social Regeneration in the Argentinean Andes

Olivia Angé

With much admiration
and warm wishes.

Olivie

berghahn
NEW YORK · OXFORD
www.berghahnbooks.com

First published in 2018 by
Berghahn Books
www.berghahnbooks.com

© 2018 Olivia Angé

**Library of Congress Cataloging-in-Publication Data**

A C.I.P. cataloging record is available from the Library of Congress

**British Library Cataloguing in Publication Data**

A catalogue record for this book is available from the British Library

ISBN 978-1-78533-682-9 hardback
ISBN 978-1-78533-683-6 ebook

To Maywa,

a daily *alegría*

# Contents

# Illustrations

# Acknowledgements

After centuries of abuses of all kinds, Indigenous people in the Argentinean puna have learned to be suspicious of strangers' gazes. They have become experts in the art of conducting confusing interactions by which they avoid complying with others' expectations without any confrontation. This is how they have been able to transmit cultural practices that were mocked, sometimes even forbidden, on the national scene. In such an interethnic context, I received every sign of trust and care as an important benefaction. And I received many. In the hope that this book will honour the original gift, I took the greatest care to remain faithful to my hosts' discourses and experiences, shared in the intimacy of courtyards, or publicly at the fair. I am aware, however, that this is a debt that I would hardly be able to cancel; I will better keep it alive in memory and enduring reciprocity.

There are some houses in Chalguamayoc (Jujuy, Argentina) where I was constantly welcome. At the home of Telesforo Benitez and his wife, Sylberia, as well as Justo Benitez and Isabela, I could find warm refuges when wandering in the highlands. I want to thank them for their unconditional hospitality. In Yavi, my neighbour Lola Tintilay and Mariel, her daughter, befriended me. I am indebted to the staff of the local NGO. They accepted my awkward presence in meetings, and they satisfied my curiosity about their affairs, while my interventions ended up being of little use to them. In particular, Lucio Martinez, and his wife, Julia – they are not only leaders, they are exemplary.

Fairs are settings of very rich sociability. I would not be able to name all the people who helped me to navigate the fiesta, through the masses, barters and balls. But I do remember them, with immense gratitude. Some of them came from the village of Chosconty, such as Perfecto and Simona, Genoveva and Masimo. Thank you for never failing to rendezvous at the Yavi and Manka Fiestas. Thank you as well for initiating me to the elder's measures.

Further away, Anne Marie Losonczy from the Université libre de Bruxelles and Gilles Rivière from the École des Hautes Études en Sciences Sociales also helped me to apprehend fairs and look at them with new eyes. Their teaching stimulated my interest in these complex transactional scenes. They are outstanding thinkers, meticulous ethnographers and generous supervisors, and I feel very fortunate to have had them close to me throughout. While continuing this investigation as a postdoctoral researcher, I received the beneficial support of my sponsors Laura Rival at Oxford University, Anne Christine Taylor at the Musée du quai Branly and Alberto Arce during the Marie Curie Intra-European Fellowship at Wageningen University. I thank them for hosting me in their departments, for nurturing my thought and for giving me the opportunity to pursue my research in new directions.

Throughout the years spent in these institutions, I met some particularly inspiring scholars: Sasha Newell, Joël Noret, Pierre Petit, Daou Joiris, Maïté Maskens, Marc Brigthman, Perig Pitrou, Julien Clément, Jessica de Largy, Emilie Stoll, Élise Demeulenaere and Maité Hernando Aresse are great friends and colleagues. I have learned a lot while thinking with them. Thank you very much. Giovanni da Col, Inge Daniels, Emilia Ferraro, Tristan Platt and Nico Tassi read my work and provided helpful advice to disentangled theoretical conundrums. We did not know each other personally when they accepted to help me. Likewise, I received comments from two wise anonymous reviewers who thoroughly read my manuscript. The free gift exists in academia, and I very much appreciate it.

Last but not least, David Berliner is the one who has been present at all stages, since he shared with me his fascination for nostalgia. His teaching is huge, and it extends beyond academia. He is a guide, a fruitful and funny one. Thank you for clearing up my many, many doubts, for being kindly critical and for taking an interest in my life, even when you could not pay much attention to yourself.

I am very thankful to Marion Berghahn for considering my manuscript and for making this book become a reality; to Lizzie Martinez, Amanda Horn and Harry Eagles, who have demonstrated treasures of patience in bringing this book through the production process; and to Nora Scott, who impressed me by scrupulously translating my thought.

I also want to express my gratitude to non-academics who were life companions while I was writing this book. Javier Briones has devoted a great amount of energy to this research. I want to thank him once again. I am grateful to Silvia, Raul and the Briones family for genuinely opening their arms. Thanks to Martin Maïnoli for his good-hearted creativity. All of them, as well as Chris and Rafa, were generous in giving me a taste of the joys their Argentinean livelihood offers. Experiencing their cultural intimacy was a transformative learning process that I mostly enjoyed. I am deeply thankful as well to my Belgian *comadres*: Mélanie Van Pelt and Julie Callebaut. They are a constant source of social effervescence and affective relief. My brother, Mikaël has been a master in restoring ontological security. My sisters, Marine and Chloé, have spent extended periods in the puna, helping me to assemble my life dispersed across the continents. Thank you for being as you are.

Since I have been back in Europe, my liveliness has been enhanced by the daily care of my beloved partner, Thierry de Crombrugghe. From him, I received the supreme gift, a flourishing life.

# Introduction

This book explores how barter creates social and economic values by addressing a particular kind of Andean exchange: *cambio*. This trade is a core transaction in fairs that gather lowland cultivators and highland herders in the Southern Andes. Such fairs are usually embedded in the celebration of a Catholic feast day, which also entails sportive, religious and political dimensions. Similar festivals are held throughout the cordillera, where fairs arise in conjunction with religious ceremonies, many times constituting a fundamental asset of the celebration. In fact, this case is not peculiar to the Andes, as the condensation of economic transactions in the frame of a religious celebration is found in many cultural and historical contexts.

Anthropological theorisation of ritual practices has nonetheless been built on a conceptualisation of religious practices as disjoined from mundane economic interests. The opposition is based on the premise that the formalities of ritual revere the collectivity, while exchanges of necessities are chiefly individual. Anthropologists have crafted the concept of ceremonial exchange to account for those transactions at the interface of the economic and the ritual. Ceremonial exchange was the cornerstone of Bronisław Malinowski's detailed account on the Trobriand kula, in which he argued against the stereotype of the primitive economic man. In his typology of local forms of exchange, Malinowski opposes the pure gift to 'trade pure and simple' as extremes of a continuum of transactions that are not always clearly distinguished. Adjacent to trade, he identifies the category of 'ceremonial barter with deferred payment'. This includes the *wasi* that he defines as 'a ceremonial form of exchange of vegetable food for fish, based on a standing partnership, and on the obligation to accept and return an initial gift' ([1922] 2002: 143). He thus describes these ceremonial barters as made of 'payments' and 'gifts', stressing that they are compulsorily accepted, without negotiation over the terms of the transactions. Malinowski adds that huge quantities of fish obtained through *wasi* are

**Figure 0.1.** Panorama of the main fair in the Argentinean Andes: the Manka Fiesta in La Quiaca, Argentina, October 2007. Photograph by the author.

intended for ceremonial purposes, thereby suggesting a nonutilitarian character of ceremonial exchange. This character is prominent in the case of the prestigious shell ornaments circulating in the kula, which he posits as the other instantiation of ceremonial barter.[1]

In contrast, cambio is an exchange with a strong utilitarian dimension. Its core goods are meat from the highland and maize from the lowland, two keystones in the exchange partners' diet. The instrumental purpose is manifest in cambio interactions, which typically unfold as follows:

> Cultivator, handing out a sample of maize grains, calls to a herder offering meat: Shall I take one [lamb] for maize? Let's take it? For maize, that one?
>
> Herder: Go and bring then; bring maize.
>
> Cultivator: Of course, I will bring you a complete [measure]. Me myself I will bring [the maize] to you. How would you bring it? Give me a little one [lamb]. I will bring you [the maize], madam.
>
> Herder: Go for the maize. Go for the maize. Go to bring it. Bring more [maize] and I give you the lamb.

Cultivator: Show me the lamb. Is it fat? More or less?

Herder: It's a lamb! Bah, these people. With them . . . no! Your [maize], is it big? You must give me a bag full and a bit more. . . . The lambs are fat; they are big.

Cultivator: Now, if you want roasted maize, I also have.

Herder: No, no, no. I want white [maize].

Cultivator: Pure white. Let's go then. I will 'invite' you extra fruits. Sure, let's go. I will give you some fruits, so that we will know each other for the next year.[2]

This book sets out to examine the embeddedness of such barter within a broader religious celebration. In this light, cambio practices challenge the distinction drawn between ceremonial barter and trade pure and simple, outlining a notion of ceremonial exchanges that includes overtly instrumental transactions of necessities and involves negotiation.

Since Malinowski's ethnography of the kula, ceremonial exchanges have attracted much attention and played a key role in the building of economic anthropology. Marcel Mauss's ([1925] 2002) seminal essay *The Gift* further stressed the relevance of those transactions framed by social obligation to understand the fabric of 'primitive' societies. For this purpose, Mauss systematised Malinowski's ethnography, with data from disparate cultural settings ranging from ancient Hindu or German law to the North American Kwakiutl or the New Zealand Māori. But Mauss himself never used the term 'ceremonial exchange'. He instead described these economies using terms such as contractual and economic rituals, rituals of hospitality, ritual services of honour, rituals of giving, rituals of reimbursing, rituals of compensation, rituals of payment or rituals of the purchase. Claude Lévi-Strauss ([1947] 2002: 68) aligned himself with Mauss in using 'ritual of exchange'.[3] The notion of ritual exchange, favoured by these French thinkers (see also Maunier [1927] 1998), is nonetheless used to refer to the transactions called ceremonial in other instances.

Most scholarship on economic anthropology has used the term 'ceremonial (or ritual) exchange' as a synonym for Maussian gift-giving, leaving aside Malinowski's interpretation of barter with deferred payment. The term has been used to describe material circulation across the continents, such as the Kabyle *taoussa* in North Africa (Maunier [1927] 1998), the Gunwinggu *dzamalag* in Australia (Berndt 1951) or the Tikopia rituals in Polynesia (Firth 1939). Still, after Malinowski, Melanesia became a hot spot for ceremonial exchange studies, accounting for complex systems of material circulation to such an extent that the kula, the *moka* or the *tee* have come to epitomise this concept (e.g. Godelier 1996; Leach and Leach 1983; A. Strathern 1971; M. Strathern 1988). In their entry in *A Handbook of Economic Anthropology*, Andrew Strathern and Pamela Stewart draw exclusively on Melanesian data to define ceremonial exchanges as 'systems in which items of value are publicly displayed and given to partners on a reciprocal basis over time. Typically, these occasions are marked by dancing and festivities' (2006: 230). The authors later analytically differentiate this mode of exchange from trade, outlining a distinction between 'trade (= barter, commodity exchange) and gift exchange (= ceremonial exchange)' (2006: 235).

This typology prevails in most scholarship on economic anthropology. In her theoretical model of barter, Anne Chapman states that 'barter is of an entirely different nature than ceremonial gift exchange because, precisely, it involves no extra-economic factors' (1980: 35). In one of the very few sustained ethnographies of barter, R. H. Barnes and Ruth Barnes observe a direct transaction of necessities that they exclude from the category of barter in virtue of its ceremonial character. Celebrating the launch of a newly built boat, they affirm that the exchange of fish, meat and salt for agricultural produce, 'without bargaining or set rates, is ceremonial in character and thus strictly speaking not barter' (1989: 412).[4] Jonathan Parry and Maurice Bloch also take this association for granted in their penetrating introduction to *Money and the Morality of Exchange*. They argue against the opposition between gift and commodity exchange, pointing to the possibility of 'a shift from barter to ceremonial exchange', and vice versa (1989b: 10).

This book sets out to challenge this polarity by exploring the unfolding of ceremonial barter in an Andean ethnographic context. Thereby, I side with a still-emerging body of literature that has recently called our attention to the transcendental dimensions of essentially instrumental economic transactions (Gudeman and Hann 2015; Højer 2012; Miller 1996; Tassi 2010). My purpose is to question a well-established opposition between economic interests and religious abnegation, which is not relevant to understanding economic morality and practices in this Andean context.

## The Barter Myth and Its Reality

In the commonly accepted sense of the *Oxford English Dictionary*, barter is an 'exchange (goods or services) for other goods or services' – that is, a modality of exchange that unfolds in all kinds of societies.

Ethnographic studies mention barter transactions as part of economic systems on all continents. Malinowski's ([1922] 2002) description of a Trobriand trade expedition, Paul Bohannan's (1955) study of the Tiv economy, Lévi-Strauss's (1943) account of exchange meetings among the Nambikwara and Caroline Humphrey's (1985) examination of direct Lhomi transactions have become classic examples. Barter documentation also covers temporal depth. Archaeological data speak to the existence of barter networking in old civilisations across the world: from the Andes to the Amazon, in pre-Columbian Mesoamerican societies, between North American native peoples, across Australia and Melanesian archipelagos or from central Asia to Siberia. Used with different intensities, barter was combined with other modalities of exchange and distribution. Yet, in Greek antiquity, it has been appraised as a key ingredient in satisfying domestic needs under the division of labour, paving the way for Plato's ideal Republic (see Humphrey 1985: 48).

Far from being a feature of ancient economies, nonmonetary trade also flourishes in industrial societies. Direct transactions that were recurrent in postcommunist societies have attracted the attention of regional specialists (see Cellarius 2000; Hivon 1998; Humphrey 2000; Seabright 2000), who have acknowledged that barter practices existed before the fall of communism. The huge barter network that flourished in Argentina in the aftermath of the 2001 crisis offers another example of direct exchange becoming structural in a society facing economic rupture (Ould-Ahmed 2010; Pearson 2003; Saiag 2013). Although their scale is incomparable to the Argentinean case, analogous initiatives mushroomed throughout Latin America from Mexico to Chile, including Brazil or Peru, around the same time. They shared similarities with the local exchange trading systems (LETS) that develops in Europe (Latouche 2000), the United States (Gudeman 2001: 160; Hart 1986: 642) and other capitalist centres (Servet 1999). While it might be worth discussing the relevance of a barter appellation for each of these transactions, we nonetheless notice that barter not only continues in subsistence societies but is also used to overcome money's scarcity and instability within advanced capitalist economies.

Yet nonmonetary transactions are not restricted to contexts of crisis and marginalised spheres of exchange. Websites flourish to facilitate interpersonal swapping[5] in industrialised societies, or even to boost companies' business.[6] In the United States, Bartercard's homepage proudly invites its visitors to 'join a business network with 54,000 cardholders worldwide who trade over $40m every month'.[7] As suggested by this headline, nonmonetary business also entails international transactions. The United Nations in the late 1970s acknowledged the latter as an 'important means of global trade' (Horowitz 2010: 112). In the 1980s, Keith Hart referred to a Group of Thirty report which estimates that barter at that time represented 8 to 10 per cent of international transactions and half of the arms trade (1986: 642). Nonmonetary business involves national states themselves. Today, such trade is notable between developing countries that lack dollar reserves. These strategies spread during the 2008 world food shortage and ensuing inflation, resulting in massive direct exchanges of grains between countries in the South. Clearly, direct exchange unfolds in all kind of economies, involving actors from any social and cultural profile.

However, the pervasiveness of barter is overlooked by a still-prevailing imaginary of barter as a feature of 'primitive economies'. This representation, within and beyond academia, is anchored in an established 'myth of barter' as the savage origin of money – the famous story of the universal invention of money by exchange partners striving to overcome the impediments of barter transactions. The myth narrates an earlier age when people started to specialise in a given productive activity in which they proved particularly efficient. Wanting to exchange their products with their neighbours, they faced the so-called problem of the double coincidence of want. Not only did they need to find someone who wanted their goods. That person also needed to offer something they were interested in. From this age of barter emerged the use of monetary devices intended as a medium of exchange that the seller would accept and be able to use once the coveted goods was available.

This myth crystallised in the eighteenth century, notably under the influence of Adam Smith. In the *Wealth of Nations*, first published in 1776, Smith offered a classic version of the story, positing a propensity to barter as a universal feature of human nature. 'Nobody ever saw a dog make a fair and deliberate exchange of one bone for another with another dog', he famously observed. Smith saw this inclination to exchange as the drift towards the division of labour:

> This division of labour, from which so many advantages are derived, is not originally the effect of any human wisdom, which foresees and intends that general opulence to which it gives occasion. It is the necessary, though very slow and gradual consequence of a certain propensity in human nature which has in view no such extensive utility; the propensity to truck, barter and exchange one thing for another. ([1776] 1991 1:12)

However, from Smith's point of view, barter 'naturally' entangled with the division of labour was inefficient in circulating surplus production:

But when the division of labour first began to take place, this power of exchanging must frequently have been very much clogged and embarrassed in its operations. One man, we shall suppose, has more of a certain commodity than he himself has occasion for, while another has less. The former consequently would be glad to dispose of, and the latter to purchase, a part of this superfluity. But if the latter should chance to have nothing that the former stands in need of, no exchange can be made between them. ([1776] 1991 1:20, quoted in Graeber 2011: 26)

The story ends with people starting to stock things that they know others will want to purchase, transforming these objects into currencies.

In this tale, Smith and his followers depicted a sphere of economic transactions evolving independently of any social or political influence. While downplaying the role of politics and other institutions in the creation of money, they legitimised the emergence of a new discipline that would be concerned with disclosing stable and universal rules (Servet 1994). In this light, it is the very myth of barter that gave rise to the autonomous discipline of economics. To date, this narration on the origin of money is still offered in handbooks on economy and circulated by government and public institutions (Dodd 2014: 20). As David Graeber affirms in his monumental volume on debt, 'the story of money for economists always begins with a fantasy world of barter' (2011: 23).

The myth of barter is a fantasy in the sense that we have no historical evidence that any barter society ever existed. Caroline Humphrey introduced her seminal article on barter in 1985 by refuting the veracity of the barter myth: 'No example of a barter economy, pure and simple, has ever been described, let alone the emergence from it of money; all available ethnography suggests that there never has been such a thing' (1985: 48). Anthropological and historical accounts of premarket societies describe a variety of systems of exchange, but nowhere was barter the chief modality of economic integration within a given community. Anthropologists have described an array of economies of distribution and redistribution such as collective food stocking, compulsory game sharing and inter-ecological displacement, where the direct exchange of goods was only one form of transaction in a broader economic system. Furthermore, while the barter myth puts forward the double coincidence of wants as the main drawback for Homo economicus, this is not a universal dilemma. Studies in small-scale society show that people know what kind of goods their fellow needs and offers (Dodd 2014: 19; Heady 2006: 266; Humphrey 1985). Graeber further observes that, when people are known to each other, the double coincidence of want is easily overcome by deferred counter-prestation (2011: 36).

There is thus no convincing argument that barter should provide a ground for the emergence of money.

## Barter and the Creation of Social Ties

Even though the asocial feature of barter has been empirically challenged, classic anthropological literature depicts barter as being restricted to punctual exchanges with strangers and potential enemies. The image of silent trade in which two unknown persons swap their goods without exchanging a word encapsulates this idea of barter requiring no social foundation. While this figure of transaction has come to epitomise the asocial aspect of barter, nonverbal barter transactions are rare exceptions. In fact, this stereotype is empirically denied by ethnographic descriptions of intense bargaining preceding barter. Malinowski gave a detailed description of straightforward haggling in *gimwali*, in contrast to the more distinguished kula, where the exchange partners pretend to not even notice the counter-gift thrown on the ground with disregard ([1922] 2002: 145).

In all events, classic scholarship dismisses barter transactions as happening at the margins of social groups. Some even see it as intrinsically embedded in agonistic interactions. Lévi-Strauss's (1943) portrait of the Brazilian Nambikwara's encounter has become exemplary of alterity in barter transactions. In this Amerindian society organised in small communities, Lévi-Strauss described how material transactions occasionally happen between two unrelated groups. Once a messenger settles the meeting point, men of both sides hide their women and children in the bush. The two chiefs proceed to a ceremonial speech praising the other camp. Afterwards, the men lay down their arms and start singing and dancing together. Only then are the exchange negotiations launched, taking the form of intense haggling. When equivalencies are agreed upon, the goods are hastily seized. According to Lévi-Strauss, these interactions are fertile ground for conflicts, often degenerating into fights. The trade meeting nonetheless closes with a festival, where women are welcome. Yet, Lévi-Strauss notes, interplays of seduction triggered by dances and chants have been known to trigger quarrels in which people have been killed. Lévi-Strauss concludes that respecting ritual prescriptions aims at securing a climate of peace and trust for conducting safe trade. Conviviality is intended to reduce the chances of war, which could break out at any time between the barter partners who, it is assumed, have every reason to struggle in order to increase their personal benefit.

Such descriptions converge within classical texts in anthropology, classifying barter as an expression of commodity exchange deemed to prevail at the edges of social communities, in contrast to reciprocated gifts, which are embedded in kinship and stable alliances. Already supported by Karl Marx ([1867] 2013) and Georg Simmel ([1900] 1990), this approach pervades *The Gift*, in which Mauss ([1925] 2002) contends that, in so-called archaic societies, exchanges underpinning social structures do not take the form of barter. They take the shape of gifts that are 'apparently free and disinterested but nevertheless constrained and self-interested' ([1925] 2002: 4). Mauss famously argued that social ties in 'primitive societies' are structured by the constant circulation of goods and services, governed by a threefold obligation of giving, receiving and giving in turn. When postulating the necessity of a counter-prestation, Mauss emphasised that these transactions are not done for material benefits; they are instead expected to foster enduring social alliances between people who themselves stand for broader communities.

As opposed to Maussian gifts, barter is depicted as an asocial type of instrumental transaction. Marshall Salhins (1972) defends this perspective in *Stone Age Economics,* in which he classified barter as negative reciprocity, which corresponds to the strict defence of self-interest – along with cheating, bargaining or theft – and is opposed to generalised reciprocity driven by generosity and sharing. In his social geography of economic exchange, barter is posited as 'the most economic. The participants confront each other as opposed interests, each looking to maximise utility at the other's expense' (1972: 195). In her attempt to establish a universal model of barter, Chapman followed this current. According to her theoretical abstraction, a transaction corresponds to 'pure barter' if 'an economic interest creates the relationship between the two parties which are trading, and if no third factor intervenes' (1980: 40). Here, barter interactions are regarded as being driven strictly by economic ambitions and lacking social consideration. Generalising Karl Polanyi's ([1944] 2001) famous formula to all barter exchanges, Chapman describes it as 'not embedded in society' (1980: 49). In his book elaborating the argument of a heuristic polarisation between gifts and commodities, Christopher Gregory takes a similar approach: 'The simple barter exchange of commodities presupposes . . . that the transactors are strangers, aliens' (1982: 42; he refers to Marx).

In his important volume on *The Social Life of Things,* Arjun Appadurai draws on his predecessors to advance a definition of barter as 'the exchange of objects for one another *without* reference to money and with maximum feasible reduction of social, cultural, political or personal transaction cost' (1986: 9; emphasis in original). He thereby intends to distinguish barter both from commodities that refer to money and from gifts with increased social cost. More recently, Graeber, who devoted a chapter to the fallacies of the aforementioned myth, affirmed that barter 'ordinarily . . . takes place between strangers, even enemies' (2011: 29; corroborated by Dodd 2014: 20). The few anthropological textbooks that address barter also put forward this analysis. Patrick Heady's entry on 'barter' in *A Handbook of Economic Anthropology* reads: 'the prime focus of interest for the exchange partners is in the goods and services themselves rather than the social relationship arising from the exchange' (2006: 262). In this vein, 'barter' is understood as an interested transaction strictly aimed at acquiring necessities, while 'gift' emphasises generosity, as the donator gives up wealth in order to nurture social ties.

While we are warned that intellectuals in the eighteenth century made up the story of barter as a strictly economic transaction devoid of political and social component, anthropologists still seem to struggle to extricate their conceptual tools from the foundation myth of the discipline of economics. Many ethnographic examples that describe barter as imbued with conflict and hostility are available, yet the analytical focus on conflict should not be allowed to obscure the climax of festivities that features the meetings at stake as well, many times also involving feasting, dancing and sex. That barter involves strangers is an interpretation that the empirical data do not support. Does the shared participation in complex rituals in which barter is embedded, such as those described by Lévi-Strauss, not suggest that the exchange partners share a common set of norms and values? That barter happens between acquainted persons is a fact that Humphrey has already stressed: 'The most important fact about barter is that it takes place between individuals who are socially "understood", whether they belong to the same or different "ethnic groups"' (1985: 60). Barnes and Barnes corroborate this observation in Indonesia. Taking an ethnohistorical approach, they document a narration that locates the origin of a weekly exchange meeting in the migration of a villager who settled on the coast after he got lost during a fishing expedition (1989: 404). Once established, he urged cultivator relatives from his homeland to come and exchange their produce for fish. In this case, barter emergence is thus entailed in community ties.

In their groundbreaking collection, Caroline Humphrey and Stephen Hugh-Jones draw on ethnographic data from disparate cultural contexts to demonstrate that barter partners tend to nurture enduring social relationship: 'As our papers show, this "sociable" or non-commercial aspect is a prominent feature of many non-Western barter exchanges too and one which goes against the popular anthropological stereotype' (1992b: 6). When insisting on the social dimension of barter, Humphrey and Hugh-Jones not only acknowledge social ties pre-existing the transaction. They further contend that barter 'is one kind of exchange which creates social relations in its own mode.' Yet, sustained anthropologies of barter are scarce, and we still lack ethnographic descriptions that carefully set out the array of relationship that barter creates. Pervaded by the assumption that barter takes place between poorly articulated or hostile communities, existing literature largely fails to account for the nature of the social relationship that bind those who partake in barter or for the unfolding of social life as it relates to barter transactions.

This book tries to fill this gap, explaining how social relationships are created through direct instrumental transactions and how these relationships differ from those produced by other kinds of material transfer. Therefore, it documents the social fabric in which barter networks are enmeshed in the Argentinean cordillera, where direct exchanges are at the same time antagonistic and creators of enduring social relationship. Because cambio partners are in principle quits at the end of their transactions, it provides a fruitful case that sheds light on the concrete practices through which social bonds are woven through instrumental and immediate reciprocity. This enquiry further shows that, in this Andean setting, barter participates in the constitution of a new kind of relationship, which is conceived in the idiom of kinship.

## Barter and Value Creation:
## Crafting an Anthropological Category

While scholarship in economic anthropology continues to elude their conclusion, Humphrey and Hugh-Jones's contention that barter and gift share more commonalities than had previously been acknowledged has been accepted. The problem is that, seen in this light, barter constitutes a highly contextual category beyond any definition – except the core acceptance that it is a 'direct exchange of goods or services for each other without the use of money' (Heady 2006: 262). Hence, in the literature, the absence of money remains the major characteristic of barter. The heterogeneous range of transactions embraced by this conceptualisation runs the risk of making barter a blanket category filled with forms of exchange specific to every locality. Indeed, one wonders what the commonalities are between, say, swapping yam for fish in the Amazon and Yugoslav Airlines procuring airplanes for jewellery and fabric worth millions of dollars.[8] What do these transactions share besides the fact that they do not involve the circulation of cash? Are so-called barter systems about barter at all when they are based on the use of local paper money or credit cards? Said otherwise, is the very notion of barter a useful anthropological concept by which to grasp all these transactions, or shall we better read some of them as a nonmonetary expression of commodity exchange?

This book coincides with Humphrey and Hugh-Jones in deeming a notion of barter necessary to disentangle the complex diversity of material transactions. In contrast to these authors, who refuse any fixed definition (1992b: 1), I think that semantic precision is required to build a pertinent concept. An essential feature of barter, as pointed out by Humphrey and Hugh-Jones, is that 'objects exchanged have direct consumption values for the participants' (1992b: 7), so the transaction fulfils reciprocal interests that each partner has for the other's object. The relevance of this feature has been underestimated in the anthropology of economic exchanges. Yet, this book argues, it allows one to conceptually distinguish barter from commodity exchange and the reciprocation of gifts. Furthermore, the understanding of the value system that emerges from this particularity provides a way to grasp its social dimensions.

Although Andean ethnography has rarely contributed to anthropological theories of economic exchange, studies such as those carried out by Olivia Harris (2000) or Tristan Platt (1988, 1995, [1982] 2007) indicated the potential of Andean data for contributing to these debates. Scrutinising Andean types of reciprocity, these authors delineated local shapes of trade and their articulation with social relationships. In her essay on the sources and meanings of money, Harris refutes any systematic difference between monetary transaction and barter in the Bolivian highlands, affirming, 'only the context will determine which it is, and this context includes both the social relationship of those exchanging and, more importantly, where the transaction takes place' (1989: 243). Emilia Ferraro continues this argument in her recent examination of *trueque,* an Ecuadorian type of barter between peasants and personalised traders who use money and agricultural produce to establish the exchange value of their commodities. She argues that the use of money is not the most relevant feature for grasping the particularities of this transaction, which stands 'between barter and commodity without fitting comfortably into either category' (2011: 172).

As announced at the outset, this ethnography focuses on another kind of Andean direct exchange known as *cambio*, literally 'exchange' in the Spanish spoken in the Argentinean cordillera.[9] The examination of cambio stresses the significance of the nonmonetary character of the transaction. Although I agree with Harris and Ferraro that the material use of money does not determine a transaction per se, money rarely has direct use value. Monetary exchange thus departs from the consumption purposes of barter highlighted above. Further, the study of cambio shows that money's rejection as a main scale of value is a fundamental issue that needs to be addressed. The rejection of monetary calculation opens the field for another regime of value, which compares two different goods with respect to internal balance, with only minor reference to an external, abstract scale of measurement. Internal balance has been pointed to as another feature of barter. Humphrey and Hugh-Jones warned us that consumption value in barter is negotiated 'but not with reference to some abstract measure of value or numeraire' (1992b: 1). However, bemused by the common meaning, scholars continue to classify as 'barter' direct exchanges that follow market prices. In this regard, Andean ethnography can make a significant contribution towards delineating the concept of barter.

Furthermore, examining barter's regime of value proves fruitful to tease out its social dimensions. In cambio, social ties are enmeshed in the restriction this model of value imposes on the nature of the products that enter this sphere of exchange. Indeed, cambio's scale of value relates to a reciprocal transfer of agricultural products that circulate in opposite directions and shape the identity of the partners who consume identical food. This social performativity also relates to the sources of morality embedded in cambio equivalences, which are said to be inherited from ancestors. In this light, the following exploration of Andean exchange shows that, as well as epitomising interpersonal complicities and ensuing obligations, this modality of barter enacts a sense of a shared descent between the partners. This examination of the regime of value posited by cambio partners suggests that this transaction manifests an implicit ethnic identity that is not verbalised by existing categories (whether claimed or assigned). Hence, this book contributes to an understanding of how groups create themselves through economic exchange and underscores the importance of barter in this process. This aspect has hitherto been underestimated in the literature, where such social performativity remains attributed chiefly to gift-giving.

My analysis of the cambio regime of value draws on Nancy Munn's (1986) work on value transformation in Papua New Guinea. In this masterpiece, Munn identifies the act of food giving as a most basic value template in the creation of subjectivities, based on the potentiality of nurturing guests in establishing one's fame beyond the here and now. She then goes on to describe more elaborated practices of value transformation such as kula expeditions. Her dynamic theory of value builds on Charles Sanders Peirce's phenomenological notion of qualisigns, referring to embodied qualities imbued with moral values in a given social context. This concept shall help us to understand how qualities of agricultural produce at fairs are icons of the virtues of the people who produce and consume them, and how subjective qualities are collectively acknowledged through their public circulation.

Munn's theory has been recently singled out for its fruitfulness in thinking values as, ultimately, the appreciation of acts (Graeber 2001: 50). Munn clarifies that values are determined by an act's potential to extend intersubjective space-time – that is, the space-time of influence opened between self and others. Accordingly, extension refers to 'the capacity to develop spatiotemporal relations that go beyond the self, or that expand dimensions of the spatiotemporal control of an actor' (1986: 11). Those practices involving extended displacement in space, and possible connection to past and future times, are particularly prone to trigger value transformation. In Melanesia, gifts of food and shells during kula maritime expeditions are one such privilege media of value creation – shells still more so, Munn explains, because of their material qualities: as compared to perishable food destined to rapid disintegration, kula valuables are enduring materialities, which are charged with their own biography through time.

I argue throughout this book that, in the Andean context, instrumental exchange of edible goods between people coming from an array of ecological niches constitutes a value template comparable to the gift-giving explored by Munn in the Massim society. Unlike Gawan sailors to whom elevation to fame is the ultimate purpose (see also Damon 2002: 107), these Andean peasants do not verbalise fame as a target when they transport their harvest to a fair. Displaying plentiful and desirable produce on such a public stage nonetheless contributes to raise one's renown as a prolific cultivator, or herder, and generous kin. Andean peasants associate this potential chiefly with the *fuerza* (strength) encapsulated in both human and nonhuman organisms: the quality of their produce instantiates the vitality they have been able to devote to agricultural labour, which is a morally loaded activity in this rural society. An analysis of the circulation of agricultural produce at fairs from this perspective reveals that cambio items are appreciated in light of qualities that index their producers' and consumers' value.

Beyond subjective virtues, material circulation at fairs produces values that entail collectives in their totality, notably by positing a community as a fertile terroir for the production of any desirable good. We shall see that, in their encounter, the protagonists assert shared social values that draw their society together. This ethnography thereby contributes to the ongoing debate in the anthropological study of value, on the possibility of arriving at a theory that would encompass its moral and economic dimensions (Graeber 2001; Lambek 2008, 2013; Otto and Willerslev 2013). I see the study of agricultural produce's value as particularly revealing in this regard because it stands at the intersection of natural resources and crafted objects.

At fairs, regimes of value are paradoxically tangible through the expression of a 'structural nostalgia' for old reciprocities that the vices of modernity are believed to have corroded (Herzfeld 2005). During their negotiation, the protagonists regularly allude to the equity that featured in their elders' transactions, whom they refer to as *abuelos* (grandparents). Yet, these lamentations also epitomise a gap between present barter, and an ideal one attributed to the elders – that is, a process of social change. I will use nostalgic tropes to tease out the morality of cambio at fairs. Such tropes are not only descriptive; I will also bring out their performative effects. Drawing on Edward Casey's (2011) phenomenological approach to commemoration, I will discuss the new form of sociability created by this specific kind of recall. In his landmark book, Fred Davis (1979) underscores the propensity of nostalgia to sustain social identities in a context of rapid social change. In the same vein, nostalgic utterances at fairs delineate social belongings, drawing the lines of an 'ethnic economy' (Harris 2000: 112) that experiences growing regional integration.

## Barter in the Ritual Economics

So, this book furthers Humphrey and Hugh-Jones's claim to the social anchor of barter by examining the relationships that are created through material circulation. Yet, cambio does more than establish a relationship between human participants. It further contributes to social regeneration by virtue of its communicative engagement with Catholic saints and ancestors incarnated in the environment, a fact that I will highlight by exploring fairs' embeddedness within religious festivals. Ethnographic examination of fairs' interactions shows that cambios are also addressed to nonhuman beings, thereby participating in the reproduction of the cosmological order.

The cosmological dimension of economic interactions has already been documented in different Andean contexts. Harris's (2000) work on the exchange system of the Bolivian Laymi people was conclusive in this regard. Observing the role of reciprocity in securing propitious interactions with ambivalent nonhuman entities, Harris emphasises the importance of exchange in enhancing fertility. Chief among offerings by Andean peasants are the *pagos* (payments) to telluric entities. These consist of the most 'cherished' foods and drinks, together with coca leaves and other ritual ingredients, which are buried in sacred sites. That the very word pago refers to offering is revealing of a conception of exchange as a vector of communication with nonhuman beings. It is noteworthy that, in the Argentinean cordillera, *pago* is barely used and instead replaced by the word *invitación* (invitation).

Harris, as well as Platt (1995), has also pointed out the cosmological dimensions of monetary transactions. Recent ethnographic insights from disparate Andean contexts have confirmed the cosmological entailment of commodity exchanges. Cecilie Ødegaard's (2011) work on the sources of danger and prosperity in Peru throws light on how people and material circulation bears cosmological implications. In a context where the landscape is imbued with an agency of its own, she emphasises the importance of reciprocal transfers to negotiate with these ambivalent forces and transform estranged spaces into benevolent places. Drawing on ethnographic data from La Paz in Bolivia, Nico Tassi (2010) argues that cholo[10] traders posit abundance as a cosmological value, which is used to establish fertile communication with nonhuman beings and to stimulate productivity.

In the 1970s and 1980s, several specialists in Andean economies used the concept of ritual to underscore the peculiarities of the instrumental transactions they wanted to describe. However, their allusions to ritualised exchange have taken on multiple, and sometimes incompatible, acceptations, which I will introduce in chapter 5. In all cases, this notion is used without conceptual clarification as though its meaning went without saying. Such semantic fuzziness reflects a broader theoretical lack in economic anthropology. This failure was already noted in the 1950s by Ronald Berndt regarding another geographical area of studies, as he deplored: 'The term "ceremonial exchange" has, from time to time in Australia, been loosely used' (1951: 156). The confusion addressed by Berndt relates to the fact that not all transactions performed in the course of a major ceremony are ceremonial per se. For more conceptual rigour, he urges reserving the term for describing systems of exchange in which 'the goods themselves are an integral part of this manifestation.' Others, like Christina Toren, opted for a broader sense, 'to cover all exchanges that are accompanied – as it were compulsorily – by ritual formulae', ranging from effusive thanks to imposing speeches (1989: 148). She insists that money can be involved in such transactions. Salhins stressed yet another dimension of ceremoniality related to the sacrificial dimension of gifts that are addressed to non-human beings. In his famous interpretation of *The Spirit of the Gift*, he contrasted secular exchanges with ceremonial transactions involving priests who are responsible for the forest's abundance (1972: 158).

Alongside the ceremonial context, another widely accepted feature of ceremonial exchanges is that they are not intended for economic purposes. Lévi-Strauss concludes about the reciprocal pouring of wine in a French restaurant, apprehended as a ritual of exchange, that 'from an economic perspective, nobody wins, nobody loses' ([1947] 2002: 69, my translation). This point is epitomised by the similarity of the objects featured in ceremonial exchanges: usually the same kinds of items are reciprocally given. These are not swapped immediately, however. Delayed counter-gift endows same-for-same transactions with a sense of generosity, and the time interval provides an opportunity for trust to be manifested (an important point in Pierre Bourdieu's perspective on the gift, already pointed out by Malinowski [1922] 2002: 143). All authors agree that ceremonial exchange is not intended for material profit, but aims instead at strengthening the social fabric underlying the ceremony in question. Strathern and Stewart state that 'the main point here is that delayed exchanges of wealth maintain relationships' (2006: 230). The purpose of ceremonial exchanges is to build alliances. This point is corroborated by Hart, who conceived ceremonial exchange as 'a temporary social framework created in the relative absence of society' – a transaction that he contrasts to barter as 'an atomised interaction predicated on the presence of society', thereby reverting to the idea of barter as a stranger's contract (1986: 648).

Yet, the opposition between trade (with or without money) and ceremonial exchanges is not consensual. As mentioned earlier, Malinowski listed 'ceremonial barter' in his typology of Trobriand exchanges ([1922] 2002: 143). He had been careful to provide a definition, to avoid the drift nonetheless lamented by Berndt a few decades later. In a footnote, he clarified himself, writing that an act is ceremonial if: '(1) public; (2) carried on under observance of definite formalities; (3) if it has sociological, religious, or magical import, and carries with it obligations' (2002: 73). He posited kula transactions in this category of ceremonial barter while also qualifying them as gifts. Mauss strictly classified kula transfers as gifts, and it is under this category that the kula became a keystone in the emergence of an economic anthropology. The idea of ceremonial barter was not addressed in his *Essai*, and after him, the discussion has hovered between gifts and commodities, the notion of ceremonial exchange being associated with the former.

Despite Berndt's call for theoretical clarification, the dzamalag performed by the Gunwinggu people in Northern Australia whom he described also resulted in further incoherent interpretations. In the 1940s, he observed it as fellows. When Gunwinggu people host visitors for trading purposes, they gather together and sing and play music to initiate the dzamalag. Women from each community successively offer fabrics to the men from the other moiety, hitting them as an invitation for sexual intercourse. After having sex, men please their welcoming hosts with beads and tobacco that women deliver to their husbands. Then comes the local men's turn to be invited to sexual relations through erotic jokes and gifts made of fabrics. They also gratify their partner with tobacco and beads, which the visiting women hand over to their spouses so that the goods have come back to their original givers. After a collective dance mimicking warfare, the men put down their arms and share a feast. In addition to this exchange of same for same condensed within a ritual meeting, dzamalag are composed of giving ceremonies of utilitarian goods, for which no immediate return is expected (1951: 160). Berndt is rather vague about the concrete modalities of dzamalag transactions, which he qualifies as 'exchange' or 'distribution' without clarifying how equivalencies are agreed upon.

Graeber emphasises the relative lack of sociability during these meetings. He classifies them as 'ceremonial barter' and uses them to develop his argument that barter takes place between strangers (2011: 32). Stephen Gudeman also acknowledges dzamalag as a form of 'ceremonial exchange', but he develops a more ambivalent analysis of its social fabric. 'The community aspect of the exchange as an end itself yet for the sake of ensuring trade; carrying out trade is also an end, yet for the sake of making community' (2001: 124). Gudeman admits that this figure of trade creates a new community, albeit an evanescent one that is doomed to disappear soon after the exchanges are concluded. I wonder, however, if Gunwinggu people are performing barter with their visitors or whether dzamalag is not a ceremony of reciprocal gifts. Berndt never uses the word 'barter' in allusion to what he calls 'ceremonial economics'. Hence, we find here a confusion similar to the one found in the kula, whereby ceremonial exchanges are understood as barter or gift according to the author's interpretation.

Further confusion stems from the fact that, while ceremonial exchange is sometimes used as a synonym for systems of reciprocal gifts, it has been demonstrated that not all gifts are in fact ceremonial (Yan

2006: 246). In contrast to the kula, the potlatch or the moka, which are typical examples of ceremonial giving, regular presents between kin, or blood gifts, are not regarded as such. In his article published in 1938, Homer Barnett already drew a distinction between formal gifts composing the potlatch and 'informal gifts expressive of friendship and goodwill' (1938: 353). Although widely used by anthropologists, the concept of ceremonial exchanges indeed constitutes a fuzzy category that refers to an array of transactions peculiar to each author. Some even consider commodity exchanges as potentially ceremonial. From his symbolic study of a rural market in Madhya Pradesh, India, Alfred Gell concluded that 'market is a ceremonial as well as a commercial occasion' (1982: 471). Other authors share his view, although the criteria sustaining their argument are not always congruent (see Angé 2018; Miller 1996; Tassi 2010).

This book brings together insights from religious and economic anthropology to better frame the concept of ceremonial exchange. Herein lies another important contribution that Andean data have to offer to the understanding of economic exchange.

## Barter as a Civic Ritual

As I announced at the outset, this book aims to contribute to a still-marginal body of literature addressing the ritualisation of nonetheless instrumental transactions. It should now be clear that I am not primarily interested in the economy of ritual addressing the kind of expenses involved in ceremonies and how they are distributed among the participants. Rather, I am concerned with how economic actions are ritualised. As they are embedded in religious ceremonies, barter fairs illuminate the relationship between mundane instrumental transactions and cosmological concerns. However, I am convinced that the theoretical framework outlined here should also be capable of accounting for secular ritualisation of transactions imbued with political or social concerns. I thus take rituals not only as repetitive acts composing religious rites but also as 'acts of commitment' (Gudeman and Hann 2015: 6) to religious, political or social values that transcend individual concerns.

To develop this argument, I will compare the fairs emerging as part of a religious celebration with those organised by development and heritage institutions. This comparison shows that these fairs, which I propose to call institutional, produce civic value related to the reproduction of national ethnic groups. The last section of this book thus sheds light on another process whereby barter participates in the creation of social fabrics, partaking in national formation. According to Rodney Harrison, official heritage refers 'to a set of professional practices that are authorised by the state and motivated by some form of legislation or written charter' (2013: 14). These practices are framed by the authorised heritage discourse, unravelled by Laurajane Smith, which 'takes its cue from the grand narratives of Western national and elite class experiences, and reinforces ideas of innate cultural value tied to time depth, monumentality, expert knowledge and aesthetics' (2006: 299). Following these authors, I will view heritage not as a restricted set of material and immaterial items but instead as a stance towards objects that are considered the embodiment of the past and thus are the target of particular management and representations. Here, again, I will examine nostalgic tropes to enlighten discrepancies on the transmission of barter. Comparing longings verbalised by heritage stakeholders with those mentioned by cambio partners will allow me to grasp the cultural interplay at stake in institutional fairs.

As Smith convincingly argues, heritage must be apprehended as a performance 'that embodies acts of remembrance and commemoration while negotiating and constructing a sense of place, belonging and understanding in the present' (2006: 3). However, as she further notes, in existing literature, the link between heritage and identity is usually taken for granted, and the mechanisms through which this link is established still need to be clarified. The case of Indigenous barter in Argentina shows how the performance of heritage concretely contributes to the crystallisation of ethnic identities and to the display of multicultural objectives.

The turn towards multiculturalism, common to many Latin American nations,[11] intends to reverse previous policies of forced cultural assimilation in the interests of a new appraisal of ethnic identities asserting pre-Columbian roots. Effective or not, discourse on the composition of ethnic nationalities destabilises prevailing cultural configurations as well as mutual esteem between different social groups. In this sense, advocacy of a multicultural nation prompts a sense of cultural uncertainty that Harrison (2013) has identified as a driving force in the modern proliferation of heritage creation. The heritagisation of barter sheds light on how some forms of economic exchanges are used for displaying national multiculturality and hence constitutes one of the means through which these cultural tensions are expressed and negotiated. Linda Seligmann has unravelled how linguistic and material exchanges in the Peruvian marketplace 'constitute a politics of culture and ethnicity' participating in the formation of national and subnational identities (1993: 187). We will see that barter fairs, including their safeguarded expressions, indeed provide a case in point, for examining the devices by which the state intends to assert social categories, as well as 'the creative appropriation of constitutional multiculturalism' by concerned populations (Wroblewski 2014: 78).

## People in the Book

In January 2005, I moved from Belgium – my native country – to the *puna*, as Argentineans call the extension of the altiplano on their territory. This highland steppe spreads over five departments in the province of Jujuy[12] and extends towards the provinces of Salta and Catamarca to the south. With my partner at the time and our newborn daughter, we settled in a small village presented on the welcome sign alongside the main access road as the 'native community of Yavi, legal person n°002260bs'. In most Argentinean highland departments, Indigenous communities (as they are legally called) are uniformly listed as belonging to the Kolla[13] people.

The legal status of Indigenous emerged in Argentina with the amendment of the national constitution in 1994, consequent upon previous acceptation of the International Labour Organisation Convention 169 on Indigenous and Tribal Peoples, with which the Argentinean government recognised the juridical existence of native groups on its territory. In the 2001 population census, the Kolla people numbered 70,500 citizens. They are the second largest of the thirty native ethnic groups whose legal existence was legally recognised, after that of the Mapuche. In this context, Kolla is a microethnic referent encompassing all pre-Incaic local communities, and therefore it is a 'generalised designation for the whole native population of the Andes in Jujuy' (Karasik 2010: 258, my translation).

Apart from the juridical status, and the subsequent right to own land, the nation-state was to assert its intention to recognise Indigenous communities as legal entities, with their own identity and history.[14] As the first sentence reads, the constitutional amendment aims at 'acknowledging the ethnic and cultural pre-existence of Argentinean Indigenous peoples.' To date, the constitution of this multicultural society is still in progress. Relations between Indigenous communities and the state are conflictive, and Indigenous communities remain politically and economically marginalised. Large areas of Indigenous land still need to be delivered, while Indigenous policies aimed at reducing exclusion in terms of health, education and economic opportunities remain 'protectionist and tutelary, which ultimately infringes upon respect for these populations' autonomy and auto-determination' (Mombello 2002: 11, my translation; for cultural and symbolic exclusion, see Karasik 2010). The legal recognition of Indigenous People's preexistence to the Argentinean State should nevertheless be considered as a key turn in the national cultural politics, where the state has historically attempted to erase Indigenous strands of the population through physical extermination or cultural assimilation (Sturzenegger-Benoist 2006), focused as it is on its European components.

In this southern Andean region, ethnicity in the countryside is framed by people's belonging to kinship-based communities, which facilitate land use as well as access to an array of shared resources like water, wood or medicine plants. Even though some 30 per cent of registered Kolla people dwell in urban areas,[15] ethnic identity remains associated with the countryside and agricultural production. Such an association between indigenousness and agricultural activities is also a self-ascribed characterisation, as attested by Telesforo Benitez, an elderly shepherd from the Chalguamayoc community, when a journalist asked him what it means to be Kolla: 'Kolla agriculture, we will never abandon it, he concluded, because we really are Kolla.'[16] As is common in the Andes (Harris 2000: 30), attachment to land also points to its existence as an incarnation of remote ancestors, among which Pachamama, or Mother Earth, is an overarching feature. She is regarded as the mother of every earthly being and as the force that keeps them alive. Telesforo vividly explained: 'The earth is like a mother's breast. The baby sucks it and that's how he grows', he told me. Furthermore, Pachamama encapsulates peasants' notion of historicity and spatiality, since she is conceived of as the time and space in which human life unfolds. According to this social geography, common in the Andes (Radcliffe and Westwood 1996: 109), indigenousness relates to the countryside.

Public discourse wipes out the heterogeneity of Kolla people, drawing fixed boundaries at odds with the actual fluidity of ethnic configuration. 'Indigenous people' is a legal status resting upon self-identification and direct Indigenous descent.[17] This classification stands in contrast to the category 'Creole', which is not a legal status but a social category. Following Gabriela Karasik, a Creole is someone who 'is neither a descendant of immigrants, like most rural villagers in the country, nor Indian, although he has an Indigenous ascendant somewhere and is usually dark skinned; it involves a sense of métissage' (2006: 469, my translation). As used in northern Argentina, this term is similar to the concept of mestizo in other Andean regions. Even though Creole and

Kolla people use racial tropes to identify each other, there are no biological boundaries between them. Most of the peasants registered as Kolla trace Spanish descent, as attested by their Castilian patronyms. Nor are evidently cultural practices and cosmologies objective criteria, since people who reject Kolla identity worship Pachamama, while members of Indigenous communities make pizzas and appreciate tango music on the national radio. For decades, state-sponsored acculturation strategies have attempted to smooth over ethnic particularities by means of symbolically and physically violent campaigns. Many citizens have come to see themselves as Creole because they have set aside practices they associate with the indigenousness of their ancestors. The border between these social categories is thus highly subjective and shifting, as ethnic configurations usually are (Banks 1996). In this context, fairs are outstanding instances where ethnic categories are played out through social interaction.

Among Creole populations, those whose direct European filiation is attested by the whiteness of their skin are categorised as gringos. However, there are very few of them in this northern region of the country, and they are mostly migrants who have settled in the main towns for professional reasons. This is how people in the village identified me, as well as my daughter and her father, who is from the province of Salta. This transcontinental category imbued with distrust refers to white people. When I arrived, my neighbours in Yavi thought I was a Porteña, as inhabitants from Buenos Aires and the region around La Plata River are called. Porteños epitomise the idea of whiteness, as do, by extension, inhabitants from southern cities chiefly inhabited by descendants of European migrants. In the nineteenth century, national policies triggered important waves of immigration from Europe in view of occupying sparsely populated territories. Prosperous Argentina attracted hordes of migrants having suffered political and economic crises on the Old Continent.[18] The massive arrival of foreigners, coupled with the disastrous demographic decline of Indigenous peoples, resulted in the proudly claimed picture of Argentina as a white, European nation. According to government statistics, more than 80 per cent of present-day citizens are direct descendants of Europeans.

If we were the only gringos in Yavi, we were not the only foreigners. Situated at five kilometres from the international border, the village also features an important population of Bolivian origin. Migration from Bolivia, particularly from the nearby provinces of Tarija and Potosi, has been constant in regional history since precolonial times. The numbers are hard to estimate, since most migrants have adopted Argentinean nationality. In most cases, even local people have lost track of these flows. National identities are complex and nonexclusive in this border region, where double nationality is a common strategy for Bolivian people who want to benefit from Argentina's welfare programme. Women frequently cross the border to give birth in Argentinean hospitals so they can register their children in both countries.

As well as referring to members of rural communities in the Argentinean cordillera and to urban migrants who manifest Indigenous filiation, the term *Kolla* is also used in Bolivia as a pejorative term for highland people, in contrast to those living in the lowlands, who are called *cambas* (Karasik 2006: 477). Yet, Kolla is assigned to all Bolivian autochthones when they are in Argentina – a common situation, as Bolivian peasants constantly travel across the border for economic or social obligations. Argentineans are also keen on crossing the border in search of economic ventures. They keep an eye out for any opportunities international trade may provide. At the end of the twentieth century, Argentinean herders engaged in a highly profitable traffic of Bolivian cattle, which they drove all the way through the puna. Most common are shopping trips by border dwellers who cross over to find cheaper commodities, mostly coca leaves, but also foodstuffs, clothes, household utensils or mobile phones. Although their intensity depends on the exchange rate between Argentinean and Bolivian pesos, the international flow of people and commodities is constant. I used to cross the border myself at least once a week to purchase exotic fruits and coca leaves. I always enjoyed spending time in the market of Villazón, especially on Sundays, when I used to sit down and knit with cultivators coming from surrounding communities to sell their harvest. It was a meeting point for acquaintances from the community of Chosconty, situated in the *quebrada* (valley) at 2,500 metres above sea level on the bank of the San Juan del Oro River. I knew these women from Argentinean fairs, where they brought their fruits and maize.

However, I did most of my fieldwork in Chalguamayoc, a village of herders standing some 4,000 metres above sea level, 25 kilometres east of my own domicile. I decided to centre my research there, as I was intrigued by their economic life: they continued to practice semi-nomadism within the territory of their community while simultaneously being constantly connected with the nearest city of La Quiaca. Because they were so devoted to their flocks, my neighbours in Yavi depicted them as the archetype of the *gente del campo* (people from the country) and exceptionally attached to the *costumbre de los abuelos* (habits of the ancestors). An NGO with which they were affiliated also painted them as such. During the first two years of my stay in the puna, I worked as a volunteer in this NGO dedicated to the commercialisation of agricultural products from the puna. It is in this context that I first met people from Chalguamayoc. The staff proudly pointed out that this village was the first provider of meat for the association's butcher shop, but at the same time jealously complained that some of the members were keen on selling their meat at the market. True or not, this stereotype of traditional *campesinos* (people from the country, small peasants) firmly inserted into the local trade network caught my attention, and from February 2007 onwards, I spent most of my day-time hours in the community.

There were a few households where I knew I was always welcome to lend a – clumsy – hand with their daily tasks, and I liked to drive my hosts to the city whenever they needed to sell meat and stock up on commodities. The house of Telesforo and his wife, Sylberia, was my favourite place. I met this old couple in February 2007 when I was invited to celebrate Carnival with them by the head of the community, who wanted me to witness an authentic festival. Their four daughters had come all the way from Buenos Aires and Salta to participate in the seven-day Carnival merrymaking and to help their parents with the hard summer job of cattle branding. At around 70 years of age,

**Figure 0.2.** A flock of sheep in their pen adjacent to a household in the highlands of Chalguamayoc. Photograph by the author.

the couple was used to living on their own, taking care of two herds of some hundred llamas and sheep. I also enjoyed spending time with other families, whom I will introduce, as well as my neighbours in Yavi and friends in Chosconty. This multisite fieldwork, which took in the Bolivian lowlands, the intermediate zone surrounding Yavi and up to the Argentinean highlands, opened a perspective on communities from the three main ecozones represented at fairs.

## Outline of the Book

Chapter 1 outlines the ethnographic context in which fairs are deployed. Drawing on Chalguamayoc, I focus on those features of peasants' daily life that are significant for understanding the sociocultural dimensions of Andean barter. With this aim in mind, I explore the polymorphism of the idea of community, which refers to a kinship network, a territorial space, a legal status, an economic institution and shared nonhuman partners. I then trace the network of material transfers in which households from the Chalguamayoc community take part. This includes valley people and city dwellers, who also meet at fairs. The last part of the chapter addresses aspects of the local economy, highlighting peasants' conceptions of growth and prosperity and how they strive to establish benevolent relationships with nonhuman beings that participate in the regeneration of life forces.

Chapter 2 is a historical chapter, which takes us back to precolonial times, briefly recalling the frame of pre-Hispanic economic organisation in which markets were negligible. I trace the origins of contemporary barter fairs, underscoring their European roots. The last historical section outlines the ongoing process of heritagisation of barter, pointing to the current appraisal of fairs as an Indigenous cultural practice that needs to be safeguarded against the threat of modernity.

I then provide, in chapter 3, a panoramic view of a contemporary fair in the village of Yavi, attended by Chalguamayoc herders and Chosconty cultivators. A description of the spatiotemporal setting stresses the embeddedness of fairs within a broader religious celebration. I also examine the social identities that are played out at fairs. And finally, I describe the types of produce that are put in motion, as well as their entanglement in the identity of their producer and consumer.

Chapter 4 examines the different transactions that compose the fairs. Following local categories, I distinguish between *cambio* (exchange), *negocio* (business) and *invitación* (invitation), the latter being either consumed by humans or offered to deities. For each modality of material transfer, I discuss the regime of value and underlying social interplay. While tackling different types of transfers at fairs, this chapter delineates the emic notion of barter.

Exclusively focussed on cambio, chapter 5, the final one, explores the different ways in which barter contributes to the production and reproduction of social life. I first tease out how this specific transaction participates in the formation of subjectivities, both physically and symbolically. I then point out the cosmological dimensions of cambio at fairs and its potential to substantiate transcendental value. In so doing, I propose to see it as a form of ritualised barter, aimed at producing material and cosmological values. While referring to the enactment of a code of exchange inherited from ancestors, the use of the notion of ritual does not mean that cambio is an untouched tradition inherited from ancient times. Fairs are embedded in a broader socio-economic environment that directly impacts barter practices. In the last section, I shed light on the process of heritagisation of fairs, showing how they are used to shape new sociocultural configurations by negotiating Indigenous people's integration on the national stage. For this purpose, I examine nostalgic tropes used by heritage partakers and compare them with peasants' nostalgia, thus unveiling the nuanced moralities of barter.

## Notes

1. Malinowski nonetheless acknowledges the specificities of the kula as a 're-markable form of trade' that would deserve its own category (2002: 144).
2. This dialogue was recorded at the 2008 Easter fair in Yavi, a village in the Jujuy Province of Argentina. The original language was Spanish. All dialogue translations are mine.
3. Note that Lévi-Strauss uses 'ceremonial exchange' as well as 'rituals of exchange', contrary to Mauss, who does not use the former.
4. That money can both be physically involved in barter (Humphrey 1985: 62; M. Strathern 1992: 175) and circulate as a gift is not specific to Andean economies, as has been observed in diverse cultural settings. Such works challenge most basic definitions of barter as an exchange of one thing for another without the use of money.
5. See e.g. U-Exchange, http://www.u-exchange.com.
6. In France, see e.g. France Barter, https://www.francebarter.coop; in the United States, see e.g. Barter Business Unlimited, http://bbubarter.com
7. See http://bartercardusa.com.
8. This example is mentioned in Andrew Horowitz (2010: 112).
9. In her Ecuadorean fieldwork, Ferraro (2011: 172) mentioned a kind of barter called cambeo, the local pronunciation of cambio. Although she

did not dwell on that specific transaction, the few features listed match the Argentinean cambio discussed here.

10. The term cholo is used in different regions of the Andes to refer to urbanised Indigenous people.

11. See e.g. Garcia (2005) and Wroblewski (2014) on the Peruvian and Ecuadorian situations, respectively, or Sieder (2002) for a regional overview.

12. Yavi, Santa Catalina, Rinconada, Susques and part of Tumbaya.

13. Colla, Coya and Qolla also exist in Argentina. Kolla is the official spelling used by state institutions. In keeping with their option, I acknowledge that the state originally imposed this ethnonym on defeated populations.

14. Information from the webpage of the National Institute of Indigenous Affairs (INAI).

15. According to the government's 2001 census, which is the latest to date (see www.indec.gov.ar).

16. Extract from *Pueblos originarios. Kollas.* http://www.descargas.encuentro .gov.ar.

17. http://www.desarrollosocial.gob.ar/Uploads/i1/Institucional/6.Informacio nEstadistica.pdf.

18. Between 1857 and 1930, the national population grew tenfold, reaching twelve million by the end of this period (Sturzenegger-Benoist 2006: 85, 95). Most of the settlers came from Italy and Spain, but every European nation took part in this movement, from Portugal to Russia, including Greece and Belgium.

# CHAPTER I

# Household Economy in an Argentinean Highland Village

The puna is known as the 'abandoned region of the country'. Rugged roads, rudimentary means of communication, sparse electricity, restricted water supply and poor education and healthcare facilities attest to the state's disengagement. The visitor's feeling of remoteness is further accentuated by a landscape of arid steppe overlooked by snow-capped peaks. Although the inhabitants of the puna describe their life in the countryside as lonely, this does not mean they are disconnected from regional life. Herders keep up a relationship with the national society, in which they participate in their own particular way. On the one hand, they sporadically take part in public institutions that are nonetheless present in the village, such as school, church, development NGOs and state programs, or the local council established in the nearby village of Condor. These institutions influence local social, political and economic configurations, which herders shape at the interface of the state's expectations and the communal autonomy they strive to maintain. On the other hand, herders participate in urban life through constant trips to nearby towns or the provincial capital. In the course of their journey, intended for either economic, political or social purposes, they circulate material and intangible assets that contribute to the reproduction of domestic and communal lives. This chapter outlines the aspects of the domestic and communal lives in Chalguamayoc which instantiate the ethnographic context in which the fairs unfold.

## Composing a Herder Community in Contemporary Argentina

### A Blood Community: 'Here We Are All Related'

The village of Chalguamayoc numbers some thirty households[1] distributed among four main patronyms.[2] Alongside these major divisions, there are ten or so other names represented by only one or two households. This group of inhabitants recognises itself as a unit by virtue of a generalised bond of kinship: 'Here we are all relatives'[3] was a regular response when I asked about relations between people. The community is not explicitly endogamous. Although there is no formal prescription to marry within the community, most couples are nonetheless from the same village. The continuity of patronyms within the group is bolstered by the virilocality of couples of different origins. However, contrary to the elders' memories of a former matrimonial order, virilocality is no longer necessarily respected. This discrepancy correlates with the dramatic drop in the ritual institution of the couple by marriage and with the relative volatility of marriage alliances throughout the puna (Göbel 1998: 160). The last marriage celebrated in Chalguamayoc seems to have been some fifteen years ago, but no one remembers exactly.

The simple fact of being born in the community's territory gives one the right to claim membership in the group. But the constant migrations contribute to weakening the leavers' ties with their native land and its inhabitants. Among those who return regularly, those who return sporadically and the few who never return, it is hard to establish with precision the effective number of community members. Migrants regularly come back to their village after several years of absence and take possession once again of their fallow grazing lands or move onto the lands of a deceased elder relative, so migration does not in fact mean exclusion from the community. Carnival, the festival of the patron saint, Easter and All Saints' Day are the main times in the year when migrants return to their land, at that point manifesting the extension of the community network beyond its territorial boundaries. Through speeches, offerings and dances on these occasions, they mark their ties with their relatives who have stayed in the village.

It is noteworthy that this kin network is extended to Pachamama, who, as mentioned earlier, is conceived of as the primordial ancestor, mother of every living being inhabiting the landscape. All living organisms are indeed acknowledged as 'children of Pachamama', ideally extending kinship networks beyond the human. Humans are aware that they depend on other species for their reproduction, just as other species – especially the domesticated ones – need humans' care in order to thrive. The latter thus experience their relationship with surrounding plants and animals as framed by normative mutual responsibility for caring for each other and thereby enhancing Pachamama's fertile power. I shall return to this later. Pachamama is a complex concept hinting at the space-time in which human and nonhuman life unfolds. While Pachamama is an entity encompassing all space and time, she manifests herself in a unique way in every locality. Peasants' connection to their daily environment is therefore entailed in an affective connection to their own Mother Earth.

### Shared Land

Shepherds in the Argentinean cordillera share a conception of an animated landscape imbued with its own agency, a view common throughout the Andes (e.g. Allen 1988; Harris 2000; Ødegaard 2011; Wachtel 1990). However, unlike the kinship network, the community's territory is fixed and clearly delimited. Chalguamayoc stretches to the intersection of the adjacent community lands of Cholacor to the east, Suripujio and Casti to the west and Barrios to the south. The community legally owns the territory, which is divided into lots, the use of which is transmitted within households recognised as owning the land at the communal level. The community's territorial sovereignty nonetheless prevails over individual will, as attested by the fact that any handover of lands to an outsider requires the group's approval. This consent becomes all the less likely as the degree of otherness increases. As a rule, it is explicitly forbidden to sell land to someone *de afuera* (an outsider), even though there is no legal framework to stop those deciding to do so in the teeth of the community's opposition.

The community space is divided into three zones: the *pueblo* (village), the *cerro* (highlands) and the *campo* (plains). The *pueblo* is typical of the villages in the puna and materialises their national integration: the cement public buildings in the centre of the village housing the church, the school, the nurses station, and the community hall contrast with the mud-brick houses. Vehicles pass through the village on the single track – sometimes blocked by weather conditions – heading to neighbouring communities and the urban space. The rest of the territory is impracticable to travel by motorised vehicles. School activities break the daily silence of this seemingly deserted space: the thirty or so students who live there, the teacher and the people responsible for the upkeep regularly walk around the grounds. This institutional core is encircled by several scattered hamlets within a two-kilometre range;

there the herders have their main house, but it stands empty for the better part of the year. The monthly meetings of the 'community' and the religious services draw people to the village, which at those times becomes extraordinarily animated. The herders divide the rest of their time between the highlands and the plains, where they own one or more secondary residences, which they occupy in turn as they shift the herd in search of favourable ecological conditions.

In the summer, the grazing herds spread out over the plains, which they must abandon before the last rains to be sure of finding grass to return to in the depths of winter, when the cold makes the highlands too inhospitable. Between Easter and Saint John's Day (24 June), the shepherds live in their stone huts situated at one or two hours walk from the centre of the village on the steep trails that lead to the swamps and the high springs (some 5,000 metres above sea level); these sources of water are crucial for getting through the dry winter season. Between June and September, when the temperature gets colder (usually dropping to below 20 degrees Celsius at night), the animals are taken back to the plains, where they graze on the fields they left at the end of sum-

**Figure 1.1.** Landscape of the puna in Chalguamayoc, Argentina, where ecological conditions are propitious for the breeding of llama and sheep herds. Photograph by the author.

mer. Secondary residences in the plains are inhabited the better part of the year. They are surrounded by several areas reserved for crops, which receive water uniquely when it rains. When the grass runs out at the end of winter, the herders take their animals up to the highlands, which they again leave after the first Christmas rains announcing the appearance of the new summer growth in the plains.

While living in the puna, I had the feeling that the constant mobility between houses spread over such a large space complicated my fieldwork. I have spent hours walking through the mountains only to end up in front of closed doors in the remotest part of the territory. In retrospect, I realised I was experiencing the particular environment in which the herder's life unfolds. I sometimes benefited from unexpected opportunities to meet up with neighbours, who were happy to break the loneliness of the countryside with my visit. Many were impressed that a skinny gringa like me could stride along inhabited spaces without being afraid. In Chalguamayoc, the uneven distribution of life forces through space and time outlines a geography of cosmological forces concentrated in the higher area, represented as potential contact points with the remotest ancestors connected to the past (similarly to Ødegaard's description [2010]). This explains Sylberia's preference for grazing on the high summits overlooking the village. There, she says, she can hear her divine protectors more clearly (she referred to God and Mother Earth). Because they incarnate ambivalent powers, high pastures are also experienced as dangerous spaces that the herder needs to tame with careful prayers and offerings. Sylberia's neighbour in the highlands of Chalguamayoc, was afraid to walk on her own until, spurred by her faith, she stopped drinking and started to lead a better life: 'Before, I used to walk in these meadows, and I would fall down. There actually are demons (*demonios*) living in these obscure locations', she told me, warning me to be careful on my way home. Like the Peruvian migrants Ødegaard worked with, herders in Chalguamayoc associate their environment with ambivalent forces that need to be harnessed through praises and material reciprocity in order to become sources of prosperity. Later we shall see that prayers and offerings to landscape entities shore up all kinds of economic ventures and connect the peasants with the different places they pass through as they constantly move their herds.

## Economic Destiny: Collective Use of Natural Resources

As suggested earlier, the needs of animal husbandry oblige herders to constantly move around the community territory. Three kinds of recurrent movements can be distinguished. First are the daily movements by which the herders lead their animals to the pastures. Each herder is intimately acquainted with the boundaries of the space reserved for their household, and these limits are precisely where the grazing land of their neighbour begins, in accordance with the customary distribution. Early in the morning, the herders drive the llamas to grass. Later in the morning, they accompany and watch over the sheep until the sun goes down, so they will not wander off. The llamas often go back to their enclosure on their own; however, when they do not, the herder must go and get them. In addition to these daily movements, the herders come and go regularly between their grazing site and the village to get supplies, water their vegetable garden or join the youngsters or the elderly people who live in the main house. Finally, there are the seasonal movements, taking the form of transhumance within the communal territory, which mark most acutely the interdependence of the villagers. The rhythm of these movements stems from power relations between the shepherds and their flock, a relationship that is subjected to weather conditions, reflecting Mother Earth's whims.

Good shepherds must be able to circumscribe their animals' movements, but they sometimes find themselves outmanoeuvred or *vencido* (defeated) by a flock that heads for new pastures. This happens particularly when the first rains of December fall in the plain and attract the animals looking for food: 'When it rains, they know there is grass and they head for the plain', lamented Isabela, a woman some forty years old, coping with the displacements of her frenzied llamas. When herders are 'defeated' by their famished herd, they can draw their neighbours into the same path because the latter will eventually be defeated as well, thus setting off a collective movement to the lowlands. The last one will willingly leave for fear of remaining alone in these silent lands, at the mercy of pumas and other ecological dangers. One feast day, when the whole community was gathered together, two drunken veterans narrowly escaped the scuffle threatened by the premature departure of one of their herds for the plain, a sign of the collective handling of shepherds' control over their animals within the community.

Alongside the recurrent mobility, the sporadic displacement for pumas and fox rodeos further exemplifies the necessity for the community members to join forces in view of collective prosperity. The date for such gatherings is set by common agreement when several pens have suffered attacks within a district of the community. That day, a group of volunteers meets on the edge of the territory to comb the area in search of the predators. The team is ideally composed of a member from each household, since the risk represented by the presence of puma and fox hovers over the community as a whole: any pen can potentially be the next victim of an attack.

The life shared in the territory thus binds the group together in an economic destiny entailing a synchronisation of the various households' movements. The centrifugal movements whereby the herders periodically return to the village and the vertical movements whereby each season they go up to the highlands or down to the plain unite the members of the community in a shared geographical pattern.

### Congregating around Spiritual Partners: Saint Mark's Protégés

Each village in the Argentinean puna has a patron saint to whom its inhabitants pay homage every year on the saint's feast day, which is set by the Roman Catholic calendar. The entire year is thus punctuated by a succession of saint's day celebrations. The saints are appreciated for their specialty in a particular domain, which reflects significant aspects of their life as related in the liturgy: Saint John protects the shepherd's flock, Saint James ensures the docility of horses, while Saint Isidore is responsible for strong oxen, to mention but a few. Alongside these associations inspired by European Catholicism, others have appeared in the New World, as is the case of Saint Barbara's capacity to protect people from lightning.

Saints are represented by wooden or porcelain statues, which incarnate their holy power. This material *imagen* (image) is usually housed in a box decorated with pictograms recalling the emblematic events in the life of the saint. The box is equipped with two panels in the front which, when opened, allow the statue to look out and enjoy the spectacles offered by his or her custodians. Among such spectacles, the masses and processions are certainly the most appreciated. *Hacerle escuchar misa* (have him/her hear mass) is part of the extraordinary caring of the *santito* (little saint), as is taking him for a walk during processions on the annual feast day, the sumptuousness of which depends on the economic and political prosperity of his custodians, as well as his regional renown. These public displays contrast with the everyday gestures made to the effigy, such as the offering of spoken prayers, tapers, flowers, incense, holy water and the regular cleaning of the saint's housing. These both common and exceptional attentions demonstrate the people's devotion to the saint and express a double message: gratitude for favours and protection granted, and an appeal for future favours and protection, particularly in the area of the saint's recognised specialty. Some figures are intensely venerated throughout the region, as is the case of the Our Lady of the Purification, Saint

John, Saint James or the Our Lady of the Rosary. In contrast, only the inhabitants of Chalguamayoc celebrate the feast day of Saint Mark, whom they venerate as their patron saint. No other festivities occur in the vicinity, which shows the narrowly local character of this devotion.

Under the eye of the patron saint around which they are gathered, the villagers are also determined to show the community's cohesion beyond the everyday tensions and conflicts that occupy them. The quality of the festival's organisation acts as a barometer by which the different communities compare and vie to demonstrate their unity. The two years I took part in the celebrations in Chalguamayoc, the first calls for 'collaboration' raised during the community meeting failed, spurring Francisco, the leader at that time, to strategically activate the register of the ideal of community cohesion:

> Let's make a good impression. People from the outside [are] going to come. Everyone united, that's a community. Otherwise, we will be divided and we won't do anything. As if it was an ordinary day. . . . If there are people who come, we must receive them. Otherwise everyone acts individually and each takes care of his own affairs.

Francisco then wanted someone to organise the festivities. Presenta, who had inherited an effigy of Saint Mark from her father, volunteered. Seeing her neighbours' lack of enthusiasm, she became indignant and deplored the lack of involvement on the part of the young villagers, who, in her opinion, should take charge of the organisation: 'Otherwise, when we leave [die], nothing will be left.' Francisco agreed: 'The veterans disappear, the culture disappears, the festival disappears. The young people don't want to participate. They don't even come here [to the community meeting].' As though revived by these speeches, one after the other the participants to the meeting made a show of their good will. A monetary contribution per household was set in addition to which each household proposed its collaboration in kind: two packets of rice, three kilos of potatoes or a sack of beans, for instance. Francisco proudly declared his intention to give a llama from his herd so as to receive the guests with grilled meat, the most prestigious meal that can be served on such an occasion. The municipality was solicited to help fund the trophy for the football tournament and additional food. As usual, the group of young men – none of whom were at the meeting – took charge of preparing the two soccer fields.

On the eve of the big day, Isabela and Teresa – Presenta's sisters – assisted by a few neighbour women, met in the community hall; they took care of preparing the food every year. In the dim light of the candle-lit hall, Teresa received the contributions of food as they arrived;

she weighed them and wrote the measurements down carefully in the treasurer's account book. That same night, following the closing prayers of the novena, a bonfire was lit in front of the chapel in honour of the saint, whom the flames are meant to illuminate. Among the twenty-some faithful who answered the invitation to venerate the saint, some had brought a *cuartito*, a lamb that has been gutted, decapitated and cut in half. The halves are blessed and placed on the altar until the next day, when they are cut into quarters during the *cuarteada* dance. The year before, only Sylberia had sacrificed an animal, in addition to the two Presenta had given. According to these women, such gifts are becoming increasingly rare. 'People want to sell. The only thing that matters to them is money. Relations, love, happiness don't matter to them. Our spirituality', Presenta deplored. These complaints are voiced in a recurring register in which the new generations are blamed for not reproducing the idealised behaviours of their ancestors.

Religious celebrations consistently trigger nostalgic narratives of the golden age of the *abuelos*. Laziness, venality, egotism and disregard for spiritual concerns are all mentioned as vices separating contemporary society from the ideal order that is said to have prevailed in olden days. Some cast their glorious retrospections back to the more distant past of the *tatarabuelos*, the ancestors whose deified figures are embodied in the environment. In any case, these narratives refer to a time outside any historical situation and conjoined with a mythic time when fundamental reciprocities went without saying. They present the twofold aspect identified by Michael Herzfeld as specific of 'structural nostalgia'. On the one hand, the narratives are replicated by every succeeding generation, each cohort blaming the following for modern degeneration; on the other, they relate to the damage done to a once-perfect reciprocity by the self-interest of modern times (2005: 149).

Nevertheless, Saint Mark was celebrated with the joy expected. Each of the activities that make up the patron saint festival in the puna was organised for him: the mass, the procession, the civic speeches, the communal meal, the sports tournament and the dancing. Though on a very small scale, different kinds of instrumental exchanges were also part of the festival. Several women set up makeshift stalls at the centre of the village, where they sold hot dogs, hamburgers, sweets and other festive foods. Others, fewer in number, were looking for partners with whom to barter products brought by visitors. After having been ceaselessly told that there was no cambio at Saint Mark's festival, I was surprised to hear two women talking between two *cuarteadas*: 'That man from Yavi has brought some maize. Who will be able to kill an animal? Do you think Doña Anastasia might?' The common thread of these different activities is the adoration and entertainment of the saint, whose fundamental vehicles are the contemplation and joy of his flock. These were the terms the village priest used when opening the mass for the patron saint of the village of Cusi Cusi: 'Some come to play soccer, others to dance, but what brings us together is our devotion to the Lord.'

## Emergence of 'Indigenous Communities' within the Nation-State

The provincial authorities' waiving of their ownership of Indigenous lands is an outcome of the amendments to the national constitution recognising the existence of pre-Hispanic peoples in Argentina. In order to lay claim to their land, each community has been obliged to demand the status of 'Indigenous community organisation' from the National Institute for Indigenous Affairs (Instituto Nacional de Asuntos Indigenas – INAI). The new legal dispositions are a reversal of the process designed to exclude the pre-Hispanic peoples from national politics, a policy that was inaugurated with the Constitution of 1830, when the community-based political structures were proscribed by the legal ban on the institution of caciques and collective ownership of lands (Madrazo 1981: 215).

To be officially recognised as a *comunidad* (community) and to obtain the status of civic association endowed with a national identification number, all registered members (*sensados*) were also obliged to elect a *comisión aborigen* (native commission), to be renewed every two years. The commission is to be composed of a treasurer, a secretary and a president, usually called *presidente*, although they are sometimes also known as cacique or *curaca*, an allusion to the pre-Columbian chiefs. In the process, the village must become a collective actor, whose official representative is authorised to dialogue with the municipal and provincial political authorities.[4] The first point to address was the return of the land to the communities, based on their choice between private or communal ownership. Like the vast majority of the highland villages isolated from the main roads, Chalguamayoc chose collective ownership, meaning that the comunidad is legally acknowledged as proprietor. The official appearance of native communities encourages their representatives, state officers and the actors of civil society, to regard the very existence of the 'communities' as the happy outcome of this legal process. We can hear these people asserting that 'before, communities didn't exist', or that 'communities were invisible until the Kolla people appeared'. Although they sometimes corroborate these tropes, shepherds nonetheless remember that their 'community' has always existed.

To understand the coexistence of these apparently contradictory discourses, it is useful to distinguish two senses of the term 'community'. One of these refers to the total institution built around the double descent system, outlined earlier, involving family and territory. I propose to call this 'kinship community', keeping in mind the filiation herders maintain with their land. The other, which I propose to call 'administrative community', refers to the new figure adopted by the village political organisation as a consequence of the change in the national legislation. As the herders describe it, the administrative community that emerged at the end of the twentieth century on the initiative of the Argentinean government is a continuation of the *centro vicinal* (neighbourhood association). The latter was promoted, under the dictatorship of the 1980s, as a political and social mode of organising local circumscriptions by the national apparatus. In the puna, it functioned as a communication point with the herders who, owing to their continual mobility, masterfully avoided government encroachment on their freedom.

Unlike their pre-Hispanic precursors, and as is still the case in many communities of the Bolivian altiplano (see esp. Rivière 2007; Wachtel 1990), today's community leaders do not possess an increased cosmological power. Their central role is still to promote the political and economic well-being of the community, but this no longer demands that they create favourable communications with deified powers in order to attract their good will. Instead, they strive to establish favourable communications with the political powers within and outside the government, which intervene in the region. As I was asking an inhabitant of Chalguamayoc in his twenties, about the qualities required of a 'good' president, he said in the first place: 'Of course, working for the village, that's what a leader must do, obtain projects.' Julian used the word *proyectos* to refer to material support from any kind of institution, intended for raising villagers' economic well-being. In fact, the leader's ability to attract resources to his community supports his precarious authority. These resources are redistributed at monthly community meetings, which provide crucial incentives for herders to come through the centre of the village that day.

After the historical disengagement of the state in the puna, several programmes are now in place to promote rural development. Indeed, some initiatives are especially targeted at Indigenous communities. These are led by state agencies such as municipalities, provincial branches of the ministry of social affairs, the National Institute of

Technology for Agriculture (INTA) or the INAI. Other programs are launched by NGOs managed by the church or by agronomists who have come from cities in the south to see to the well-being of Indigenous communities. Both governmental and nongovernmental initiatives are tainted by a similar ideology, since they share common stakeholders, among whom the World Bank features prominently. Their idea of indigenousness coincides with that constructed by international agencies, where it is associated with imaginary pristine communities living in harmony with their natural environment, whose productive activities are intertwined with ancestral cosmologies.

These interventions revolve around three main lines of action, which also prevail within international mainstream development programmes: fighting poverty, empowering civil society and safeguarding ancestral cultural heritage. Since they have been granted the status of civil association, Indigenous communities have become potential collective beneficiaries of these programmes. Apart from economic development, these institutions have been involved in lifelong education plans aimed at training peasants to take on leadership roles. Many of those involved in development programmes have participated in *escuelas de dirigentes* (leaders schools), where they have been taught how to manage their community and to articulate it with extra-local politic players. The most successful have become regional Indigenous leaders, hired by NGO and state programmes to implement their projects in the communities. Their role is vital to the implementation of proyectos, since initiatives led by foreigners arouse suspicion in the villages. Contrary to what has been described in other Andean contexts, these rural development leaders remain under the influence of external activists, categorised as gringos, at the head of NGOs and state programmes concerned with Indigenous integration.

Aware of this hierarchy, peasants make a strictly selective use of the projects they are offered and are reluctant to participate actively in the training that usually conditions access to material benefits. Tania Li observed in Indonesia that resource distribution fosters articulation of peasants' behaviours with providing institutions' expectations (2000: 164). In the Argentinean puna, monthly community meetings are key concrete loci where this articulation operates at the local level. In the course of these meetings, peasants become aware of the appearance of a national context, in which they can use an Indigenous identity to access material resources. As we shall see later, fairs organised by these same institutions provide another locus where administrative and local cultural identities are articulated.

Legal recognition of the existence of Indigenous peoples thus gave rise, in the rural areas of the puna, to the superposition of an administrative community, grouped around development projects and constituted under the impetus of outside organisations, upon the already-existing kinship community, focussed on the organisation of economic and religious life. These two facets of the 'community' cannot always be separated, as illustrated by the case of the president, whose status is also recognised by those villagers who had refused to be registered as members of the administrative community. In the same manner, the monthly meetings organised to meet the expectations of national institutions are often co-opted by herders for the purpose of resolving problems pertaining to the kinship community, such as preparing the patron saint's festival or a puma hunt. In all events, by creating the context for interactions between herders' social organisation and government expectations, the administrative community operates as the nexus where Argentinean herders' 'indigenous citizenship' (Garcia 2005) is constructed.

## Social Affinities and Economic Complicities

### The Household as the Basis of Daily Economic Activity

Beyond the difficulties posed by the definition of this concept, the household is recognised as the primary socio-economic unit throughout the Andes (Mayer 2002; see also Weismantel 1995). In the Argentinean puna, the household revolves around a couple, their children and, sometimes, disabled ascendants. In principle, the daughters leave the family home and move with their companion into one of his family residences. When they are unwed mothers, they stay at home and receive help from their elders in raising their children. A household can therefore often have four generations under the same roof.

Many homes also contain the statue of a household saint, whose protection ensures their prosperity. A sanctuary may be reserved for the saint inside the home, eventually occupying a chapel in the case of well-to-do families. This sacred effigy must not leave the household before the death of the principal couple. At that time, it is passed on to one of the children, who will care for it, thus honouring the deceased parents and other ancestors. In addition to the statuette, each nuclear family keeps a series of stones called Pachamama, which embody the engendering power of the household. They stand discretely on a shelf and, when it comes time to sow, they are placed on the sacks of seed

prepared for sowing so that they will transmit their fertility. To ensure their fertility, their owner periodically makes offerings to them: he
sprinkles them with alcoholic beverages, decorates them with bits of
paper and offers them incense. These stones, also called *tierra* (earth)
are similar to the *illas*, whose presence has been observed elsewhere
in the Andes (see e.g. Allen 2016; Harris 1989: 256; Sillar 2012). The
household saint and the stones thus embody a fertile energy that binds
together the members of the household in a shared domestic economy.

In addition, animals are recognised as fully fledged members of the
family. As elsewhere in the Andes (Rivera Andia 2005: 144), herders
in Jujuy use the vocabulary of kinship to describe the bond that con-
nects them with their herd: 'The flock knows us. We talk to them. They
hear our voice and are already glad. I follow my flock, and my flock
follows me. They are our children; we raise them. When we go away,
we miss them. Of course, if we are their mothers!' glossed Sylberia
proudly on her sheep and llama flocks. Kinship tropes are enacted by
daily care imbued with intense affect. The affection with which animals
are treated is posited as a condition for a smooth interaction with them.
Each species is believed to communicate in a language of its own, the
mastery of which is part of the herder's package of skills. Beyond the
effect of sound, affectionate care is recognised as a key vehicle of mutual understanding. Lola, who was my sixty-something neighbour in
Yavi, gave me plenty of advice on how to properly care for animals.
She was always complaining about how exhausting and unprofitable
herding her sheep was. She constantly threatened Mariel – the young-
est of her five children, and the only one who has not migrated to the
city – that she would sell the herd if she did not help her with the
daily grazing. But when I left the village, Lola had not carried out her
threat, because she cared for her animals too much to get rid of them.
While teaching me how to milk a recalcitrant goat, she recommended:
'You must appreciate them. You must talk to them, and then they will
follow you. They know that you love them and they respond to your
commands.'

Herders who spend their life with their herd know every animal in-
dividually. Some of them are given a name; otherwise, they are identified by a physical particularity. Aware of their habits and character, the
shepherd may also qualify them as *flojas* (lazy), *chúcaras* (indocile),
*mañeras* (vicious) or *guapas* (brave). Herders are concerned with their
animals' emotions, scrutinizing their experience of sadness, boredom,
happiness, loneliness or tranquillity. They are so constantly mindful
of their animals' mood that their own affective state is bound up with
their animals'. I remember a conversation with Gabina, whom I had

met in the village early in the morning. She was complaining about having insomnia because her flocks were in the highlands:

> I cannot live without my sheep. When I have to leave them, I cannot sleep. I lie down, and I stay awake until the sunshine. I am wondering: 'What will they be doing? Where will they be?' With my sheep, I go to their pen, I talk to them for a while. I also tell them off when they make me curse. And then I sleep straightaway, peaceful. When Lazaro [her son] is at home, then I sleep. We stay chatting until late and I fall asleep, but alone, I can't.

Gabina's words instantiate the domestic animal's status as part of the family.

Her words also attest that herding activities are not strictly instrumental. Herders do not take care of their animals thinking of the tasty meat they will procure. They enjoy their relationship with them as an intrinsic dimension of their daily herding practices. Their animals' well-being is indissociable from their own. This is, at least, how a good herder is conceived of. In this light, herding is a practice of virtue in the Aristotelian sense, which means that these are autotelic practices composing a good life (Lambek 2008: 138). Herders agree that their herd brings them happiness. Further, I was told that herding should be performed cheerfully, as should agricultural tasks. The experience of long-term happiness, Joel Robbins points out, is fuelled by 'a steady flow of effervescence by virtue of moving regularly through a wide range of successful interactions across the life-course' (2015: 226). This makes sense in these Andean plateaus, where a flourishing life is indeed composed of a succession of successful interactions. What is particular here is that this interactional sequence includes human and nonhuman actors, among which domesticated animals are most significant.

The moral appreciation of herding practices nonetheless mingles with instrumental consideration, since the herd also is a mainstay of the livelihood in the puna. In addition to providing meat, sheep and llamas provide wool, fat (in the case of llamas) and milk for cheese (in the case of ewes). Formerly in decline because of its lack of monetary value, the llama has regained considerable importance in the domestic economy since the end of the twentieth century: today, llama meat finds outlets on the regional markets owing to the joint influence of promotional campaigns conducted by rural development organisations and of demand from the booming tourism sector. A local survey carried out in 1986 showed that the herds of Chalguamayoc had five times as many sheep as llamas. Today, their numbers are roughly equal, thus showing the influence of market outlets on herding strategies. At present, the herds of the most prosperous families have no more than 400 head of animals, all species combined. Medium-size herds have from 100 to 150 head. Below 50, the animals' rate of reproduction barely suffices to feed a small domestic unit (a couple with one or two children); above 200 head, the herd becomes difficult to manage and endows its owner with a privileged social status.

Although animal husbandry is their mainstay, households usually combine several productive activities – farming, crafts and sale of labour – all of which manifest an ideal of self-sufficiency. This is a strategy to cope with the risks of bad weather conditions or an unfavourable economic context. It was to ensure such economic security that my neighbour Lola constantly insisted that I grow some vegetables: 'Sow! That way, when you don't have any money, you still have something to eat.' Nevertheless, in the higher lands of Chalguamayoc, weather conditions threaten vegetable growing, with the exception of root crops, quinoa and broad beans. These are cultivated in small quantities during the wet season. Weaving and knitting wool from llamas and sheep is widespread. It is nonetheless in regression, first because the new generations prefer synthetic clothing imported from the urban market to garments made from natural wool, but also because the extremely long process of production turns out not to be profitable for sales on the regional market. Furthermore, the many public allowances provide households with a minimal stable financial income,[5] which makes extra craft or agricultural efforts not worthwhile to shepherds. Such public allowances are massively criticised, since domestic production is appreciated as part of a broader social obligation to perpetuate 'the elders' customs'. As a result, people see themselves as becoming *vagos* (lazy), a dangerous vice to which I shall return later.

Although the composition of the household shifts according to life cycle and the productive capacities of each member, it is always possible to identify who is part of it at a certain point in time: *compartir la hoya* (share the pot) is the key act in epitomising household membership. Shared consumption in this light is posited as an instantiation of family ties, and indeed repeated nurturing with identical food creates kinship. As essential practices in the formation of self, what and how much people eat daily is a basic act also framing their relatedness. In the country, Kolla are very keen on insisting that they eat a lot. They comment on the huge meal they ingest for breakfast, which features dishes that are served as lunch to Creoles. Eating abundantly potentially produces fat, which is seen as the prime sign of good health, while thin people are regarded as weak and prone to sickness, if not already ill. Plump persons are qualified as *guapas* (lit. good looking or brave), which encapsulates an aesthetic appreciation imbued with moral value and productive potential. This is a requirement for being a good peasant, since the value-loaded activities of taking care of plants and animals all day long require expending the energy needed to hike the mountains and resist climatic instabilities. The moral and physical values of the herder are indeed entangled with the *fuerza* (strength) he is able to devote to the growth of other species. Beside quantities, peasants also insist that they consume food primarily from their own production. Ingredients grown locally are seen to be more healthy and nutritious than those coming from industries or extensive agriculture in the lowland. When eating their own meat and vegetables, people consider that they are making the most of the energy they have spent in their fields, thus accumulating fuerza to raise further plants and animals.

### Indispensable Alliances within the Kinship Network

Every domestic unit is embedded in a network of allies composing what Nathan Wachtel identifies as 'the first circle of gift-giving and reciprocity' (1990:112). Among these, some may have been affiliated with the household in the past, as in the case of brothers and sisters. Nephews, uncles and direct cousins make up the group of *parientes* (kin) among whom these alliances are established by preference. Unlike the household, this network of privileged relationships is more shifting and diffuse: new members may be brought in, while others may leave, according to the evolution of the quality of social and economic complicity. The kinship relations at the source of these networks confer on the patronym an effect of aggregation. Even if these allies do not bear the name directly, they can trace a genealogical link back to a common ancestor, thus establishing different poles of preferential cooperation within the community. The death of an elder brings together the alliance network that has been established in the defunct's line. At this point, the allies find themselves gathered to ensure, through the funeral rites, the diffusion of the energy of the deceased's person among their membership.

Blood ties can be vehicles of both animosity and indulgence and thus constitute a potential but not obligatory channel for social and economic affinity. In a tone of confession consented to by his guests, Nicolás, who had kin in the country but had himself settled in La Quiaca, sadly observed: 'Relatives are worse [than strangers]. There seems to be a sort of egotism between people. If someone has [something], the others are going to want to take it away.' Companionship between kin is thus initiated on a personal and voluntary basis. When descent or alliance kinship serve as base for social and economic complicity, the partners call each other by their kin relationship: *Tío* (Uncle) or *Tía* (Aunt), as well as *Abuelo* and *Abuela*, are used for naming cherished elders.

Between such privileged allies, there grows a generous reciprocity thanks to which goods and services circulate without need for strict accounting. It is through *ayuda* (help) that gifts of labour are made. No retribution is stipulated, but social etiquette calls for an equivalent availability when the partner requests it. Yet, when prestations are transgenerational, elders are not expected to reciprocate equivalent effort. There is no deadline for the return, which does not necessarily consist in an identical job. A festive meal tops off these jobs, preferably composed of grilled meat and maize beer, known as chicha. On these occasions, the household head also provides coca leaves and wine designed to replenish the workers' energy and to please the telluric forces invoked for the successful realisation of the task at hand. This provides a festive connotation to collective work. The entanglement of collective work and celebration is verbalised by the use of the term *invitación* to refer to the request made by the beneficiary of the work. The allies who answer the call are indistinctly termed *ayudantes* (assistants) or *invitados* (guests). This is in contrast to potential ayudantes who are contracted for the day and remunerated in money. The latter are not invitados; they might be called *peón* (labourer) instead. They do not necessarily enjoy the festive meal with the guests, eating as they do when they are allowed to take a break.

More exceptionally, invitation between these cherished kin involves raw food transferred through reciprocal gifts of the partners' respective productions. Isabela, who used to give food to her impoverished sister-in-law, glossed: 'I give meat to Angelica. Sometimes she comes and asks for her children. So I invite her . . . Afterwards she offers what she picks.' However, invitation made of raw food is secondary in this circle of appreciated kin within a shared community. Because they engage in broadly similar productive activities, they usually do not covet their respective produce.

Even though invitation and ayuda are favoured, monetary exchange is not precluded between kin. It is even most appreciated when one of the parties trades in commodities; his partner will do him the favour of buying from him first. In turn, the seller will try to place these transactions in a general framework of generosity. For instance, when we were celebrating Carnival at the home of Telesforo and Sylberia, the sister-in-law Andrea appeared looking for alcohol. To get to the house, she had taken a path that was twice as long as the one that would have taken her to Aurelia, who sells a few items from her house in the middle of the village. When she arrived, Sylberia served her a dish of stew, and when she left, she gave her a few stuffed buns to share with her children. Andrea in turn took a few camomile flowers from her bundle because she knew that Sylberia had not planted any that year. In this context, monetary transactions are engaged as a favour to the seller. Harris describes an opposite situation where cash is accepted from kin as a favour to them. However, both examples speak to the fact that that the circulation of money between kin is not a moral infringement. The clientele networks of the grocery stores officially installed in the countryside – in contrast to those in Chalguamayoc, which strongly resemble a household larder – also overlap with the alliance network. Social affinities largely influence the choice of one or the other, giving rise to an economic cooperation that in turn fuels these alliance networks.

Being able to gather an important crew of allies, for feasting or working, is the means and the sign of a household's prosperity. It is morally appreciated as the manifestation of their members' virtue as good persons. Although the circle of allies hints at positive moral values, social interactions are of course less predictable than this portrait suggests. Conflict is another dimension of kin complicities, aroused by possible stinginess, laziness, incest, domestic violence and other blamed behaviours. While normatively proscribed, *envidia* is always susceptible to come out between relatives. Envidia can be translated as envy or jealousy, but in this context, it refers to a political act intended to diminish the potential of a prosperous person. Sabino, who wanted to start a business selling llama 'ham' using the money he had saved from his most recent stay in Patagonia, preferred to move away from Chalguamayoc and set up his business in La Quiaca for fear of incurring such a fate. When I asked why he intended to leave his flock to settle in the city, he replied: 'It's hard to prosper here [in Chalguamayoc]. Envidia interferes.' Because of the malicious words it sparks, envy is said to be the cause of *mal de aire* (lit. bad air). Through a powerful stare, or a malignant blast of air, victims of envidia will become unlucky, weak or ill, or even die. In addition to curses and stares, jealousy can be enacted through refusal to cooperate or engage in material transaction, which has the direct effect of shrinking the victim's space-time of influence. Envidia thus provides a template of subversive value transformation, in the sense of Munn (1986).

In this light, envidia stands in opposition to the circulation of labour and agricultural produce and, to a lesser extent, manufactured

products that bolsters favourable kinship. As a mark of trust and subjective appreciation, material transfers are fundamental components
of a positive sociability. This is of course the case of reciprocal invitations, but it is also true of selling and barter, in so far as they arise as
a sign of generosity prompted by the quality of the underlying social
relationship. In contrast to envidia, such generous transactions oper-
ate a positive value transformation as they create moral subjects and
flourishing economies.

### The Community: Collective Labour and Rivalries

Like other peasant communities, those in the Andes are usually depicted as clusters of cooperation. In the Argentinean cordillera, communal belonging involves a series of economic rights and obligations
that gather its member into a shared social entity. As described earlier,
herders and cultivators are bound together by the rhythm and movement drawn by their daily activities of care for the human, vegetal and
animal kin within their domestic units. Being part of a shared community involves sharing common natural resources such as water, grass,
trees or fish. It also involves facing common adversaries like pumas,
glacial winds, overflowing rivers or contagious sickness. In order to
cope with these aggressive opponents, co-villagers join their energies
to build infrastructure, draw limits, or organise missions to protect
cherished beings from potential dangers.

The president of the community is entitled to rally their people to
partake in collective labour intended to cope with adversities. Importantly, such intensive collaboration usually concludes with festivities
where the participants share food and music. The organisation of the
patron saint's celebration described earlier is an example of such collective work. Yearly rodeos to round up escaped donkeys or pumas
and foxes provide other exemplary manifestations of communal mobilisation, when neighbours patrol the edges of their territory to expel
unwanted visitors. Herders also agree on dates for parasite removal,
when all the llamas are forced one by one to enter the communal bath
reserved for this purpose. The community regularly gathers to maintain their path, river bed, herd vaccination bath, rodeo enclosures and
the like. The cleaning of irrigation canals is another task requiring collective efforts for shared benefits. It is nonetheless noteworthy that,
in these herding communities, canal cleaning does not have the ceremonial and political importance it bears in the lowland. Communities
also engage in the building of major constructions such as schools,
chapels, roads or assembly halls.

Nowadays, such constructions are triggered by programmes channelling the public budget to the community in the form of wages and materials. Generally, the distribution of government allowances and resources made available by development institutions plays a crucial role in the organisation of community work. This circulation engenders instrumental relations with the administrative community, giving rise to serious conflicts between potential beneficiaries, who thus find themselves vying for funds. Via the distribution of resources he has managed to attract to his village, the president builds a clientele that he will be able to mobilise when the time comes. Inversely, dissatisfied members may turn their back on him. I remember hearing that a community member had refused to cook for the Saint Mark's feast because the mattresses she had been promised in the end went to a neighbour. Critiquing dependency to the state for engaging collective tasks, elders complain that the younger generations fail to collaborate on communal work, recalling proudly how their generation built important infrastructures without waiting for government support.

Community presidents also complain that it is becoming increasingly complicated to gather a workforce within their community. This is, they say, because communities are not as united as they used to be – a social value they are keen on mentioning to convince reluctant people. Francisco motivated the assembled villagers, hesitant to commit to a collective construction, in the following terms: 'Each person must do their bit. Each person must get involved. We are a community. You know very well what that means. It doesn't mean each person doing their own thing. We must work together.' Working together is thus not only a way of getting an infrastructure built. Such activities are also appreciated as an instantiation of social values. Beyond their economic instrumentality, the accomplishment of collective activities also participates in the creation of the community's renown, triggering the admiration of other localities. I mentioned earlier that one of the stakes involved in the patron saint's feast was to demonstrate the community's prodigality by inviting people, and this required joint efforts in logistics, cooking, dancing and sporting events. While this is a remarkable occasion to display communal unity and performance, other less notable cooperation also raised comments in surrounding villages. Everyone knows where people gather for rodeos, canal cleaning, Mother Earth offerings and the like. Such communities prompt regional admiration, and their names circulate as an example of social cohesion.

Social cohesion within the community is indeed a force that is constantly undermined by political competition and inter-domestic attacks because the community is also the theatre of daily conflicts around the management of economic resources. Clearly, even though the community crystallises around the key value of cooperation, it is also penetrated by conflict and enmities. These sometimes oppose kin groups articulated around a family name. They also bring into conflict household descendants with the same surname. Since, as mentioned earlier, close parents do not necessarily get along, filiation does not involve socio-economic complicities. So, while the community is seen as a homogenous entity from the outside, it is actually composed of an array of social relations varying in their affective and economic potential. In this sense, the community's boundary cannot be identified with a specific way of circulating labour and goods. The sense of solidarity and generosity crumble at the boundary of the circle of allies described above. This circle can, however, extend beyond the community to include friends and kin from other villages.

### The Intercommunity Space and Valley Partners: Measured Reciprocity

The zones specialised in the production of food products lacked by the herders lie beyond the community space: to find the maize that completes their daily diet and the ritual dishes, herders are obliged to leave the puna, cross the transitional zone and enter the adjacent lowlands. Among the places around Chalguamayoc, Barrios, Suripujio and Inti Cancha are known as villages of herders; Casti, Lecho, Yavi and San José, for growing cereals, fava beans and potatoes; Yavi Chico, Portillo, La Falda and Yanalpa, for growing maize. Each sector also engages in the activity of the adjacent zone as a secondary practice. The success of these subsidiary undertakings is nevertheless limited by the ecological restrictions that increase the risk of bad harvests and discourage increasing the scope of these residual activities. In order to obtain the complementary goods, herders instead have recourse to networks of barter embracing the different production zones. Since each community produces a distinctive speciality, the peasants move around from village to village in search of these valuable goods. That is where they can be sure of finding the most advantageous exchange rates but also the greatest variety and quality of products. The peasants' recognition of these specialisations shapes the local monopolies of the goods that flourish in each sector, thus contributing to create relations of preferential dependence and in turn the economic identity of each community.

The inhabitants of Chalguamayoc take their cheese and meat to Casti and get their cereals and potato there; they also go to Yavi Chico

**Figure 1.2.** Landscape of the quebrada in Tupiza, Bolivia, where ecological conditions are propitious for the cultivation of maize and fruits. Photograph by the author.

for maize. In each of these villages, specialised in products they consume, they have preferential partners owing to the favourable conditions of exchange they are offered. These exchange circuits piggyback preferably on permanent alliances. Julia, a well-known cultivator in Casti, is part of an extensive network of exchanges: her commitment to satisfying those who exchange with her is unanimously appreciated. She explained to me:

> People give me meat, cheese and money too. If I am not at home, they leave the meat so I will pick vegetables, maize, potatoes. I know who it is right away; I start preparing for him. It's because we have acquaintances, friends.

When increased complicity develops between faraway relatives or friends, their ties might be strengthened through the institution of *compadrazgo* (co-parenthood). This is a figure of voluntarily composed kinship network that was imported from Europe to Latin America (Gudeman 1975; Mintz and Wolf 1950). It is usually described as a 'form of ritual kinship established through the rites of the Catholic

Church . . . between a person, his or her biological parents, and his and her godparents' (van den Berghe 2010: 145). Throughout the Andes it became a core institution with important social and economic implications. In the Argentinean cordillera compadrazgo relates an adult sponsor (*padrino* or *madrina*) to a child who becomes his or her *ahijado*. Still more significant is the relationship between the sponsor's couple and the child's parents who become *comadre* and *compadre* to each other. Catholic rituals, such as baptism, confirmation and marriage, are the main opportunities for establishing such ties but other nonecclesiastic opportunities also exist, such as the baptism of a baby bread at All Saints' Day, the first hair cutting or school graduation. Compadrazgo is usually engaged with cherished people who are not closely related by blood filiation or matrimonial alliances (although direct kin are not necessarily precluded). It transforms friendship into a form of kinship expressing the affinities of the couple. In virtue of compadrazgo, people are expected to treat each other as their most cherished kin.

This institution has been qualified by Andean ethnographers as fictive (Mayer 2002: 11; Weismantel 1995: 88), spiritual (Gudeman 1975; Molinié 1975: 42) or ritual (Harris 2007: 74; Lehmann 2007b: 5; Murra 1992: 143; Platt 1986: 244), as compared to the 'real' kinship. I don't see this as a convenient terminology, omitting as it does the practical, and indeed, real dimension of compadrazgo. Compadrazgo is by no means a social fiction, neither is it restricted to a ritual act. We shall see that such ties bear important implications in peasants' social and economic life, which cannot be reduced to a spiritual, ritual or fictive form of relatedness. These qualifications align with a Western perception of a 'real' kinship restricted to genetic filiation and sexual reproduction that is not universal (Carsten 2012) and does not fit with the experience of kinship in the puna.

This voluntary form of kinship is expressed in social relations through the respect conveyed by the use of a specific appellation, through warm interactions and through material generosity. Here is how Mariel described it:

> If you are compadres, you have to show respect. When you see them, you greet them: 'Hello, comadre! Hello, compadre! How are you?' You invite them. If you give a party, you say: 'Fine, let's invite the comadre.' But not because you have to. Or if your comadre needs something . . . For example, my mother's comadre doesn't have a vegetable garden, so she gives her [vegetables]. But naturally, not because she has to. It's to show respect, to ask her for help, to be more sociable. It's like being part of the family.

As Mariel's words suggest, these social relationships are highly praised, and their emotional weight is entangled with the indispensable economic aid they provide in reproducing the household. Like in the circle of close parientes, invitation ideally prevails within compadrazgo. Marcos, a Bolivian cultivator I was in the habit of meeting at an annual fair, explained to me: 'You have to give everything to the comadre. You even take it to her house. You offer beverages, grilled meat. You help her. For instance, if you have many sheep, you take her some wool. And she will give you what she has.'[6] Beside invitations, barter is another appreciated modality of produce circulation within a compadrazgo network. I shall examine this further when addressing the social fabric of fairs.

Although these intercommunity exchanges are regular and common, the portion of produce reserved for direct exchange is residual. In the case of cultivators, half of the harvest is sold on the urban market, 10 per cent is reserved for sowing and the remaining 40 per cent is consumed by the household. It is from this last share that the peasants take what they barter. These goods come to ten or so fifty-pound sacks of potatoes and vegetables. In the case of herders, a household of six consumes a dozen llamas a year and sells around fifteen. A further three or four heads can be reserved for direct exchange for maize, fruits, a few vegetables and chiefly potatoes. These rough figures of course depend on the composition of the households and the complementary resources they have at their disposal.

Labour is another resource giving access to agricultural products not harvested by the household. For instance, some Chalguamayoc villagers walk the four hours to Casti, where they take part in the potato harvests in full swing, while the potatoes planted higher up are still growing. In February, Isabela usually helps harvest potatoes for Julia, who is the wife of her cousin Lucio, so she does not have to buy potatoes while waiting for her own to be ready, in April. On our way back from La Quiaca, where we had gone for supplies, Isabela explained to me: 'People in Casti sow a lot. The neighbours don't want to help [Julia]. Whereas we [in Chalguamayoc] sow little. So, it is in our interest to help. That way, you eat potatoes for free; you don't have to buy any.' It is very common for people of Chalguamayoc to be hosted by kin for several days so that they can participate in agricultural tasks. Their compensation is not calculated according to the labour market. At the time of my research, one day of labour in the field was worth a wicker basket of potatoes at harvest time – the monetary value depending on the potato variety, many of which were just not available on the market. Sowing is not as labour intensive as harvesting, and inter-ecological collaborations are less frequent at this stage. When it happens, one day in the field gives claim to the right to harvest one row of potato plants. While also qualified as ayuda, that kind of collaboration involves an etiquette different from the ayuda described above whereby services are not remunerated in agricultural produce – and reciprocated in labour instead. Because they do not produce likewise, peasants from different communities usually have strong interest in acquiring raw food from their partners, and they usually receive some in gratitude for their help. At the same time, ayudantes from further communities who are tied with compadrazgo receive plenty of cooked food and partake in the festive expression of collective work. They are treated with the same largesse as the local kin.

Shoring up the exchange of agricultural produce with labour is a strategy documented in other cultures, where the economy is marked by ecological specialisation (Barnes and Barnes 1989: 407; Cellarius 2000: 85). Across the Andes, labour is used to access goods that are not produced in one's own ecological tier, or goods that are produced but grow slowly according to climatic conditions. Harris (2007) has described similar modalities of circulation of labour between ecological tiers in the Laymi territory in Bolivia. In central Peru, Cesar Fonseca observed a collective duty to offer hospitality to members of other ecological niches looking for products lacking in their own territory (1972: 330). This involves welcoming their help in the fields in exchange for raw food. Likewise, Enrique Mayer describes services of *allapakuy* ('to help harvest', in Quechua) as a moral obligation between peasants of different ecological tiers (2002: 149). These are long-term agreements between communities, whose members gain the possibility to access the produce of the other community in times of need. In the contemporary puna, the agreement is not established at the communal level: it is an inter-household system of complicities based on friendship, possibly but not necessarily articulated on kin networks.

Adults remember having seen their elders leave the village with their donkeys loaded with meat and wool and then come back several days or weeks later with a selection of fruits and maize. They also remember partners from the valley coming to their house to propose their goods. Local hospitality included feeding the partners and their animal companions during their stay. Equally important was accepting to slaughter a few animals to exchange for the cereals and fruits brought by their valley partner so as to provide them with the meat that motivated their expedition. In this respect, Telesforo told me proudly that he was known beyond the puna to be predisposed to slaughter animals and make visitors' endeavour successful. He saw this as a way of appreciating their effort to travel from distant ecological niches. Willingness to barter in this context is depicted as an act of generosity and hospitality. Conversely, some valley people were remembered as good persons for being eager to welcome herders' help on their parcel when the latter would travel at harvest time to obtain maize or potatoes in exchange for labour.

These long trips have become the exception, owing in particular to the increasing number of motorised vehicles that make it easier to travel to the market in the city. As the elders tell it, these exchange trips were what remained of bigger caravans that, until the mid-twentieth century, connected the puna with the Bolivian valleys of Talina, the tropical forests of Santa Victoria and the salt flats of Susques. Telesforo evoked such spectacular journeys with emotion when recalling how many households he was acquainted with in regions as far away as the Salinas of Susques or the lower valleys of Santa Victoria, insisting that he had even gone as far as the city of Orán in the province of Salta. Older and mature men's reminiscences of the journey they engaged in decades ago speak to their pride of having travelled across great distances, experiencing an array of climates and ecologies – the further the village, the higher the appreciation of the venture. Differences in landscape, altitude or administrative jurisdiction are mentioned to highlight the alterity of the places reached. These narrations further account for the social complicities they were able to establish in unknown communities, where year after year they were hosted. When complicity intensifies, partners could agree to extend their networks of compadrazgo to faraway zones where it was possible to produce different foodstuffs. These inter-ecological alliances will be explored further when examining the social fabric of cambio, and its potential to extend subjectivities in space and time.

Since llama and donkey caravans aimed at procuring exotic items have nearly disappeared, these cambio take place exclusively through isolated inter-household exchanges or during the fairs that will be described later. Although they are relatively insignificant in terms of the amount of produce involved, they remain fundamental to how peasants conceptualise their regional economy. This is illustrated in the following extract from a speech given by the leader of the valley community of Chosconty during the monthly meeting: 'The quebrada has always needed products from the puna. And the puna needs the quebrada as well . . . We share the same culture, the same tradition and the same customs.' This dependence confers a sense of moral duty to inter-ecological exchanges. It also hints at the prevalence of a dualist conception of economic and social organisation, in which highland

and lowland economies are complementary. This complementarity between ecological niches is acknowledged in the literature as the cornerstone of the Andean economy (Lehmann [1982] 2007b; Masuda et al. 1985; Murra 1972a). However, in the Argentinean region, where peasants regularly participate in a market economy, inter-ecological reciprocities no longer constitute the mainstay of rural organisation.

## The Markets beyond the Peasant Economy

Although people in the countryside continue their agricultural activities, and their economic identity stems from this production, domestic units also derive a steady income from periodic migrations and public allowances. Moreover, in the highlands, herders regularly travel to the nearest town to sell llama and sheep meat at the market butchers', while, during the harvest season, cultivators bring their vegetables to the central market, where they improvise stalls.

Usually, the money earned is immediately exchanged for the industrial foodstuffs that have become part of the peasant diet over the course of the twentieth century (mainly dried pasta, rice, wheat flour, sugar, tea and oil). These products, called *mercaderías* (lit. merchandises) are purchased in the shops surrounding the market. Many shopkeepers in town have kin relationships with the rural Argentinean and Bolivian communities from where they, or their parents, originally come. However, their urban settlement and economic ascension distinguish them from their rural kin, and their ethnic identity is particularly vague. Although the term cholas, who as 'sellers appear Indian to whites and white to the Indians', is not part of the local repertoire of identities, I could see many commonalities between the mainly female sellers in the markets of La Quiaca and Villazón, and the social configurations outlined in other Andean markets (Weismantel 2001: 90; see also Seligmann 1993). In the country, they usually have the same poor reputation as other urban merchants. Peasants consider their market transactions to be unfair because they have no say over the value of their meat and must accept the prices dictated by the vendors.

Growing inflation in Argentina makes these prices volatile, which is interpreted as a great injustice: herders always wonder how much their meat is worth and whether they will be able to fulfil their basic needs with their earnings. However, national inflation does not in itself justify peasants' reluctance towards market transactions since, in the past decade, the price of llama and sheep meat has risen more than that of other meats and vegetables because of increased demand from tourist markets. If peasants continue to interpret market transactions as asymmetrical, it is because they observe that merchants enrich themselves more than they do, while at the same time they struggle to produce food in the harsh living conditions of the countryside. Moreover, stories about shopkeepers cheating constantly circulate in the village: peasants are aware that they are seen as illiterate and simple minded when they navigate the market, and therefore they feel like they are a target for the vendors' chicanery. With this reciprocal stigmatisation as a backdrop, interactions in shops are usually furtive, and verbal exchanges are restricted to basic economic considerations. Barter is not accepted at grocery shops, although some market sellers engage in barter when only small quantities are involved. In this case, equivalences are established based on market prices. Note that such transactions are not acknowledged as cambio. Until I observed nonmonetary transactions myself, I received many negative replies when enquiring about the possibility of engaging barter at the market.

In the midst of this suspicious environment, some merchants prefer to establish long-term relationships with their regular clients. To this end, they treat them as *caseros* (lit. from the house), ideally situated at the interface between clients and friends.[7] They wrap the economic interaction in friendly conversation aimed at personalising the relationship. In this context, the merchant may also do his client favours by selling on credit, making special prices or accepting barter. Such was the case of a coca seller from La Paz, who had furnished her cramped store with small chairs on which her clients were invited to sit until she served them. Even if she sometimes mixed them up, she tried to greet her clients by name and ask about their family. Her guests would do likewise.

When I accompanied Telesforo and Sylberia to do their shopping in town, we always stopped by her shop. 'Hi, casera. How is your grandson doing?' Telesforo would ask, sitting happily surrounded by huge bags of coca leaves. They continued chatting as the woman carefully packed the portions ordered by her clients. In the meantime, the latter chewed coca they had received when entering the shop. A few weeks later, when looking for Telesforo, I asked his casera: 'I'm looking for Telesforo Benitez. You know who I'm talking about?' 'Yes', she replied. 'I know him; he's my client.' This reciprocal relationship entails mutual fidelity between the partners. The day we found the door closed, Telesforo was worried about where else he could purchase his monthly provision, even though several shops displayed huge bags of coca leaves in the very same street.

With this personalised treatment, the sellers nurture their business, while the buyers protect themselves against being cheated, a permanent threat weighing on economic interactions between strangers. The resulting relational figure contrasts sharply with the 'impersonal, stereotypical, brief and strictly business oriented' (Mayer 2002: 163) relationship binding those transactors who do not know each other. Such kindness confers a positive moral value on market transactions and transfigures the imaginary of the greedy merchant prevailing in how peasants view the extra-ethnic economy.

While people in the country travel regularly to the city for economic, health and administrative purposes, many Kolla people have settled in cities all around Argentina from the closest, Jujuy, to Buenos Aires or Comodoro Rivadavia in Patagonia. Many stayed in the lowland of Salta and Jujuy, voluntarily working on plantations after forced labour was abolished in 1950. Others migrated more recently in search of the greater comfort and consumption promised by urban life. Some travel for seasons of agricultural harvest or for temporary contracts in factories or on construction sites; others have accepted a permanent job and only come back to their home village for holidays. Furthermore, common among those who have resisted the massive movement of urban immigration are members of the community who divide their time between the village and the city. Most families living in Chalguamayoc own or rent a home either in La Quiaca or on the outskirts of San Salvador de Jujuy. These places of passages enable the peasants to sell their produce or carry out administrative processes. In addition to their sporadic use, these dwellings are generally occupied by adolescents attending school in town.

Migration is such an important part of Kolla social fabric that every household spreads ties thousands of miles away from their house. Even though they miss the people who have left, they are very proud to mention the remote cities where they could find refuge in case of need. And indeed, many country people come to need it at some point, either to gather money for their young people or to consult doctors for their elders. Kolla identity therefore entails 'a complex continuum of urban-rural life ways' that prevails in many Andean contexts (Wroblewski 2014: 67; see also Colloredo-Mansfeld 1999; Ødegaard 2010). Even if they are constantly in contact with urban life, those who keep their main residence in the country lament the desertion of their kin and the new lifestyle they adopt in the city, which they see as overwhelmed by immoral ecological, material and social values. Notwithstanding a fascination for imported fashion and technologies, the agricultural lifestyle remains an economic and ethical ideal for most country people.

## Criar and Practices of Prosperity

### Pachamama, Holy Earth

Throughout the Andes, peasants pay homage to Pachamama. An ambivalent telluric deity, purveyor of the life force, she is both the Earth[8] and the liveliness that makes it fertile. In the Argentinean cordillera, she is the emblematic figure of the telluric powers, and all offerings designed to regenerate the life forces are addressed to her. Unlike other parts of the cordillera, the communities here no longer worship Pachatata (Father Earth) or the powerful Apus who are mountain deities incarnated in the summits overlooking their territory. If the surrounding mountains are effectively imbued with agency, it is under the generic name of Pachamama that these forces are worshipped. Other deified figures – some of which are recognised by the Catholic Church – are nonetheless engaged in life flourishing and prosperity in the puna, alongside Pachamama. According to Lola's list, one can beg the favours of 'the Earth, God, the Virgin, the saints and the little souls [of deceased ancestors]'. People pray to one or another, depending on their preference and on the circumstances prompting their orisons. The only requirement is to formulate one's request con fe (with faith).

God, Jesus Christ and the Virgin Mary are solicited for everything. I mentioned above that the saints are preferably called forth in a chosen field indicated by wonders ascribed to them in accounts of saints' lives. Nevertheless, the respective identifications of these figures are not mutually exclusive. Some saints protect animals, which are also the responsibility of Mother Earth, while others are associated with natural phenomena embodied by the figures of the Andean pantheon. God is regarded as the universal Father. A father, he is called Tata (lit. patriarch), like the sun, who was a powerful god from whom the Incas claimed to descend. Beyond this diversity, Mother Earth, closely associated with the image of the Virgin Mary, remains the divine figure emblematic of fertility. She appears as the vehicle of all forms of fecundity considered to result from the diffusion of the breath of life; this is why prayers and offerings are made to her at the different stages of production, consumption and distribution.

The challa is the primordial offering to Pachamama, expressing gratitude and a request for abundance. It can be a few drops, preferably of alcohol, discretely sprinkled on the ground before drinking. Or it can be a series of more liberal libations: in this case, the object one wants to grow is sprinkled with beer, wine or chicha by the protagonists, who

chew coca while making their wishes known. Bigger celebrations require a *corpachada,* an offering of food and drink poured into a hole in
the ground. Commensality with Mother Earth is continued by a meal
shared among the participants, who partake of dishes defined by the
specific ritual context. Grilled meat with kernels of boiled maize (*asado
con choclo*) are served at Carnival and Christmas, the same grilled
meat (*asado*) with boiled kernels of dried maize (*mote*) for the branding of animals and patronal feasts, the feet and heads of sheep or llamas with boiled kernels of dry maize (*tistincha*) for family saints and
soup made from dried meat (*charqui*) and pounded maize (*kalapurca*)
for All Saints' Day and the feast of Pachamama. Strikingly, all these
meals combine produce from different ecological niches: meat from
the highlands, maize from the lowlands and potatoes from the intermediate zone. The combination of meat with maize and potatoes to
produce ritual meals is recurrent throughout the Andes (Fonseca 1972:
330; see also Harris 2007: 82). Ideally, these collective meals precede
the dancing and singing of *coplas* (couplets) designed to delight the
fecundating powers. Spurred on by the effects of alcohol, the passion
of the valiant, light-footed dancers appears as a mark of generosity,
a gift of themselves in return for the life-giving power dispensed by
Pachamama. The stamping dances are therefore designed to stimulate
her fertility, thus using the entertainment to channel economic prosperity to the benefit of the festivity's organisers.

Successful offerings also require the circulation of nonmaterial values. Worshippers must be affectively engaged in the ceremony. *Alegría*
(joy) is a key ingredient of most rituals intended to regenerate life forces.
'Pachamama likes everybody to be cheerful. That's what is needed for
Pachamama', I was told when helping Lola to make her offerings. Body
movement and vocal sounds are essential carriers of alegría. Their most
appreciated expression is dancing and singing, acts that are both enhanced by the consumption of food and alcohol. Harris observed in her
Bolivian fieldwork that the combination of antagonistic emotions is a
common ritual prescription (2000: 42). Harris's point takes on relevance
when scrutinising the gloomy tone and lyrics of the coplas on death,
broken couples and lost countries. The *contrapunto* style, whereby a
man and a woman successively reply to each other, is explicitly meant
to arouse gender oppositions. However, in contrast to Harris's point on
the combination of opposite emotions, the display of sadness remains
an exception, prescribed in mourning or ecclesiastic processions, and
alegría is emphasised as a necessary ingredient to all offerings.

In any case, challas and corpachadas are intended to increase the
prosperous potential of Pachamama's dwellers, including human. Peo-

ple have an individual *fuerza*, which is a life force enabling them to perform an activity with assiduity and perseverance. Such strength is similar to the flows described by Gudeman with the same words, in Panama and in the Colombian cordillera, where it 'is the energy that people need and use in all of life's doings. . . . the energy of life – that humans must have to live' (2012: 60). Strength is maintained by the daily ingestion of different kinds of ingredients. Alcohol and coca leaves are seen as very powerful in this regard, along with local foods such as meat, maize and potatoes. This is in contrast to industrial foods, decried for only providing reduced energy resources and therefore not adapting to agricultural labour. A more stable flow of strength is expected from worshiped spiritual and telluric entities, including God, Pachamama and closer ancestors. As Harris (2000: 28) noted, since precolonial times, ancestors have ranked high in the Indigenous pantheon, and they bestow strength, good fortune and prosperity on those who worship them.

Lack of strength, by contrast, causes slackness and the incapacity to bring energy to productive tasks. Such a vice is collectively acknowledged as provoking discontent in telluric beings, who might in this case absorb the lazy person's vital forces, resulting in a negative impact on their daily economic productivity. In this respect, resting in a field instead of caring for animals and plants is seen as potentially dangerous, since people might be *agarrado* (caught) by the Earth during their sleep. If not *comido* (eaten up), they will at least be *asustado* (scared) by Pachamama via a nearby natural entity (a tree, a stone, a pond). *Susto* is a very common pathology throughout the Andes, wherein the victim loses their *ánimo* under the assault of another living entity. Commonly used throughout the Andes, ánimo refers to both spiritual and physical forces. It is thus the source of personal agency and productive potential; not specifically human, all living beings capable of growth and reproduction are imbued with it.

Pachamama is not the only one who can extract ánimo from human beings. Any angry ancestor can diminish a person's vitality if they feel offended by the person's behaviour. As a result, ánimo is extracted from the body, progressively depriving the person of physical energy and social identity, and eventually leading to death. The relationship between laziness, telluric beings' retaliation and physical health points to a moral economy whereby working for the growth and reproduction of the Earth's inhabitants is not merely an economic necessity: it is also a moral duty to fellow humans and other living organisms, including powerful beings incarnated in the environment. This conceptualisation of human vitality underscores humans' relatedness to their environment, seen as the chief source of both 'danger and prosperity' (Ødegaard 2011), of life and death. In this sense, the distribution of the life force ultimately depends on unpredictable powers; 'it is a contingent gift of the Divinity' (Gudeman 2012: 62).

## Pachamama's Areas of Influence

Herders in Chalguamayoc lean on Pachamama for the success of all activities connected with the growth of beings in the world. They use the term *criar* (to raise, cultivate, nourish) to refer to those practices that maintain or increase the vitality animating the entities that compose Mother Earth. Those who want to win her favour diligently cultivate this vitality by maintaining the diversity of these entities and ensuring their well-being. Peasants' economic and physical welfare is bound up with their willingness to care for beings around them; to generously nurture the mutual relations with the entities that contribute to a sound physical and social life. When a person cares for those beings and phenomena that descend from the original ancestor, Pachamama, they also ensure that she will care for them in return. Failure to take care is, on the contrary, a threat to human life. As the saying goes, 'the Earth breeds us, the Earth eats us'[9]. Pachamama is an ambivalent power indeed, which increases the urgency to maintain smooth relations with her.

Among Pachamama's descendants are the different animal species, including those bred by the herders. The worshipful gestures prescribed at the critical junctures of the breeding cycle attest to this. The newborns are welcomed by a challa aimed at promoting their growth. Likewise, slaughter is a time for offerings and prayers designed to revive the herd's fertility despite the consumption. The suited gestures for this differ from one family to the next. According to Sylberia and Telesforo: 'Before slaughtering, you have to pour a bit of wine on the enclosure gate. Then we drink and that's it. Catch [the animal] and kill [it].' Lola, on the other hand, proceeds as follows: 'You chat a moment with Pachamama. You talk, you chew coca and there you have it, you go and catch [the animal].' Others make the animal drink facing the rising sun and fill its mouth with a generous bunch of coca leaves before cutting its throat. Wishes can be expressed at that time, such as 'may we have a better herd' or 'may [animals] cover the mountain'.

In addition to being expected to reward those who raise their herd with diligence and affection, Pachamama is a privileged interlocutrice for entering into communication with the animals: she acts as a mediator each time the herder needs to ensure their tranquillity. For their undertaking to meet with success, the herders solicit the Earth so that she will promote the docility of the herd. Before starting to vaccinate his llamas, Telesforo assured me: 'Yesterday evening, Grandma [Sylberia] has been talking with the Earth so that the animals would be docile.' In addition to talking to her, his wife had presented Earth with incense smoke, wine, alcohol and coca 'so that she would be pleased'.

The authority manifested in husbandry is a fundamental point that distinguishes humans from the animal world. 'We [humans] give the orders, not the parsley', exclaimed an indignant Lola to a balky goat, using the image of the obvious submission of the plant kingdom to affirm human primacy in the raising of stock. Nevertheless, I mentioned in the previous section that this supremacy over animals is always shaky: when a herder fails in imposing their will, they end up vencidos. Hence, the herders must constantly reassert their authority through physical exercises. The case of the llamas, living at the interface of the domestic and the wild spaces, is eloquent. They are skilled at circumventing their master's orders and, by in turn obliging him in to respect their intentions, these animals temporarily deprive him of the authority that distinguishes the status of the *criador* (lit. raiser or breeder).

Furthermore, the herders warn of telluric beings' potential to endow the llamas with their power, thus inviting humans to treat them with circumspection. 'Llamas can do *brujeria* [witchcraft]', they acknowledge. In this context, the animal's status is the equivalent of the most powerful human beings, the *medicos caseros* (lit. doctor of the house), who, too, possess powers of witchcraft inherited from ancestors and other entities dwelling in the environment. Standing at the interface between the domestic and the wild, llamas can channel forces of evil or good by means of brujeria. Earth is therefore asked for her help in taming these animals; at the same time, she is capable of punishing people who show lack of affection by mistreating them. Those who leave their animals in distress would thus run the risk of suffering in turn. As Maria, a young Yavi shepherd, warned me, if you neglect your animals, 'They become sad. They weep on you. It is as if they were cursing at you, and then, after a while, you end up sad yourself. Any time you make your animals suffer, they weep on you, they curse at you.' When an animal curses the shepherd, the latter risks losing their vitality, or ánimo. In this sense, animals impact the most intimate part of their breeders and therefore play an important role in the formation of the peasant's subjectivity.

In certain respects, the relationship that grows up with cultivated plant species resembles that between the herders and their herds. The notion of criar applies to the care of plants as well, since this requires not only daily attention in the form of watering and weeding but also affective, verbal and gestural communication. The seeds, too, are personalised. They must be sown in pairs so that they will reproduce under the joint effect of the fecundating telluric powers and the person who places them in the ground at the same time transmitting the energy of their life breath. Children are seen as particularly powerful for this task. These seeds then give birth to the plants and roots, known as *señores* or *señoras* (lit. sir or madam) when they reach a respectable size. Growers concern themselves with the welfare and feelings experienced by their plants. They pay great attention to their vegetables, cereals and potatoes becoming sad or happy, getting sick and getting well, mostly by scrutinizing the growth and colour of their foliage. In addition to composing favourable ecological conditions, growers are expected to provide a warm affective climate, even after they are harvested. Each species aspires, for instance, to be stored and cooked with others of its kind: 'Give me this lonely one. He's gonna cry', worried little Marylin as she saw we had neglected a bean while cooking a soup.

Of course, vegetal growth is also seen as resulting from Pachamama's fertilising power. Her contribution to agricultural work is solicited with offerings. Lola remembered how her grandmother used to treat the Earth:

> So nice! I experienced these customs when I was a child. My grandmother brought everything for Pachamama. With a bunch of flowers, she used to decorate everything with flowers, roses, dahlias . . . all these things she used to bring. And she gave her food, libations. Mmmm, we used to do it so nicely. . . . Now some people do it, others don't. They sow with wine, with beer, whatever. They do the challa and that's it. In the past, chicha was the main [offering]. Seeds also need a challa. You must give them good food.

As in other parts of the Andes, access to mineral resources is also recognised as depending on the good will of the telluric and chthonian powers. Teleforo's story of the shutdown of the silver mine overlooking Chalguamayoc attests to this dependence: 'The people [miners] have already gone. The Earth threw them out. She wanted the Creoles[10] to work there. They [the outsiders who exploited the mine] didn't give her what she wanted – some wine, a bit of grilled meat, everything. So [Earth] took [the mine] away.' In this vein, the discovery of raw silver is related to Pachamama's good will, and, when one acquires some, it is then treated a source of fertility: accordingly, the old people used to bury their silver in a treasure box near their house.

**Figure 1.3.** Offering asking Pachamama to protect the integrity of a truck or even to increase its value through time. Photograph by the author.

Pachamama's influence extends beyond the mineral and agricultural domain, however. She impacts the vitality of inorganic entities as well, such as manufactured goods. The common practice of pouring libations on industrial machines so that they will not break down attests to the fact that they are also endowed with some kind of vitality. A radio, a mobile phone or a car can also receive challa to keep them from deteriorating or, even better, so the household will soon have a second similar or even better one. The day Mariel saw my new kitchen stove, she invited me to follow her example: 'I sprinkle everything so that they last for years.' Such offerings take a spectacular turn at Carnival. I will describe later the festivities performed for animals at this time, but all goods can be sprinkled – whole houses and shops even. After the wine and the beer, their owner showers them with confetti, serpentines, candies, coca and talcum powder. At Mardi Gras, whole communities gather alongside their motor vehicles, which are sprinkled all over by their owners who dance around them to the music of a *cumbia* band. 'May you have a brand new one by next year!' shouted the brother of the owner of a dilapidated taxi with exaltation, when I participated in the 2008 ceremony in Yavi. 'May he have two for the next year!' added his neighbour.

### Prosperity and Material Circulation

In addition to intervening in the distribution of economic resources by influencing the growing process, Pachamama is also responsible for the success of economic exchanges. The circulation of goods is usually preceded by an appeal for the collaboration of telluric or Catholic entities designed to protect the values of the materialities involved in the exchange. These prayers concern the physical safety – of humans and their goods – endangered by the transport entailed in trade, as well as the favourable outcome of the transactions. To ensure deities look well on their undertakings, traders make offerings. When the exchanges involved long, potentially dangerous journeys through unfamiliar territory, these ceremonies used to include festive meals, singing, distribution of chicha and offerings of incense. Today, they are reduced to a short challa made for the goods put into circulation, together with formulas raising the attention of the entity called upon. For instance, I have heard: 'Pachamama, Holy Earth! Let it be a propitious time!' and 'Almighty God, let us sell everything quickly and get home safe and sound.'

Major offerings are performed annually. Every 26 July, traders worship Saint Anne by selling and giving miniatures of the goods they hope to purchase during the coming year: a computer, a car, a house, a restaurant, etc. (Angé 2016b, 2018). Mother Earth's hold over the conduct of economic exchanges is spectacularly evident at Carnival, when all the beings and objects whose proper development is to be ensured are sprinkled with drink and showered with serpentines and confetti. At Mardi Gras, the merchants call on Pachamama for her protection by setting out offerings to her in their shops. A little pile of stones is made in front of the door or in the main room. The owners and close friends and relatives gather to make a challa over this miniature mountain. Deeply faithful followers opt for a corpachada followed by a meal and dancing in answer to the bands playing in the streets of the town. In the market on the preceding Thursday, Jueves de Comadres, Earth is called upon to favour the profusion of the exchanges carried out in this essentially feminine space. On that day, the vendors gather around a pile of stones that has been constructed. After making the challa, they share grilled meat and dance until dawn to the music of a band invited for the occasion.

Not only exchanges are under the influence of Pachamama. Material circulation is appreciated as part of the interactions that please her, like the productive activities covered earlier by the practice of criar. In a region where inter-ecological exchanges have historically conditioned peasants' survival, material circulation carries a priori a positive moral value. As Harris (2000) suggests, reciprocal exchanges between ecological zones are endowed with reproductive qualities that stimulate cosmological regeneration. Figuring among the highest moral values, the propensity to accept transactions solicited by counterparts from complementary ecozones also contributes to assert ones' personal qualities. 'I am a good person, people know it. I always welcome everybody. Those who come to exchange, to harvest . . .' boasted Julia of her well-known generosity with herders from surrounding communities.

Such moral values are displayed not only to fellow humans. They are also addressed to nonhuman entities, such as Pachamama, who appreciate people's propensity to engage in fair exchanges and reward them for their generosity. Alternatively, the refusal to exchange is a cause of disgrace for the household. By refusing, when requested, to put a good into circulation, the owners expose themselves to accusations of greediness and ensuing punishment that could deprive them of health or wealth. This appreciation of material circulation includes industrial commodities. That is how Laura, a young cultivator from the community of Casti, who also worked in the municipality, narrated the selling of her car:

> People look at the coveted object. Then it starts to wear out for no reason, it falls apart totally. If they ask you [for it], and ask you again, you should give it to them and that's all. Still more so, if they agree with the price you have asked. That's what has happened with our car.

The same outcome can also be produced by the aforementioned envidia. Jealousy of someone's prosperity is considered a fundamental source of sickness and bad luck via the 'bad air sickness' that results from the proliferation of insults and rumours. Skin rashes and pains of unidentified origin are other unpleasant symptoms diagnosed as punishments for keeping back goods without reason.

## The Value of Monetary Transactions

Throughout the Andes, market exchanges have been imbued with a variety of moral connotations, from exploitative transactions associated with the Devil to a circulation of money envisioned as a reproductive force maintaining social order. Far from being systematically associated with a diabolical force, as Michael Taussig (1980) maintained based on his study of Bolivian miners, money is ascribed ambivalent powers. Michael Sallnow (1989) criticised Taussig's viewpoint, stressing that agriculture and stockbreeding do not expose one to the supernatural dangers that threaten mining, whereas their products, too, have been extracted from the Earth, and commoditised since the dawn of the colonial era. What exposes miners to retaliation is not so much the extraction of the metals as the individual appropriation of metals intended for paying taxes to the state, therefore encouraging political decadence.

Important work done by Harris (2000) has shown that the fertile power of material circulation is not restricted to direct transactions but also involves monetary exchanges. Tassi's enquiry into the cholos' market practices in La Paz also attests to the regenerative capacities of capitalist trade, which he associates with an aesthetic of material overabundance. Abundance, he says, 'becomes the constitutive principle of a form of "material teleology", which avoids the modernist divide and contradiction between the material and the transcendent, the economic and the religious' (2010: 206). He evokes the widespread tale of Ekeko, the god of plenty, materialised by the prolific figure of a smoking dwarf transporting an abundance of goods. Some market vendors in the Argentinean cordillera also keep an Ekeko, whom they worship by burning incense, sprinkling alcohol and lighting cigarettes in his mouth, or by giving him coca leaves. Peasants know about these partnerships with Ekeko, but I have never seen one in my hosts' houses.

In this southern region, monetary practices figure among those referred to as criar. While we were queuing at the bank to withdraw her meagre retirement pension, Sylberia wondered: 'Some say that money grows [*la plata se cria*] at the bank. Other say no, that it sleeps.' This reproductive force associated with money appears clearly in how peasants deal with the old coins accumulated by the elders at the beginning of the twentieth century, when they set out on exchange trips with the mining centres. In the puna, some elders buried treasure boxes near their home to activate their coins' economic fecundity. The stories I have heard about these chest discoverings, mention how the heirs, excited by the attractive idea of the immediate money they could make by converting the coins into pesos, nonetheless handled them with awe. The national currency, in contrast, is kept in constant circulation through exchange, and, as a rule, the peasants opt for savings in kind when they have the chance. In addition to being the object of commodity exchanges, the peso circulates in the form of gifts that attest the fertile power the peasants attribute to it. Indeed, money is among the most appreciated values used to congratulate the protagonists of life-cycle rituals such as baptism, the child's first haircut or the installation of a young couple.

Of course, not all kinds of monetary transfers are loaded with a positive moral valence. In the Argentinean puna, profit is approved of as long as it results from physical effort, thus referring to a sense of *sacrificio* (self-sacrifice). The efforts invested in the physical travel required by the exchange of agricultural goods justify the profits made by the traders. The peasants in this region share the viewpoints of Harris's interlocutors, who noted: 'People who make money give birth in this way are thought to perform a valuable social service. Money when it returns in the form of profit is fertile, not through the process of planting and maturation, but through exchange' (2000: 247). Travelling to take products unavailable in a place is regarded as a beneficial activity that produces value. In this case, commercial profit corresponds for the seller to the service rendered.

As a rule, peasants in the Argentinean puna denounce as an infraction of transactional morality those commercial ventures in which one party appropriates a profit at the expense of the other. They see market transactions as unfair when they consider that merchants enrich themselves more than they do, while they themselves struggle to produce agricultural goods in the remotest parts of the country, transmitting the lifestyle of their ancestors. In the end, the asymmetry is marked by the wealth appropriated by the merchant, who is then denounced for their greediness. Prosperous traders usually have a bad reputation. Amassing large amounts of money is said to make people lazy and indifferent to their relatives' needs. However, those successful merchants who remain committed to the social and cosmological reproduction of their community are not repudiated. Their commitment involves participating in communal ceremonies and in the network of reciprocities they entail, as well as not giving up agricultural production, albeit on a minor scale.

Furthermore, the demonisation of unjust appropriation is enmeshed in racial stereotypes that are common in different Andean regions. Racial tropes are explicit in the stories told about the cutthroat, known by a variety of names depending on the region: Gilles Rivière (1991) spoke of *lik'ichiri* (lit. someone who takes people's fat) and *kharisiri* (lit. someone who slashes or cuts throats for profit; a liar, an abuser) in the Southern Andes; Peter Gose (1986) talked about the Peruvian *ñakaq*; and Mary Weismantel (2001) evoked Ecuadorian *pishtacos*. These different terms refer to the same imaginary figure who adopts the guise of a man whose voracity cannot be appeased by sacrifices or offerings, as other Andean deities are. The cutthroat siphons the fat from his victim, whom he gradually empties of life force for his own benefit. The aggressor sells this substance for profit or uses it to boost his own failing health. There is no possible communication or reciprocal relationship with such a person. Rivière showed that those likely to be accused of being cutthroats are outsiders (village priests, engineers, agronomists) or local inhabitants who act like cutthroats by refusing, like the former, to submit to community norms. They instead nurture the relations they entertain with the outside world.

In both cases, cutthroats' practices are related to the greediness of outsiders, many times stereotyped by the whiteness of their skin. They are reproached with not so much the amount of wealth they have amassed as 'its quality and origin and, in particular, the strictly personal use they make of it' (Rivière 1991: 37). While most studies insist on the asymmetry of the transactions as a vice, consumption is also fundamental in the formation of the *pishtaco*'s personhood. White men are all depicted as keen on engaging in unfair transactions. As Rudy Colloredo-Mansfeld (2003: 278) has pointed out, the key difference between the gringo and this evil white figure is the inappropriateness of the food that keeps the latter alive.

In Argentina, the *lik'ichiri* is not evoked as such. Gringos are nonetheless seen as a generic embodiment of a danger of undue absorption of the peasant's vital resources for their own interests – a legitimate consideration in light of the manifold abuses Europeans and their descendants have inflicted on peasants since early colonial times. For this reason, their presence in the rural villages arouses suspicion among the inhabitants, who actively circumscribe outsiders' movement in the community space. I myself have been the object of accusations by people in Chalguamayoc, who suspected that I was walking around their territory for economic purposes. Some were afraid that I might be prospecting for silver; others thought I wanted to appropriate Telesforo and Sylberia's land. My comings and goings were hotly debated at community meetings, in the course of which denying me access to the village was discussed. As Weismantel (2001) made clear, in Andean intercultural interactions, whiteness is often associated with profit-taking and material extraction. This relation also prevails in the puna, where peasants regard their poverty as a historical outcome of these asymmetrical flows. The social relationship in which money circulates therefore shapes the moral valence attributed to it, as does the modality of the exchange in which money is involved.

## Notes

1. The population of the community is counted in households, regardless of the number of individuals in them.
2. Out of respect for the privacy of the people in the book, I have decided to keep all family names anonymous.
3. *Parientes* is the word they use in Spanish.

4. The community leaders are in turn represented at the Indigenous Participation Council responsible for talking with national authorities. At the
   time of my research, the Kolla people had the right to elect two representatives: one for the valley communities and the other for those of the puna.
5. At the time of my research, only two families in Chalguamayoc perceived
   no allowances at all. The large majority perceived several, among which
   unemployment and old-age pensions were the more common, along with
   *Madre de Siete Hijos* (Mother of Seven Children).
6. That kind of reciprocity does not manifest likewise when compadres are
   of different social status, in which case a paternalist asymmetrical largesse
   is expected from the wealthiest partner. Such compadrazgo is described
   as a 'vertical' tie, in contrast to the 'horizontal' alliance between people of
   equivalent social status (Mintz and Wolf, 1950).
7. In exceptional cases, the relation of casero evolves into the asymmetrical
   mode of compadrazgo mentioned in note 6. Peasants may ask business-
   men to sponsor their child and thereby build an alliance that crosscut
   social class and, possibly, ethnicity.
8. I capitalise Earth to stress the agency and subjectivity this telluric being is
   imbued with, as she is endowed with intentionality and affectivity of her
   own.
9. The original words are: la Tierra nos cría, la Tierra nos come.
10. Here Telesforo used the term Creoles to mean persons born in the village.
    In the same way the term can refer to those born in South America, in con-
    trast to immigrants from Europe. The expression shows the complexity
    of ethnic categories and the way their meaning changes according to the
    context.

# CHAPTER 2

# Historical Perspectives
# on Andean Fairs

The Spanish imported fairs to provision the urban and mining centres that formed the backbone of the colonial economy. The economic organisation of precolonial south Andean societies is known for its overall lack of marketplaces. Instead, domestic units procured foodstuffs from a variety of ecological niches via kinship relations that distributed their respective produce. The historian John Murra (1972a) famously referred to this strategy as vertical control of ecological niches. He proposed the model of 'archipelago' to describe the unique organisation whereby ethnic groups established permanent colonies far from their main centre of occupation in order to access produce from an array of ecological milieus.

Murra specified that, when the kin network did not include the needed ecological zones, 'barter, always present on the fringes of the system, gained in importance' (1974: 1359). The role of interethnic trade thus varied with the period and the region, particularly when the political centres expanded and extended their control over the different ecological zones. In northern Argentina, archaeologists and historians have not identified the existence of archipelagos and instead emphasise the existence of extensive inter-ecological networks of exchange. Contemporary barter is publicly acknowledged as a vestige of such ancestral inter-ecological reciprocity.

This association between barter and ancestral inter-ecological reciprocities is not specific to this meridional region. In Peru, Fonseca has affirmed that peasants, after being deprived of their maize fields in the lowlands when the government established new provincial boundaries in the nineteenth century, used barter to 'materialize again the ideal of ecological complementarity' (1972: 327). In a more general sense,

Murra expressed his surprise, for instance, that 'even today some regional exchanges follow the old caravan routes that connected the "islands" in the "archipelagos"' (1992: 134, my translation). He associated these circuits with the application of the traditional equivalences, which he saw as the expression of the bonds of solidarity between the different ecological levels they connected.

Today, the fairs at which inter-ecological transactions feature in a condensed form are also envisaged as cultural practices emblematic of Indigenous identity, despite the fact that the Spanish originally imported fairs to supply the mining economy. In the Argentinean cordillera, both government and nongovernment institutions advocate saving these gatherings, appreciated as 'ancestral' and considered to be under threat from the increasing inclusion of the peasantry in the capitalist economy. With the explicit purpose of encouraging peasants to *rescatar la costumbre* (rescue this tradition), many institutions devote funds to the perpetuation of old gatherings and to the implementation of new ones.

This chapter traces the evolution of these fairs from their establishment by the Spanish settlers down to their present-day form, inflected by the heritage policies of which they are the object. Beyond the focus on fairs, I shall outline the socio-economic history in the puna, in order to tease out long-term economic strategies in which contemporary fairs are embedded. We shall see that they do constitute a contemporary expression of vertical economy, alternative to Murra's model of archipelago that does not seem relevant to understand pre-Hispanic circulation in this southern part of the Cordillera.

## Colonial Times

### *Trade in the Vertical Economy*

Murra's (1972a) model of precolonial Andean economics was elaborated from an examination of administrative archives on the Central Andes in the sixteenth century. In his core essay on vertical control, he used his model to account for five Andean ethnic groups colonised first by the Inca and then by the Spanish. Their complexity ranges from the Quechua people of Chaupiwaranga, numbering less than a thousand households, to the Aymara people of Lupaca, reaching about twenty thousand households at the time of the conquest. He conceptualised the notion of 'archipelago' to describe these little islands of complementary production far from the political centre and populated by permanent settlers, who entertained close economic, political and social ties with the city. The goods where then transported in caravans and distributed between parents of the highland metropole. When this system was in force, kinship relations were thus the preferred vehicles of vertical transfers of goods.

In the case of large-scale ethnic groups, these colonies were settled in remote territories, situated at a distance of up to a two-week walk. Some of these colonies were multi-ethnic settlements gathering people from diverse horizons, a model that was maintained under the Inca Empire. But the Incas gave it new expressions where the settlement of islands was related not only to ecological specialisation but also to arts and crafts, administrative or military purposes (Murra 1972a: 465). Since his model embraces policies spread across the cordillera, differing in their scale and political organisation, Murra saw it as an ancestral Andean pattern. He nonetheless identified core transformations provoked by the Inca conquest first and by the Spaniards afterwards.

When the Spanish first arrived, there were two principal economic circuits. Besides the aforementioned circulation within the ethnic group, based on the vertical exploitation of a maximum number of ecological levels, the second circuit was devoted to those products absorbed by the Inca state: essentially maize and prestige goods, whose distribution was a monopoly of the imperial authorities.[1] The European settlers dismantled both circulations. Alongside these two circuits, the marketplace played a subsidiary role, and the emergence of specialised merchants was the exception.[2] As Carlos Sempat Assadourian has noted, in the Tawantinsuyu 'there were exchanges of "food for food in small amounts" among producers themselves, without this relation creating the specialized function of the merchant' (1995: 103). When merchants did exist, they did so precisely in those regions where the vertical exploitation of a maximum of ecological levels was limited by either environmental or political constraints (see Rostworowski 1999; Salomon 1978).

Murra himself acknowledged that the model might not be generalised to all Andean spaces and times, calling for careful investigation in all localities (1972a: 444). Maria Rostworowski (1999: 302) has pointed to an example of alternative organisation when documenting coastal societies. Drawing on the example of the Canta region, she described another model of social organisation intended to control multiple ecological niches. She observed enclaves that were not multi-ethnic and not related to ecological tiers as Murra's archipelagos usually are. She stressed that 'the Peruvian coast offers an environment quite distinct from the mountains, and therefore its socio-economic organization is also different' (1999: 305, my translation).

Although studies addressing the southern cordillera are still scarce, archaeologists who have worked in the area have advanced the existence of economic systems departing from Murra's archipelago model. Mariet Albeck concluded her article stating that the 'archaeological history' of the puna of Jujuy departs from the altiplano (2007: 141). It is important to bear in mind that we still lack fundamental knowledge of the political and social organisation of this meridional zone of the cordillera. What is known, however, is that the region was dominated by policies crystallised since before the Tiahuanaco. Their inclusion in the Inca Empire provoked a significant reconfiguration through the massive displacement of the population. The granting of land ownership to newcomers has been a source of interethnic tensions since before the Spanish invasion (Lorandi 1992: 144).

Archaeological excavations attest the importance of the cordillera's ecology in the circulation of goods and individuals and thus in the organisation of the Andean economy, as has been the case since hunter-gatherer times. Albeck's investigation depicts the puna as an immense herding zone, where only resistant crops (quinoa, papa, oca and olluco) could be cultivated as a subsidiary activity. The immense plateau is surrounded by valleys – San Juan de Oro, Quebrada de Humahuaca, Quebrada del Toro, Valles Calchaquies, Oasis Atacameños and Rio Loa (Albeck 1992: 127) – where the bulk of vegetable crops, including maize as well as other subsistence and ritual goods, were procured through exchange. While inhabitants of the Humahuaca valley were, before the Spanish arrival, mostly self-sufficient in the production of vegetables and meat, they nonetheless needed salt harvested in the puna, from where they also imported wools, fabrics and ceramics. Besides salt, Albeck pinpointed wood from the lowlands and stones from the highlands as monopolies of specific loci, involving interethnic relations of dependence.

She therefore concluded that these regions would not fit Murra's model of vertical control. These populations instead engaged in exchanges (1992: 104), composing a dense interethnic network of trade connecting the Chichas living in the zone of Yavi, the Cochinocas and Casabindos occupying the central puna and the Omaguacas settled in the homonymous valley (1992: 133). It is noteworthy, however, that a few corners of the puna enjoyed a local microclimate in which the cultivation of maize and other less-resistant vegetables was possible, thus providing increased independence to these zones. This is the case of the hamlets around the Yavi River, which were connected to the fertile lands of the Sococha valley unfolding to the north, in present-day Bolivia. In fact, this valley was part of the Chicha territory, an ethnic group differing from the Cochinocas and Casabindos in the central puna. In 1650, the Spanish moved most of the chicha population to the present-day Bolivian region of Sucre, while people from other areas were brought to occupy the emptied space. Likewise, the Atacamas in the south of the puna are thought to have been settled there after the Spanish conquest (1992: 128–129).

Lautaro Núñez has proposed the notion of 'gyratory societies' to emphasise the importance of displacement in the configuration of puna societies. This variation of the vertical exploitation model is based not on the permanent control of remote archipelagos but instead on the recurring movement of part of the population. Based on research in the area of the Atacameños, Núñez advanced the hypothesis that their displacement took the form of llama trains, conducted by 'traffic lords' ordered by a political elite, in a process that would have created 'embryonic merchants' (2007: 35, my translation). The latter were in charge of the distribution of the excess of subsistence products as well as goods symbolising the power of their lord. In addition to exchanges between the puna and local valleys, trade routes linking the puna to

**Figure 2.1.** Llama trains suggest that contemporary fairs stem from precolonial inter-ecological trade routes. Today, they have become exceptions but persist in some meetings like the Santa Catalina fair. Photograph by the author.

the western coast and eastern rain forest, existing from before Christ, are attested by the presence of ritual objects (2007: 42). Núñez specified that these caravans were more than mere strategies to access subsistence goods. Examining the nature of the goods involved and the modality of the journeys, he stressed their political stakes and argued that they entailed 'rituals shared beyond the different ethnic belongings' (2007: 35, my translation), a point that he later generalises, stating that 'caravans emerge between herder societies across the Andes with a very similar rituality' (2007: 38, my translation). However, his article does not provide much detail about the kinds of rituals these caravans were embedded in.

Although we lack details about the modality of exchange through which the produce of the different ecological niches was circulated, the data presented above refute the idea 'that barter is not a particularly ancient phenomenon at all, but has only really become widespread in modern times' (Graeber 2011: 37). The important point to stress here is that archaeologists assume that llama and donkey trains led by peasants in the twentieth century are in continuity with these pre-Hispanic trade routes, although the latter covered a larger area, implying 'a material and ideological subordination of local elites to new political order' (Núñez 2007: 47, my translation).

### Feeding the Mining Centres

The European colonisers' introduction of the capitalist market triggered an important revolution in an Andean economy formerly articulated around kinship networks. Refuting the established idea that Indians would have been reluctant to partake in commodity exchange, the volume edited by Brooke Larson, Olivia Harris and Enrique Tandeter (1995) shows that natives were involved in the emerging market in early colonial times. However, historians do not lend major importance to the urban markets the Spanish established upon arrival to feed the urban elites. Another economic institution played a crucial role in organising the Andean colonial trade (Conti 1989: 432): the annual fair, which was imported from Europe, where they were widespread at the time.[3]

In the 'Andean economic space' established in colonial times (Assadourian 1982), the present-day provinces of Salta and Jujuy were a cattle route: the only passage between the Atlantic pampa and the highland mining centres. The animals came through by the thousands to rebuild their strength before starting the long climb up the cordillera. The trail between Salta and the towns of Potosi, Oruro and Cuzco was also marked by a network of fairs, where buyers from the north in search of cattle and beasts of burden could encounter the traders driving their huge herds up from the southern plains. These animals, the profitable buying and selling of which were monopolised by the large Spanish landowners, were the principal good organising this exchange network. In addition to the trade in cattle, merchants also proposed products from the different specialised regions in the economic space (sugar, cocoa, liquor or wax).

Their detailed knowledge of the geography combined with their ability to drive the herds, based on the practices of caravans inscribed in their economic strategies since pre-Hispanic times, gave the Indigenous people a capital role in distributing the products brought to the poles of consumption. The landowners, who rewarded the traveller, usually ordered these trips to the mining centres. Although they did not have access to any large-scale trade, the native peasants took goods of their own to the fairs. Hence, the native peasants took advantage of these gathering points to exchange the surplus of their domestic production with the other peasants in the valleys, who also participated in the event. The profits of such personal trade would go to pay taxes, and to buy coca and manufactured goods (Conti and Langer 1991: 98; Palomeque 1994; Sica 2005).

This might not be true, however, for the peasants in the region of Yavi, who were under the authority of the most powerful *encomendero* (Spanish ruler) in the region. In 1674, the governor of Jujuy awarded the greatest *encomienda* of his jurisdiction at the time to Pablo Fernandez Ovando, whose son was to become the eminent Marqués del Valle de Tojo. The latter received this land as a grace from the Rey, making the previous encomienda into its own estate, which stretched from the present-day puna of Jujuy to the border with Salta in the south, as well as the Tojo valley down to Tarija in Bolivia (Rutledge 1987: 104; see also Madrazo 1982). Under these circumstances, the historian Guillermo Madrazo surmised that barter would have been paralysed: 'In fact, its importance seems to have diminished strongly after the conquest in relation to the situation of submission of the Indigenous people to their encomenderos' (1981: 214, my translation). This hypothesis is controversial, however (see e.g. Lorandi 1992: 153; Montero 2004: 150).

For those whose mobility was hampered, fairs provided an ideal setting for the gathering of representatives of numerous ecological niches, in contrast to the caravans, which usually travelled from place to place. The trips to the fair thus complemented the caravan migrations, synchronising the trips and providing the opportunity to conduct a variety of transactions. In addition to the direct exchanges, the peasants sold a few products – especially wool, valued by the prosperous merchants, who exported it abroad (Langer 2004: 12); this activity allowed the peasants to procure goods produced outside the Indigenous economy, such as knives, needles, sugar or coca leaves.

At the local level, therefore, the fairs regulated the circulation of the peasants' surplus domestic production while tying their economy into the regional trade circuit. Here, as in Europe, fairs were not only a 'higher' economic forum (Braudel 1979: 63) but also a high point in the expression of regional sociability. The fair was a festival and a party of sorts, as attested by the space devoted to games, dancing and the consumption of extraordinary beverages and foods. Fairs thus acted as a point of convergence between the commercial economy aimed at feeding the mining centres, in which the Spanish monopolised large-scale trade, and the subsistence economy of Indigenous peasants, who were secondary players in the regional trade circuit, occupying only the niches spurned by the Europeans (Conti 1989: 112; Madrazo 1982: 134).

## Independence of Nation-States and a New Configuration for Fairs

### The High Point of the Nineteenth Century

After having briefly disappeared during the wars of independence, fairs came back with new vigour with the reactivation of the regional economy and the resumption of silver mining in Bolivia in the second half of the nineteenth century. In continuity with the colonial era, the north of newborn Argentina acted as a purveyor of the animals needed by the mining centres (Rinconada in Argentina but also Tupiza, Lipez and Oruro in Bolivia). These animals were used as a means of transportation and as beasts of burden (mules, donkeys and horses), as well as a source of food (sheep and cattle). Again, the trail linking the Argentinean lowlands with the various urban centres in the altiplano guided the establishment of the network of fairs, remodelled based on the new distribution of mining activities. From the Salta fair and the important Tablada in Jujuy to Huari (Bolivia), numerous commercial gatherings marked the road through the mountains: among the most important were the fairs of Tilcara, Humahuaca, Cerrillos, Iruya, Abra Pampa, Cieneguillas, Yavi, Santa Catalina, Atocha, Ayoma and Uyuni. The merchants who travelled to the Tablada, on the outskirts of San Salvador de Jujuy, usually continued northwards, visiting the fairs along the way and ending with the Huari gathering. Described at the beginning of the twentieth century as the principal fair in South America (Conti 1989: 441), this gathering was attended by merchants from Argentina, Chile, Bolivia and Peru.

Cattle sales – at the time conducted by big traders as well as small merchants – were always the focal point of the fairs specialised in one or another species. The meeting calendar was structured by the circulation of the stock, which could be driven up into the mountains only in the spring, before the summer rains, and after the severe winter cold. This season of harvest and abundant pasture, which made it possible to fatten up the animals, was also a time of opulence that favoured peasants' exchange of agricultural products among themselves. In addition to the lucrative transactions that provided revenue for a class of prosperous traders, the local peasantry continued to occupy the fringes of the fair to dispose of their surplus domestic production in exchange for goods from complementary ecological niches.

According to historians, the simultaneous transfers of goods that took place at fairs were still structured by the pre-Hispanic relations of reciprocity between peasants from complementary ecological zones. In those regions where the circulation of goods were once framed by the vertical model, the circulation of goods then followed the relations of friendship or compadrazgo established with the inhabitants of the complementary lands separated from their centre. Murra (1992: 143) observes the phenomenon in the following terms:

> Where direct collective ownership of ecological levels had been lost during the three centuries of colonial erosion, highland entities had succeeded in shaping an interzonal network of paths and fairs, where exchanges, usually embedded in ritual kinship (*compadrazgo*), allowed them to restore access, albeit indirect and limited, to these same resources.

In her description of the large annual Tablada gathering, the historian Viviana Conti wrote that the peasants did not aim to make a profit and that they set the terms of their transactions using traditional equivalences (1988: 78). The peasants also engaged in monetary transactions with the Creole merchants or those of European stock, to whom they would sell certain products – salt and woollens in particular – and in this way obtained the money they needed to buy what the latter were selling.

It is noteworthy that, beside these meeting points, herders from the puna continue travelling to surrounding valleys in the form of caravans. Historical data speak to the importance of these journeys in the herders' economy. The main destinations mentioned for the northern puna are the valleys around Tarija, where herders looked for maize. We can thus assume that the relationship described by Albeck between the puna and valleys in present-day Bolivia held during the colonial times, although they were complicated by the activities of the encomienda (Montero 2004: 48). These expeditions continued after the border between Argentina and Bolivia was settled, despite the taxes imposed on international trade. The historian Raquel Montero advances the conclusion that the puna was 'joined to Southern Bolivia not only through commercial relationships but also through kinship ties, through a common history, ecology, a social and economic reality' (2004: 65, my translation).

### Desertion by the Cattle Traders and Proletarianisation of the Peasantry

After a high point in the second half of the nineteenth century, the network of fairs was affected by the structural transformations occurring at the end of the century in the region and worldwide (Conti and Langer 1991: 110). The new routes travelled by food, established in the wake of the railroad lines connecting the region's recent urban centres with the port of Buenos Aires, remodelled the fairs' profile. The diffusion of agro-industrial goods by rural grocery stores undermined the reciprocal dependence between producers in the complementary ecological niches. But above all, large-scale trade was annihilated by this new means of transportation: the mining centres were henceforth supplied with industrial commodities brought in by train, and the demand for cattle as a food source and as beasts of burden fell off considerably.[4] The direct exchanges of surplus domestic production that were once a marginal phenomenon and carried out on the periphery of the exchange space (Conti 1989: 440) now came to be the focus of the fairs in this part of the Andes. If the large-scale trade circuits were shunted away from this network, the network itself nonetheless retained its preponderant role in the Indigenous economy.

The peasants of the puna, whose intervention had been crucial in the postcolonial Andean space, found themselves marginalised by the emerging new economic order at the end of the nineteenth century. Faced with the atrophy of the caravan trade, small peasants were forced to work as unskilled labourers to pay their taxes (Conti and Langer 1991: 110). Many thus provided their labour to the big mining companies that had recently moved into the puna or to the sugar industry that had developed in the lowlands of Jujuy. The sugar industry was indeed thriving, being the major economic activity there. While Indigenous people from the Chaco initially supplied the plantation labour force, the situation changed when business rocketed in the 1930s. The powerful owners, in search of more workers, developed networks throughout the puna, where *contratistas* (recruiters) sent peasants to the fields. Many times, the former were owners of local groceries who recruited indebted clients to repay their debts.

At the beginning of the twentieth century, landowners in the puna were eager to find a profitable way of managing their properties, at that time rented to the peasants. While the national state had refused to acquire these remote territories, another client appeared in the early 1930s: the head of the sugar industry purchased – or leased – large estates in the puna, forcing the inhabitants to cut sugar cane for them six months a year by way of paying their rent. In his book on the history of the development of capitalism in Jujuy, Ian Rutledge gives a detailed description of the sugar industry's extension in the department of Yavi. As mentioned earlier, this territory was part of the encomienda of Tojo, established since the beginning of the eighteenth century. After temporary expropriation between 1877 and 1893, the property had subsequently been taken over by the Campero family. Around 1930, they decided to rent it to the owner of the second major sugar company in Argentina at the time, San Martín del Tabacal. A *contratista*, who later became deputy to the provincial government, was in charge of gathering native workers and sending them to fulfil their duty at the beginning of the sugar harvest. The abominable treatment inflicted on the tenants is documented, and still alive in the memory of the elders, who were transported in cattle cars under threat of the whip to carry out painful and intensive labour in the tropical climate of the lowlands (Rutledge 1987: 200). The forced labour was later replaced by more voluntary salaried relationships, under the pressure of the 1944 legislation by President Juan Perón, in favour of the protection of labourers.

Karasik (2006) has identified the inclusion of puna people in the labour market, in the mines and plantations, as a keystone in the crystallisation of ethnic identities. Racial discrimination, economic subordination and physical mistreatment merged in the construction of identities, articulating ethnicity with collective suffering. In this regard, it is important to note that both in the mines and on the plantations, Bolivian migrants were assimilated to Argentineans from the highlands. They bore the same work conditions and were assigned shared accommodation sectors, until the Peronist government voted laws that did not apply to Bolivian workers. At this point, citizenship and integration in the nation-state came to be experienced through differentiated labour conditions.

When the herders migrated to the mines and sugar plantations in the 1930s, it was the valley inhabitants' turn to seek out their highland partners, who had deserted the transaction spaces they had once shared. The patronal feasts, inevitable opportunities for migrants to return home, guaranteed these cultivators a successful trip to the otherwise deserted highland communities. A new calendar of meetings, based on that of the patronal feasts, thus fell into place: 'Once a year, during fairs established in earlier decades, small towns host visitors with diverse festive activities, and open-air tents become the scene of an intense exchange of things for things and according to precepts of balanced reciprocity' (Madrazo 1982: 219, my translation). The pre-Hispanic migrations to the lowlands, where herders used llamas as beasts of burden, were thus reversed: now the cultivators from the south Bolivian valleys travelled up in search of their highland partners.[5]

Despite the seasonal proletarianisation, the fair kept its preponderant role in the economy of the puna, for which it was still, in the first decades of the twentieth century, a fundamental practice, completed by caravan trips (Bugallo 2009: 6; Göbel 2003; Madrazo 1981: 225). As Justo, a fifty-something-year-old herder in the village of Chalguamayoc, testifies:

> The grandparents didn't sell llamas like we do. But they did sell their wool in La Quiaca. Wool was very valuable, but hardly anyone used the money. What they earned they used to pay [the land rent], and no more. Outside of that, there was only barter. Here they spun, wove and took the blankets, shirts and socks to the valley, along with meat. And they brought back maize. That's how my grandfather would leave. He would leave for two weeks and would bring back the food for the whole year. For the fruits, they would go to Tojo for [the] Easter [fair].

With these exchanges of agricultural goods, highland and lowland peasants would ensure their mutual reproduction by providing each other with the products of their respective activities.

Here, again, the zone of Yavi deserves further comment. It is an exception in the sense that puna and valley can be reached within less than a day's walk, allowing people to cultivate plots in different ecological zones. Such a modality of vertical control strategy is documented in the nineteenth century (Montero 2004: 153). In Chalguamayoc, some elders remember when their family owned plots in Santa Victoria, where they grew maize, although they had stopped exploiting the plots at the time of my research. Other examples of double residence across ecological tiers also exist in the oriental slopes of Humahuaca.[6] In all events, such testimonies speak to the combination of different strategies of vertical control, including double residence and reciprocal exchanges.

In the second half of the twentieth century, peasants' participation in fairs decreased because of their progressive integration into the labour market. After Perón's intervention, working conditions improved to such an extent that peasants, for the first time, took the initiative to look for temporary contracts on plantations. A study carried out in Yavi in the 1970s found that 70 per cent of its population was involved in the sugar industry at that time (Rutledge 1987: 230). In this light, Rutledge posited the violent recruitment system established in the 1930s as the first step towards the proletarianisation of the puna people, to be completed by the abandonment of their agricultural activities.

Until the 1970s, their labour was mostly sold during periodic migrations to the lowland plantations or to the mines. At this point, the labour legislation produced favourable labour conditions for unqualified workers, thus encouraging peasants to settle permanently in the lowland districts around San Salvador de Jujuy. The national recession of the 1980s triggered a movement back to the puna, which revitalised the declining fairs. Meanwhile, rural economies had undergone significant transformations, affecting peasants' involvement in barter networks. Salient among these changes were public allowance distribution, increased means of communication and transportation and daily consumption of industrial foods.

As a result, peasants' will and ability to sell their crops at urban markets increased, along with their opportunity to consume items that were not produced locally. Furthermore, agricultural production had become secondary in many household economies where it was used as subsidiary activity in times of employment shortage (Rutledge 1987: 234). Barter fairs thus stopped being the indispensable setting in which peasants exchanged the surplus of their agricultural production and obtained complementary items. Although their scale varied according to economic contexts and market participation, fairs continued to be held. This fact points to the persistence of economic practices at the margins of the market, challenging Rutledge's argument of the development of a 'completely capitalist society' during the second half of the twentieth century (1987: 265). Until today, household economies in the puna cannot be reduced to a capitalist strategy (see also Madrazo 1982: 213).

## Contemporaneous Meetings:
## From Spontaneous Gathering to Institutional Event

### Feast Days and Fairs in the Twenty-First Century

Today, fairs are still a key component of the festivals by which the Andean communities celebrate their patron saints. In Argentina, the protagonists use the terms *feria* (fair) and *fiesta* (party, celebration) synonymously. Composed of dancing, political speeches, competitive sports and church rituals, these festivals are designed to please and pacify ambivalent telluric and Catholic entities. The concentration of these exchanges within a circumscribed space and time is related to the massive flow of peasants towards a ritual centre. The composition of the fair is not merely a way of taking advantage of the geographical moves dictated by the religious calendar through the circulation of agricultural goods, as noted by Deborah Poole (1982: 101). I argue that the profusion of material circulation is in itself part of the religious celebration. Today, some fairs have even outstripped the ecclesiastic rites, and most of the participants perform the fiesta only through trade. Even if they favour one or another of the economic, religious or ludic activities, these different aspects continue to be interconnected in the way peasants celebrate their deities.[7]

The most successful fairs take place in a zone easily reached from the different ecological levels, thus ensuring a greater variety of products for exchange. The importance of the fair also varies according to the match between the date of the celebration and the broader economic calendar. The main events occur at the end of the summer harvest or at the end of winter, when dried foodstuffs are exchanged to tide people over the lean season. These economic motivations are combined with social expectations, since peasants also travel to meet up with friends and kin. Moreover, a household's decision to travel is influenced by its neighbours' intentions: each community favours a few events, to which trips are organised between allies or by the community as a whole. Finally, affluence reflects religious devotion, because fairs result from the displacement of peasants coming from an array of ecological niches, towards a common centre of worship. 'This is the reason why barter has been set up: because it's the Virgin's day. We know that people are going to come together', I was told by Hilda, a herder in her fifties from the community of Yoscaba, whom I met at the Saint Catherine celebration. Hence, the transactions entailed in the festival suppose a regional synchronisation of the religious calendar.

The spatial extension of the fair and the variety of products available depend on the geographical area concerned by the meeting. The whole of the Southern Andes is involved in the two main gatherings: for the Abra Pampa Easter fair and for the Manka Fiesta (lit. pot party, in a mixture of Spanish and Quechua), participants travel south from La Paz and north from Salta. These main events gather thousands of participants. Yet, usual meetings draw on average a few hundred people. Most celebrations end after a few days; only key meetings last up to the next week.

## Fairs as Cultural Heritage

At the end of the twentieth century, development organisations burgeoned in the Argentinean cordillera. As mentioned earlier, in addition to poverty reduction, their programmes aim at empowering Indigenous peoples' communities and reviving their traditions. Agronomic engineers, supported by Indigenous leaders co-opted into their projects, began to convene new fairs, arguing that these provided effective tools for simultaneously strengthening civil society and asserting Kolla people's identity. These encounters were also, though less openly, intended for institutional promotion. I have suggested elsewhere calling these new gatherings 'institutional fairs', as compared to the more spontaneous fairs that accompany religious celebrations (Angé 2016a). During community meetings, and radio announcements, peasants are convened to the festivities in order to *revalorar su cultura* (reappraise their culture) and to *rescatar la costumbre de los abuelos* (rescue the traditions of the elders). A key purpose of such events is indeed to retrieve Kolla traditions by mitigating the erosion of Andean fairs. On the one hand, the organisers remark a decreasing trend in participation. However, this is relative, since the number of fairs is on the rise. On the other hand, they lament the massive presence of industrial commodities and the use of money at the expense of barter transactions. The latter argument is identified as a trend towards the *comercialización* (commercialisation) of fairs, which they see as a threat to the perpetuation of what they view as an ancestral practice. From there on, new encounters have blossomed all over the puna, in addition to the old gatherings, all of which results in a busy schedule for those attending fairs.

The promotion of fairs is appreciated as a successful policy by NGO technicians, state agents and other rural-development stakeholders. The diverse subventions the organizers are granted for convening their festivals testifies to this. They appreciate fairs as fruitful tools to 'organize Indigenous communities', a target that echoes the strengthening of civil society lying at the core of international development agenda.

Moreover, these meetings are seen to provide appropriate settings where to arouse peasants' experience of cultural pride by displaying Kolla cultural highlights on a public stage. Fairs' purported efficacy to achieve these development targets have enticed every institution to organize its own event and compete for attracting the greatest number of participants. Instigators admit, however, that they have fomented a mushrooming of institutional fairs in the region, which has provoked a dislocation to the barter network. Offering free transportation and gathering, institutional fairs are cheaper to attend than spontaneous one. Many peasants thus opt to save their products for the former meeting, at the expense of the latter. The new schedule of fairs therefore disrupts the old alliances between highland herders and their valley partners, who do not share the same institutional affiliations. Surprisingly, the enhancement of barter itself is not listed as institutional fairs' achievement. This transactional figure thus provides a means to strengthen civil society and crystallize ethnic identities, in tune with the objectives dear to international development institutions.

At the beginning of the twenty-first century, another wave of preservation spread out from municipal secretaries for tourism and cultural affairs. While fairs used to take place on the outskirts of cities, with little attention paid by state institutions, city councils began to invest money in promoting meetings within their district, and officials started to investigate historical contexts in order to play up any connection with past encounters. They recognise the present barter system as a vestige of 'ancestral' inter-ecological reciprocities, and fairs are therefore considered 'cultural activities' emblematic of Andean Indigenous identity. The increase in municipal attention resulted from an expansion of the tourist market related to two main causes. On the one hand, most Argentineans could not afford to travel abroad after the 2001 currency devaluation. When they recovered from the economic crisis, they spent their holidays within the country, thereby boosting the national tourist industry. At the same time, the adjacent Humahuaca valley, locally called the Quebrada, was declared a UNESCO World Heritage Site. The main reason why provincial authorities sought this label was to make tourism a leading sector for developing the regional economy (Belli and Slavutsky 2005). The declaration did indeed contribute to the tourism boom in the Quebrada. However, it is worthwhile noting that rural villages have remained on the margins of this flourishing industry. Visitors congregate in urban agglomerations from where they organise daytrips to surrounding attractions such as archaeological sites or outstanding geological formations.

Public officials in the neighbouring highlands beyond the delimited UNESCO area thought their cultural treasures also deserved attention. Thus, moves for the preservation and appreciation of material and intangible cultural assets spread towards the puna. There, fairs started to be held as a local attraction for the tourists congregating in the world-famous valley. A spokeswoman for the tourism secretary at the highland municipality of La Quiaca explicitly set out such a strategy in 2012:

> We don't want to be just a place of passage towards the [Bolivian] border to shop and go back [to the Humahuaca valley]. A few years ago, we started promoting this fair as our own heritage so that the quantity of tourists would increase. And it has been successful – advertising [the fair] is bringing in more people.

La Quiaca, as well as other councils, has formally recognised the annual fair as an event 'of municipal interest'. This new status justifies the allocation of public resources to the organisation of meetings that were once much more spontaneous. As a result, fairs are reshaped, and barter transactions are displayed in a new window. In the final chapter, I will describe some of the changes in the material decor of barter and in the discursive display that wraps it in a new morality of exchange. This will shed some light on the process by which barter became conceived of as a cultural treasure, instead of being a nonrational, inefficient and backward practice, as local Creole mainstream representations would have it.

## Notes

1. Yet, intermediate instances of power at a segmentary level, such as federations or *señorios*, also developed centres of distribution between the households and the state (see e.g. Rostworowski 1999).
2. This was specifically the case in the steeper Southern Andes, thus making possible a direct control over the ecological archipelagos, which in this case were closer together (Platt 1988: 421). Exceptions have been documented for the Central and Northern Andes, particularly in the case of coastal economies and present-day Ecuador, on which Rostworowski (1999) and Salomon (1978), respectively, worked. Salomon showed that barter expeditions in the Northern Andes gave rise to the formation of squares in which specialised traders, *mindales*, who were appointed by the political leaders, also carried out a concentration of exchanges.
3. For the characteristics of the European fairs, see the work of Fernand Braudel (1979).

4.  Train stations connected to networks of supply by pack animal, but the large cattle transhumances from Salta and Jujuy was wiped out.
5.  This is a north Argentinean pattern developed by Madrazo (1982) but should not be generalised to other regions, as a reviewer aptly noted. In Bolivia, where valley peasants from Cochabamba were proletarianised in Llallagua, herders from the altiplano travelled to mines to supply agricultural produce and work on the margins of a mining economy.
6.  I am thinking of Santa Ana, where herders cultivate plots in the nearby Valle Grande and Valle Colorado – a strategy that is still observable today, although many valley plots are abandoned (see Angé 2016b, 2018). A similar case is Aparzo, where herders exploit land near Iruya and San Andres.
7.  Fiestas also have a political dimension, expressed essentially during the speeches made by local authorities and at times accompanied by parades. Electoral candidates also take advantage of these events to campaign. Nevertheless, I will not deal with this aspect of the fiesta here, as it deserves another study on its own.

# CHAPTER 3

# The Fair

## A Religious Gathering of People and Goods

After outlining the social and historical context, I will now consider the fabric of contemporary fairs. A detailed case study of the Yavi Easter fair provides a general overview of how fairs unfold today, considering the articulation of material circulation with other dimensions of the fiesta. I focus on this particular event because it is renowned for being one of the oldest gatherings in the region since colonial times. As well as being the village in which I lived, Yavi stands at the junction between the valley and highland where I have been conducting my fieldwork. The main protagonists of this encounter include tuber cultivators from the communities around Yavi, maize growers from the Sococha valley and herders from the highlands, including Chalguamayoc. This Easter celebration therefore provided an excellent opportunity to grasp the social configurations emerging in this festive context, in comparison to the daily social fabric I was familiar with.

Despite the fundamental role of exchanges in Andean societies since settlement compromised access to products from distant ecological zones, the pre-Columbian economy is characterised by a general absence of trade specialists (but see Núñez 2007). Travellers exchanging their produce were not dealers but peasants looking for exotic products they could not produce in their own ecological niche but which they nonetheless needed to complete their diet (Harris 2000: 58). This particular kind of economic actor, who assumes the double function of production and distribution, still congregates at fairs. Alongside herders and cultivators, I will invoke other participants, thereby highlighting the extension of the economic network of fairs beyond the peasant communities. I will go on to describe the economic and social values of the goods brought by different categories of actors, in an attempt to explain how these goods take part in the construction of peasants' subjectivities and social identity.

## The Spatiotemporal Setting

### Processions

Previously an administrative, religious and economic centre of a huge encomienda, Yavi has become a small rural village, giving way to the flourishing city of La Quiaca after the railway came to the puna at the beginning of the twentieth century. The little church, famous for its gold ornamentation, still attests to this colonial past. The Marquis of Tojo, who was head of the encomienda when he initiated the first local line of nobility, built the church in 1709 (Madrazo 1982: 63). Featuring this sumptuous church, Yavi continues being a regional centre of religious activities until today. Every Easter, the village is the scene of an important celebration: peasants come from surrounding communities to weep over Christ's death, other worshippers come from La Quiaca to faithfully follow the procession of mourners and tourists come from the south of the country to watch this spectacular performance of local traditions.

Arriving from the surrounding communities in the municipal lorry placed at their disposal, the pilgrims throng to Yavi on Good Friday afternoon. The women are by far the most numerous in the growing group of followers. They wear dark-coloured dress, in stark contrast to the bold colours they usually favour. The costume consists of a shirt and a fine wool vest over a full skirt for the women. For the occasion, some affix colourful flowers to their hats, which they wear over their long braids as protection from the sun. Always fewer in number, the men wear a shirt, sometimes with a hand-knit pullover and town trousers. To keep out the cold, the women wear a blanket over their shoulders, which is held together with a safety pin; the men wear ponchos. Traditional dress is donned as a sign of respect, but it is also designed to protect the travellers from the 'bad air' that might weaken them during their trip. The faithful also transport voluminous packages full of agricultural produce.

Quickly, the newcomers gather at the church to start their praying and singing. The mourners are expected later at night. At around nine o'clock, they enter the church on their knees to the sound of their lamentation:

My sweet Jesus,
 Look with pity on

My soul lost for mortal sin
My sweet Jesus
Whom I carry in my heart,
Bleeding from his wound
Only for loving me.[1]

They are welcomed by the priest and crowds of visitors. The effigy of
a crucified Christ hanging on a replica of Mount Calvary overlooks
the nave. Those who find no room in the church attend the mass from
the courtyard, where a screen and loudspeakers broadcast the ritual.
Tourists and visitors are manifestly impacted by the deep faith displayed by the locals. The incessant flashes of their cameras speak of
their appreciation.

When the Good Friday liturgy ends, a man dressed in white representing Joseph of Arimathea climbs the artificial mount on a ladder to
take down the Christ. In 2008, the priest addressed a few words to the
Puneños at this point, lamenting the poverty of this Indigenous people,
victims of discrimination and injustice: 'For the people of the puna, for
the Kolla people, who continue suffering lack of work, lack of health,
malnutrition and child mortality'. Such a miserable trope seems to be
a constant in the Good Friday office. In 1975, the attendance could
hear a similar discourse:

> This Christ nailed on the cross is the symbol of the puna; because our
> area takes the shape of a huge cross. The Cross of our land, harsh and
> cold. The cross of oblivion and marginalisation. The Cross of the chil-
> dren who are suffering, and the men with no work. The Cross of the girl
> without illusions, nor horizon for her life. Maybe therefore the Puneño
> understands better than anyone else the mystery of Good Friday. His life
> is a continuous and permanent Good Friday.[2]

Then the first procession sets off. The Christ is followed by the effigies
of Our Lady of Sorrows, John the Evangelist and Mary Magdalene, after which come the mourners. Surrounded by the visitors, the procession follows the path delineated by the altars set up around the village
to represent the Stations of the Cross. Street lamps are extinguished,
and the procession is illuminated solely by the candles brought by the
mourners, who weep unabatedly – except when they stop at the altars
to pray, led by the priest. After the first procession, the latter returns
to La Quiaca and visitors go back to their home or hotel, while the
mourners continue their procession, ending with the *despedida* (farewell) of Jesus at the cross overlooking the village. At dawn on Saturday,
after having spent the night worshipping the Lord with prayers, songs

and processions, the faithful leave the church for the final procession, which ends at the foot of the village cross with Jesus' farewell.

The path of the procession skirts the cemetery, barely illuminated by the rising sun. There, the cultivators, who have arrived the previous day, stay each year. The first signs of life appear in the camp that will soon turn into an effervescent fair when the holy night is over. The exhausted worshippers return to the hangar the village has placed at their disposal. Before they rest, they distribute the branches of molle (a variety of pepper plant) and virreina flowers that composed the Mount Calvary. The holy boughs are preciously kept as a remedy for various diseases such as nervous trauma, rheumatism or mal de aire. The priest's benediction is expected to amplify the curative powers of these plants. Some of the exhausted pilgrims take a rest. Others, claiming that devotion conquers fatigue, head directly for the cemetery, carrying meat from their llamas and sheep, hides, wool, potatoes and fava beans, all typically produced by the protagonists of the procession.

On Saturday night, the church is the theatre of another ecclesiastic ritual. Most of the mourners have already returned home. Those attending the mass are the parents of the babies being baptised, along with the future godmothers and godfathers. In 2008, there were five waiting for the sacrament, from the communities of Yavi Chico, Casti, Suripujio, Inti Cancha and La Quiaca. With the exception of the last, all these communities take part in the Good Friday processions. Installed at the first rows, they were dressed in their finest apparel, white for the babies. Before mass started, other worshippers joined the audience, leaving bottles of water on the rostrum and sitting in the back. After having sanctified the fire and the water, the priest proceeded to the anointment of the little novices. His prestations finished with the signature of the baptism certificates. After the relationship between the baby and his new godmother and godfather has been acknowledged through their participation in the anointment, another ritual starts, which is intended to institute the compadrazgo between the two couples.

While the priest clears the altar of its ritual panoply and the attendance honour the sacred effigies before they leave the church, the couples occupy the rostrum, where they kneel facing each other in the midst of the bustling crowd. Ignored by all, they exchange performative words through which they 'receive each other as compadres'.[3] There is no specific formula stipulated; every couple chooses the terms with which they settle their union involving respect and mutual help 'in this life and the following one'. This alliance is not acknowledged by the priest, who distinguishes it from the status of the child's godfather.

For the protagonists, both alliances constitute a unique institution engaging the two households as a whole. Indeed, all the members of the domestic units are concerned by the extension of the kinship network and the implications in terms of economic cooperation. Some couples, supported by their new allies, invite their friends and family to continue the celebration at their home, where they eat, drink and dance together. Presents are given to the baptised child by its closest kin. The lamentations of Good Friday thus yield to the joy that concludes the celebration of Christ's resurrection.

### The Fair

The first cultivators also arrive in Yavi on Friday afternoon, thus completing a trip begun at dawn. They come from the valley of Sococha, on the Bolivian side of the border. They must take several vehicles so that the Argentinean state police, who have orders to keep out foreign foodstuffs, will not confiscate their goods. A very few cultivators still walk up the valley beside their donkeys loaded with crates and baskets full of fruits and maize. They unload their products on the outskirts of the fair so that their donkeys will not encumber the place of exchange. Busy with their prayers, the local breeders do not get to the plain before the following morning, at the same time as the herders who have come by jeep from remote villages, outside the bounds of those participating in the church celebration.

During the gathering, each community concentrates on a specific sector, which represents an economic activity and an ecological niche. Cultivators from the valley specialise in maize and fruits, those from the intermediate zone in tubers, and herders come down from the hills laden with meat. The participants usually unload their goods in the spot they occupy each year so that their exchange partners can find them easily. The things to be exchanged are set out directly on the ground, in wooden crates and burlap sacks. The women take care of arranging the foodstuffs, running their own display on with their neighbours so as to create rows on either side of an aisle that the public is invited to use. Since close kin lay out their wares contiguously in a shared row, this arrangement reflects the preferential alliances and facilitates their cooperation during the fair, as well as the circulation of food and gossip. Collaboration within households is also required for conducting exchanges of agricultural produce. One member stays on site while another walks around the stalls looking for exchange partners, herders mixing with the different groups of cultivators and vice versa. The adolescents form their own groups and stand around talking in the central aisles of the fair. Surprisingly similar, their outfits (jeans, hoody and cap) reveal their desire to dress in their best clothes, bought in the popular shops of Villazón. The younger children jostle around the games of chance and the football tables, interrupting their play for ice cream and sweets.

**Figure 3.1.** Spontaneously formed rows at the Yavi Easter fair in 2005. Photograph by the author.

Coming back to their stalls, cultivators who carry the finest sheep and breeders who pile up fruits and ears of corn spark comments among their attentive neighbours. Once everyone is back in place, intracommunity cooperation resumes among allies: food is shared, money is lent, supplies are watched and information is passed on. A convivial atmosphere reigns among neighbours, and they appreciate these few days of closeness. 'It's only here that we get a chance to chat. At home, we don't have the time. You've got to run around in all directions', I was told by Mirta, who was constantly engaged in conversation at the Abra Pampa fair. At midday, these allies also gather with their compadres to share in a festive meal of grilled chops, wine and lemonade, with fruit for dessert. After lunch, some of the guests go to sing in one of the two tents, which fill up as the day goes on. The older people still remember when there was singing and dancing all over the fair with no physically designated space explicitly reserved for these activities. Today, one is unlikely to see a peasant singing outside the few square metres surrounded by tarpaulins that serve as tents.

When night falls, the animation around the cemetery shuts down. The herders who arrived that morning in their vehicles full of meat leave for home with their newly acquired goods, sometimes leaving behind an adolescent bent on night-time ventures. Only the coplas singers continue, oblivious to the angle of the sun. After having heated some soup, the Bolivian cultivators once again transform the fairground into a campsite. With nightfall, the cold makes itself felt, and each family huddles in the tight resting place they have arranged to shelter from the weather. The next morning, exchanges start with first light, when other shepherds arrive with new pieces of meat, in search of their trading partners from the valley. After two or three days, the fairground is empty. The protagonists, laden with their coveted exotic products, join their relatives in the truck that will take them back to their village.

Taken as a whole, the fair engenders a twofold movement of concentration and dispersion. The peasants' gathering around a religious centre is followed by their dispersal: from the fiesta site towards the rural villages and then from the village centres towards the households scattered over the community territory. The physical displacements that structure the fair are thus composed of inverse symmetrical routes taken by the peasants from the highlands and the lowlands to meet up in this intermediate location. Foods also circulate along this route. For the herders, fruits and maize replace the meat and wool they carried on the outward journey. Unlike the people, who return the way they came, the agricultural products continue the trip begun a few days

**Figure 3.2.** A family packing their encampment and goods at the end of the Santa Catalina fair in 2010. Photograph by the author.

earlier in the hands of their producer. When observing peasants stating their journey back I was struck by an impression of identity inversion: stockbreeders loaded with maize temporarily take on the appearance of cultivators, and the latter, their sheep in hand, look like breeders. Indeed, without the least bit of meat and loaded down with a diversity of fruits and cereals, the breeders return home *lindos* and *contentos* (joyful, happy). Used to qualify beautiful produce, *lindo* can also refer to humans, indicating that they are in fine fettle.

### Dancing

On Saturday night, the nerve centre of the fiesta shifts to the *carpas* (tents). The taxis from La Quiaca arrive full and go back empty; jeeps and minibuses coming from the surrounding rural communities are also full. The rendezvous is set between eleven p.m. and midnight, which is when the musicians start the *cumbia* concerts. The renown of invited bands reflects the importance of the encounter. At the Manka Fiesta, musicians come from as far away as La Paz or Lima. The variety of *cumbia* widespread in Jujuy is the Andean one incarnated by bands known throughout the cordillera. The young people begin to party. Dancers gradually fill the tents, which are circumscribed by superposed metal sheets. The lighting is rudimentary: a few bulbs hang in the corners, and others designate the place reserved for the musicians. At the back, the bar is made of beer cases, still full, which portend a drunken night. Alcohol inevitably intensifies the affectivity of social interactions, charged with hate and love. Every ball gives rise to encounters and events that circulate as gossip the next day. It is noteworthy, however, that drunken interactions have no major consequences on daily life. Fights are a constant feature of balls, but the enmity is most likely to calm down once the effects of the alcohol have dissipated. Dancing nights also end in sexual encounters. While, during the day, bachelors form groups excluding girls, cross-gender interactions gain in intensity when the night advances. Like hostility, these interactions do not usually last beyond the party. When a child is conceived, the father is not expected to take responsibility for those qualified as *hijos de la fiesta* (children of the party).

Seductive interplay ordinarily unfolds in a circle of sociability embracing adjacent communities. This endogamy is not framed by strict

**Figure 3.3.** Teenagers' celebration in the sector of the ball tents at the Manka Fiesta in 2008. Photograph by the author.

normative prescriptions. Still, criteria of attractiveness are articulated on ecological origin. Highland and lowland people ascribe derogatory stereotypes to each other, which depreciate them as sexual partners (this is also observed by Karasik 1984: 76). Puneños are depicted as ignorant and silent, while Quebradeños are reputed to be unfaithful skirt-chasers. Paradoxically, the circulation of these clichés speaks to the inclusion of homologues from complementary ecological zones into the circle of uncommon, but still potential partners. It is unusual to hear such rhetoric about Creoles, not to mention gringos, who are not even approached.

While the road around the cemetery, too, teems with people, the fairground is now deserted. The sound of the *cumbia* can already be heard and will not stop until daybreak, so the cultivators get only a light, broken sleep. The details they include the next morning in their commentary of the night-time activities attest to this. They know at what times the power failed, how many times the police had to be called to break up fights, which of the nearby tents had been urinated on by some man who was drunk. Beyond the apparent inertia of the camp, the farmers turn a blind eye to the younger generations' merry-making.

Only the central aisle is still used by the older people on their way to the two *carpas de coplas* (coplas tents), the last remaining areas of animation in the midst of a drowsy crowd. The average age of the participants attests to the younger generations' disaffection for this activity, preferring as they do the *cumbia*. The dancers form circles as they arrive, within which they dance, sing and drink. These groupings mark affinities: the dancers gather based on extended kinship networks. Close friends and compadres are invited to join in, thus signalling their inclusion in the network in question. As they circle, the dancers sing slow songs that provide the cadence, which is akin to walking. Those who have brought their instruments mark the rhythm with tambourines and flutes. For instance, one can hear them sing:

> Pachamama Holy Earth, don't eat me yet.
> See how young I still am. I would like to enjoy life.
> Pachamama Holy Earth, don't eat me yet.
> See how young I am, I must leave some seeds.

People invite each other to partake of beverages, which are discourteous to refuse. They buy bottles of wine and lemonade, which they offer to someone of their choice as a gesture of respect and affection; the recipient must then share a round (*compartir a la vuelta*), filling the glass in honour of each member of the group until the bottle is empty.

Before drinking, the guests take care to sprinkle some of the beverage on the ground to share with Mother Earth, to whom the dancing and singing are also addressed.

During the fiesta, the consecutive shifting of the principal pole of activity attests to the coordination of the different phases of the celebration, which are separate in terms of both space and time. The ecclesiastical ceremonies take place in the church in the middle of the village. The fair and the dancing are juxtaposed and are held on the outskirts of the village at complementary times: goods circulate during the daylight hours, while the dancing gets going when night falls.

## Performing Social Distinctions

### Puneños and Quebradeños

The main protagonists at fairs are peasants, who come in from scattered communities. They rarely use the term Kolla for self-identification in their private conversations. In their daily lives, they actually verbalise more spontaneously their belonging to economic entities in terms of ecological criteria. Following a typical Andean 'vertical economy', this polarisation is mapped as follows: highland herders tend sheep and llamas in the puna lying at 3,500 metres, lowland cultivators grow maize in the quebrada below 2,500 metres, and intermediate tuber cultivators dwell in between. In the Argentinean puna, this intermediate zone has no explicit name: people are either Puneños or Quebradeños, according to whether they live in a highland community where herding is a key practice. In the zone of Yavi, this village is the articulating point above which people are considered Puneños, while below they are seen as Quebradeños. This limit corresponds to ecological criteria that shape the landscape specifically in each region. In the cold plateau, the soil is only covered by a steppe, while the quebrada features trees of different varieties, among which the *churqui* tree is emblematic.

Ecological specificities of each region are pinpointed in the pioneering work of geographer Carl Troll (see Harris 2000; Platt 1986), who associates them with tipping points in temperature. Accordingly, Troll has traced a heuristic line separating the two regions. In practice however, the border is not sharp, and an intermediate zone unfolds between puna and quebrada. Platt has extensively studied this border in the Bolivian region of North Potosi, where this zone is known as *chaupirana*. However, Platt describes practices intended for people to shrink the intermediate zone and reduce it to a simple line (1986: 232). Harris corroborates this point, noting that, despite the empirical existence of the transitional zone, 'in symbolic thought it can be "reduced" to a line which opposes and joins two halves' (2000: 105). In a similar vein, fairs contribute to the practical erasure of the intermediate zone, since these encounters display the Puneños as herders living in the high plateau, as compared to the Quebradeños, who cultivate vegetables in the valley.

At fairs, this dual representation is made manifest by the peasants' own discourse, which reifies their respective belonging to one of the two groups. Discreet comments are thus addressed to the other members of the household. For instance, Genoveva drew her husband's attention to a breeder carrying a sack of maize to his stall, followed by a vegetable grower coming for his due and carrying a sack one-fourth full: 'Look at all he has given him! And that too [pointing out the small sack carried by the woman]! Our product has value, too, not just meat!' In adding this last phrase, Genoveva is affirming her belonging to a group of maize growers, in contrast to another that produces meat. These belongings are also verbalised in the exchanges that accompany the transfer of agricultural goods, specifically when a conflict arises during the negotiation. At that point, the partners are quick to make stereotypical accusations aimed at unsettling the other, in which they identify their interlocutor with a broader collectivity. The following is an example of a herder blaming a vegetable grower: 'You must bring fat meat, not like that one.' The latter replied: 'The same for you. Sometimes you provide maize that is tough, spoilt, eaten by rats.' With these formulas, they mark a distinction between what is constructed as a community of herders and a community of cultivators.

When it comes time to exchange, the members of an economic community who are offering and seeking identical goods can also become potential competitors. The rivalry is concretised when certain products lack. In this case, to brag of the merits of their production, some do not hesitate to make comparisons with that of their neighbours or relatives, and to denigrate them. In fact, cornering goods can arouse tension between peasants who are the closest. For instance, Emilia reassured me after having quarrelled with her neighbour at the fair who was also her comadre: 'We only quarrel for a minute. And only over meat. Then we forget.' As potential competitors, members of a community benefit from distancing themselves physically to carry out their exchanges. Therefore, cultivators stride across the fair, looking for potential partners from the highlands. People from an ecological zone are nevertheless interdependent, since the image of the ones can tarnish that of the others. When they comment on the quality of the products they have exchanged, or the equivalence they managed to

obtain, the speakers refer to the quality of the work of the complementary producers as a whole, again marking a difference between 'us' and
'them', built on a residential ecological zone and on economic activities.
    Mutual regards of cambio partners are deeply ambivalent. Those
living on the highest lands of the mountains, surrounded by the most
powerful divine powers and the wild entities of their inhabited pastures, are seen as uncivilised and enigmatic people. The meat they produce is nonetheless the most appreciated. At fairs, a group of vegetable
growers usually quickly gathers around the herders as soon as they
arrive. All try to reserve a piece of meat for themselves by listing the variety and quality of the vegetables they have harvested. Thus, herders
are at an advantage when negotiating exchange conditions. They also
usually receive the *yapa*, a small amount of goods offered at the end of
the transaction to which I will come back later. Notwithstanding their
privileged situation at the moment of the transactions, they are seen as
simple minded and materially deprived by cultivators, who are keen on
reselling bartered meat and feel they enjoy better living in the warmer
valleys. In any case, the fact that they produce their own goods place
Puneños and Quebradeños within the categories of campesinos or *productores* (producers), both of which bear an Indigenous connotation
in the Andes of Jujuy.

### Bolivianos and Argentinos

Identities based upon agricultural activities extend beyond Kolla people, since they are also invoked by Bolivian herders and cultivators,
who are not concerned by Argentinean mappings of Indigenous people. As mentioned earlier, fairs in northern Argentina draw peasants
from neighbouring Bolivia. The participants' nationality is indicated
by their Spanish, which they speak with a particular accent and vocabulary. The women's traditional dress is another distinctive criterion.[4]
The Argentineans are dressed in their best clothes. The flamboyant
colours of their full skirts set off their white blouses. They wear long,
colourful earrings, and their hair is parted in the middle and hangs
down in braids, which are extended by multicoloured *tullmas*,[5] for
those who appreciate the traditional hairstyle. Some even wear a flower
on their hat. The women cultivators from the adjacent valleys of Sococha and Talina appreciate another style. Some wear the traditional,
dull-coloured pleated skirt, over a number of underskirts whose em-
broidery can be glimpsed. An apron covers their blouse and knitted
vest. They wear their traditional sandals with raised heels. Today, these
women are Bolivia's main representatives, together with a few trad-

ers from La Paz and potters from Casira. At bigger fairs, such as the Manka Fiesta or the Abra Pampa Easter fair, several Bolivian regions are represented, each of which has its own subtle dress variations: the length, fabric and design of the skirt, and the width and height of the hat are the main indications of locality.

At fairs, economic identities are grafted onto national belongings: most of the cultivators are Bolivian, while most of the herders are Argentinean. This division is because of the establishment of a national border cutting through the territory of ecological complementarity outlined by Albeck (1992) for the pre-Hispanic period (see chapter 2): accordingly, the valley zones of Sococha and Talina fell under the jurisdiction of Bolivia, while the adjacent plateaus are Argentinean.[6] Allusion to nationality in the protagonists' speech shows that it is another feature of their identity. When glossing their transactions, peasants mingle national, economic and ecological registers of identity. At the Santa Catalina fair, I heard: 'Bolivians bring maize. We, from the puna, come with meat.' These assertions only partially match reality, since some herding communities are on the Bolivian side while some maize producers come from Argentinean villages.

**Figure 3.4.** Bolivian potters from the region of Casira in Bolivia, wearing their typical clothes at the Yavi Easter fair in 2010. Photograph by the author.

Peasants nonetheless distinguish themselves according to their nationalities and ascribe established stereotypes to one another. On this basis, Argentineans are said to be lazy and simple minded, while Bolivians are accused of being cunning and deceitful. 'They are sharp. They are not dumb like us. Bolivians, it's another kind of people', Sofia, a neighbour in Yavi, glossed as we drove back from the market. When she needed labour to continue the endless renovation of her extended house, she constantly looked for Bolivians – not only because their wage is cheaper, but also because she observed that they work harder. However, this well-established image of the Bolivian as a hard worker cross-cuts the stereotype of herding in the Argentinean highlands being harsher than cultivating the valleys.

Despite this reciprocal stigmatisation of economic behaviours, Argentinean and Bolivian peasants paradoxically acknowledge a shared cultural identity. They are usually aware of the long history of population displacement from the northern altiplano, dating back to pre-Incaic times and still significant today. Indigenous people from both countries have a sense of shared cultural practices, as well as a shared history. Massive transnational migrations to the Argentinean mines and sugar plantations at the beginning of the twentieth century contributed to strengthen their sense of shared community. In the first half of the twentieth century, Bolivians and Argentinean highlanders shared tasks and accommodations, and many migrants settled permanently in the region.[7] In any case, exploitation and physical violence are still alive in the collective memory, associating Andean ethnicity with a sense of suffering shared across nationalities. Juan, Sofia's husband, thus told me while we were chatting in his courtyard, 'From there [he said pointing north to Bolivia], to all Jujuy, people are the same.'

Generally speaking, the cultural practices of the ones and the others are regarded as similar, even though contrasts can sometimes be pointed up, sometimes minimised, depending on the speaker's intentions. Bolivians and Argentinians are fond of comparing at length the offerings they perform at one celebration or another, the recipes they use for traditional dishes or the practices that promote plant growth. For instance, while we were chatting about prosperity during the Yavi fair, Genoveva explained that she praised the moon when full, for attracting money to her household. She then asked me with much curiosity what was the procedure in Yavi and if the moon was also called upon to make sure the money would not be lacking. Furthermore, the embeddedness of the temporality of fairs within the religious calendar lends itself to comments that are more specific. Preceding the celebration of the deceased on All Saints' Day, the Manka Fiesta is the theatre of discussion on cooking habits for the dead while exchanging key ingredients for their ancestor's meals.

In a more general sense, Bolivian are thought to preserve their traditions better, as epitomised by Quechua being their mother tongue (see Karasik 2010). Furthermore, Argentinean Puneños develop tropes of states officials having 'stolen their culture' by extracting archaeological remains, prohibiting the celebration of telluric entities (notably under the dictatorship) or developing denigrating education policies. In comparison, they see Bolivian Indigenous people as more apt to organise political mobilisation, defend their rights and preserve their cultural traditions. As Karasik nicely put it, Bolivia is depicted as 'a reservoir of ancestral andineanity' (2010: 276, my translation).

National belonging as a basis of identity claims is thus complex and ambiguous: sometimes peasants acknowledge the existence of a cultural, social and economic unity that stretches from one side to the other of their ecological milieu, while at other times nationality is mobilised as a register of distinction. This ambivalence contrasts with Creole Argentineans' estrangement from Bolivia, which they depict as a poor, backward and chaotic nation. The qualification of Bolivian and Kolla are used in the similar pejorative sense in interactions between Creoles and Indigenous people, be they Argentineans or, in fact, Bolivians. This confluence puts Argentinean Puneños along with the Bolivians as epitomising national alterity – a discrimination that the 1994 amendment of the constitution was meant to revert by assigning a specific form of citizenship to native communities under the status of Indigenous People.

### Campesinos, Comerciantes and Visitantes

Until the end of the twentieth century, no Indigenous peoples were formally recognised in Argentina, and there were no collective actors aggregated around ethnic identities. Andean people in Argentina were identified as campesinos, poor ones, following class distinctions. According to Karasik (2005), there was nonetheless a sense of shared identity, in contrast to 'others' who were not Puneños or Quebradeños. After decades of politics intended to erase any sense of ethnic belonging, only recently have they started to be distinguished as *indigena* (Indigenous), following ethnic tropes. The Argentinean archaeologist Axel Nielsen sums up the situation in a documentary on Kolla people on a state television channel:[8]

In the '80s, the organisation of native people, as we see it today, with the vitality of present days, a presence in the media, did not exist at the time. Most of the people in the quebrada . . . felt that they were campesinos. . . . The underestimation of Indigeneity that was the stamp of the creation of the nation-state in Argentina, was still surviving, incorporated by the people in their discourse. Only since the constitutional reform of 1994 . . . have we started to hear people calling themselves native, starting to adopt symbols.

In the Andean region, these 'natives' were thus officially recognised as Kolla people. The etymology of this ethnonym alludes to the temporary integration of this region in the Tawantinsuyu: the southeast quarter of the Inca Empire was known as Kollasuyu, deriving from the pre-Aymara estate of the Kollas. Noteworthy is that its use as an ethnonym appeared only in colonial times (Karasik 2006: 475). Before their integration in the empire, people in the puna were scattered in a constellation of political entities that were displaced and dislocated under the Incas, and under the Spanish rulers afterwards (Karasik 2010; Lorandi 1992).[9] Ethnic configurations are thus far more complicated than the Kolla category constructed by national administration implies. As the historian Ana Maria Lorandi puts it: 'To date, it is difficult to ethnically identify inhabitants of the puna and the Humahuaca valley. Present doubts are probably rooted in the Incaic intervention, which modified, at least partially, the interethnic map in the whole region' (1992: 138, my translation). She further notes that chronicles make no reference to ethnic organisation in the puna, nor in the valley; they only mention the existence of local collectives.

Ethnic configuration after colonisation was further confused by massive migration from present-day Bolivia. However, newcomers from the Alto Peru were culturally close to the Puneños, and they are said to have integrated local communities without provoking major cultural change (Karasik 2006: 468; Lorandi 1992: 153). The situation is quite unusual compared to other regions in the colonial Tucuman, where Indigenous people were disseminated either physically or through cultural assimilation (Lorandi 1992: 156). People in the puna are now publicly regarded as predominantly Indigenous, forming a unity sharing cultural affinities with Bolivian highlanders. While the category of *indio* disappeared as a fiscal status from Northern Argentina in the nineteenth century (1992: 161), it continued to be used by the administration, along with the terms *indigena* or 'native', until the end of this century (Karasik 2006: 475). Still today, *indio*, *indigena* and *Kolla* continue to be used in daily interethnic interactions, a context in which they are also used as insults.

Although Kolla are still stigmatised as backwards and uncultured, Indigenous leaders now exalt the pre-Columbian past and extol its cultural richness. In the cordillera of Jujuy, the constitutional amendment in favour of Indigenous peoples was part of a broader movement of 're-ethnicisation', as it is locally known.[10] In this context, their ethnonym is proudly circulated in the cities in the form of restaurant names, bus companies, local associations and radio programmes. However, Indigenous leaders in different departments strive to define their ethnicity according to pre-Columbian categories. In the valley, the Oclayas and the Omaguacas have been recognised and have gained independent legal status. They reject the term Kolla, not only because their rulers imposed it, but also because this ethnonym was loaded with discriminative racial value throughout colonial and postcolonial history. Like the category of chola examined by Weismantel, the ambiguous qualification as Kolla is thus a 'multivocal instrument of social intercourse' (2001: 98) that can nurture complicity or hostility, depending on who is speaking (see Karasik 2010).

In daily interactions, however, ethnic distinctions are still usually used as derogatory labels. Neither Kolla nor Creole are terms that cir-

**Figure 3.5.** Although ethnonyms are rarely used in fairs' interactions, the term Kolla is publicly displayed since the legal acknowledgement of Indigenous communities in Argentina. Photograph by the author.

culate at fairs.[11] Ethnic distinctions in this context are articulated upon economic practices. Campesinos or productores, who in fact originate from surrounding Indigenous communities, are distinguished as the social group at the core of the fair, in contrast to *comerciantes* (merchants) and *visitantes* (visitors), who come from urban centres where they are unable to produce cambio goods. The latter usually fit the category of Creole, who are not direct descendants of Europeans and do not identify themselves as Indigenous, even if some of their ascendants may have done so (Sturzenegger-Benoist 2006). Since they do have native people among their ascendants, and share cultural practices and representations with them, the Creole category suggests a process of racial and cultural *métissage*. Thus, the boundary between Creoles and Indigenous people is much more subjective and dynamic than the national census would suggest. In this northern region, to be 'Creole' is a process of becoming in which food habits, urban residence or linguistic tonalities prevail over racial criteria.

As the next chapters make clear, agricultural production and transactional interactions are also important loci where ethnic identities are played out. Creoles do not engage in direct transfers of agricultural goods from the cordillera, which do not make up the essential part of their diet. They thus come to the fair without a load and use the national currency to make their transactions. This distance from peasant affairs, which is a vector of creolisation, does not prevent their affective investment in fairs, which they acknowledge, like the church rituals, as 'being part of their culture'. These local visitors thus occupy a paradoxical position of distanced integration. The products they buy attest to this: a clay pot or a wicker basket to add a rustic touch to their home; a piece of charqui or dried peaches, the taste of which brings back childhood memories. Yet, some Creoles take an active part in fairs: these are traders specialised in manufactured products. They attend fairs to retail the goods they have bought wholesale in the urban market.

Fairs along the beaten path also attract tourists, who join the event as spectators of what they regard as regional folklore. While local Creoles are familiar with such gatherings and have known about them since childhood, tourists view them as an opportunity to see what 'Indian life' looks like. They might be interested in buying a clay pot or a wicker basket for their homes, or maybe some fruit, but they engage only in minimal transactions. Even though their mode of consumption resembles that of local Creoles, one can tell which tourists are from the southern provinces. Their hiking gear, sunglasses and cameras are all indications, while their eventual European phenotype and their accent attest unequivocally to their region of origin. They are treated as gringos,

**Figure 3.6.** A gringa buying a wicker basket from a braided campesina at the Yavi Easter fair in 2010. Photograph by the author.

although once again it is unusual to hear it verbalised in the context of the fair. While some local councils are now promoting fairs as tourist attractions, the presence of gringos remains unusual in most gatherings.

In a way, Creoles can be said to stand at the intersection between the tourists from the south and the main protagonists: from the latter's perspective, they are known 'others', in contrast to the white people, who are the extreme figures of otherness. While ethnic belongings are made implicit by the verbalization of social categories focussed on economic activities (campesinos, comerciantes, visitantes), we shall see how ethnic sense of belonging is expressed in actions and transactions at fairs.

## Material Circulation and the Fabric of Subjectivities

### Agricultural Produce

Transactions at fairs centre on the agricultural produce brought by peasants who are looking for goods that cannot be easily produced in their own fields. 'Mostly, it is an exchange of what we lack for what they lack. They don't have meat; we bring them meat. We have no flour or maize', said Griselda a young woman from the city of Abra Pampa who used to accompany her grandmother to exchange her meat at fairs. The displacement of campesinos together with their produce from the two main ecological tiers is thus the backbone of a fair.

The herders from the highlands for the most part bring llama and sheep meat. When the meat is fresh, it is sold in pieces, cut up in the case of llama meat or in *abierto* for mutton. Abierto designates the whole animal (with the wool still on) that has been 'opened' in half and gutted. In its dried form, the abierto is called *chalona*, and the pieces are known as *charqui*. The herders bring from one to five animals, each destined to obtain a particular good, depending on the composition of the household and its diet. When there are many children, the household sets aside one or two animals for fruits. A similar number is reserved to obtain maize. In the case of Justo, who lives with his wife, Isabella; his mother; two of his children and two of his granddaughters, every year two sheep are set aside to acquire maize. And Justo adds: 'It is because we eat little mote [dried maize]. We eat noodles, rice. Each week we make bread. Before, yes, we used to always eat mote. Maize was the main food.' While new ingredients have entered the daily menu, mote continues to be a classic ingredient of peasants' meal – although renown for not being appreciated by young generations. The herders also provide fat, cheese and raw wool, spun or woven. Some bring medicinal herbs from the highlands: *rica-rica, chachacoma* and *pupusa*. Lastly, the inhabitants of the puna, and more specifically the region of Cochinoca, have the monopoly on salt, which they harvest from the salt flats that cover their territory. This mineral is fundamental for cooking and is indispensable for the animals' growth,[12] which makes it a much-sought good at the fairs.

The cultivators from the quebrada arrive loaded down with a variety of maize. *Blanco* (white) and *amarillo* (yellow) maize are the principal varieties that herders look for, although one can see an array of colourful cobs featured in the cultivators' stalls. Some even offer the *morado* (purple) maize coveted for preparing a highly appreciated sweet beverage known as *api*.[13] Producers from the valley also bring fruits (apples, pears, peaches, grapes, prickly pears, pomegranates and quinces), nuts, fresh aromatic and medicinal herbs, baskets and flowers.[14] At the end of winter, they come with maize and dried fruits. The more prosperous cultivators bring a maximum of fifteen quintals of fruits and maize – any more than that and they risk not being able to exchange all their goods and needlessly to run up travel expenses.

Cultivators from the intermediate zone supply the fair with an array of potato varieties, oca (sweet potatoes), cereals (barley) and broad beans. As for potatoes, the collareja is the most widespread variety. Wuaycha, Desiré, Imilla Negra, Sani, *papa verde* and *papa lisa* are other varieties one can find at fairs. To complement the vegetable species they are able to grow at this altitude, they also raise some animals. However, craggy slopes circumscribe their narrow plots, making live-stock farming disadvantageous compared with the herders, who can graze flocks on the high puna. Because of competition from highland herders, these cultivators provide fairs with the potatoes, beans and cereals that grow in their fields, and they tend to ignore their minor activity of livestock farming. Peasants from the intermediate region therefore identify with lowland cultivators, although they distinguish themselves by trading crops that do not thrive in the lower valley. Being familiar with ethnographic literature stressing the dual dimension of Andean economies, I saw the products being exchanged during the fairs as an instantiation of the prevalence of such a socio-economic pattern in the southern part of the cordillera. From this perspective, the exchanges at fairs are part of these practices that contribute to 'perfect a discontinuity that in nature is only sufficient to suggest itself as a principle of social organization' (Platt 1986: 233).

The full range of goods the cultivators harvest is not represented in the stalls. Only those foods that are *queridos* (cherished) and *deseados* (desired) by the inhabitants of the event's zones of affluence are dis-played. When I asked Simona, a middle-aged grower from Chosconty, if she had brought some of the turnips I usually buy from her at the market, she answered: 'I haven't brought any turnips. That's because people here don't eat them. They don't know how to prepare them.' This example confirms Humphrey and Hugh-Jones's point on the im-portance of desire as a driving affect in barter. The barter relationship, they say, 'is one which defines the other party as having something one wants' – as opposed to gifts characterised by compulsion and 'con-trived asymmetry' (1992b: 18). Therefore, the existence of shared food practices among campesinos from different ecological zones condi-tions the fairs' existence.

Not only are different categories of produce compared to each other: fruits with potatoes, maize with meat, herbal medicine with fat and so on. The quality of the products within each category is appre-ciated according to specific criteria: the most coveted items are the bigger specimens. The size of the product speaks to their growing po-tential or, in other words, to their resistance to pests, rats and disease, which vitality competes with the crops. Bigness is thus a key quality. Beyond the size, every kind of fruit, vegetable, tuber or piece of meat has further criteria of appreciation: sweetness for fruits, flouriness for potato and tenderness for meat. But these are qualities that can only be appreciated through the sensitive experience of eating, which for most products require long processes of sun drying, crushing, soaking, boiling or grilling. During the fair, the key criterion used to gauge quality at first sight is thus the size of the product: sheep or llamas, potatoes, maize cobs, grapes or apples attract the consumer's eye and stir up desire when they are big, that is to say, fat, fleshy or juicy. Of course, in practice, a big specimen might not comply with gustative expectations. A tall but skinny animal hardly produces a nice meal. Taste qualities in meat in fact relate to fat content. However, because when all other variables are constant, the bigger animal will be the fatter, *gordo* (fat) and *grande* (big) are used as synonyms to qualify a piece of meat, as well as *flaco* (skinny) and *chiquito* (small). Interestingly, persons acknowledged as guapas are expected to breed animals that are *gordos*, as the herder will have a lot of energy to bring them to the best pastures and to care for them in a more general sense.

Therefore, size appears to be a key qualia for appreciating the products at fairs. Qualia is a core concept in Peirce's theory of human experiences in the world, referring to abstract properties as embodied in concrete entities. Lily Hope Chumley and Nicholas Harkness introduced this philosophical notion into anthropology, using it 'to refer methodologically to the experience of qualities as a fact of sociocultural life, rather than to qualities as purported properties of things in the world' (2013: 3). The prominence of dimensionality as an overarching repertory of qualia is epitomised by the *erracas* that are extracted of the exchange circuit and preciously kept by their owner[15] instead. Erracas are distinguished by their exceptional size and shape. Potatoes with unexpected protuberances and maize with twin cobs are common examples. When appropriately treated, erracas are expected to bring fortune and fecundity to the household. To this end, they are placed on a shelf in the kitchen, receiving incense smoke and challas during abundance celebrations at Carnival or Pachamama's day. When the next harvest comes, they can be consumed or used for offerings, in the hope that new erracas will come out of the earth and bring further prosperity. The exemplary case of the erracas stresses the relation between size and life force.[16]

### Mercaderías

In addition to providing an occasion to exchange goods produced by peasants, the fair also enables the circulation of manufactured commodities, most of them proposed by specialised traders. Among these goods, some were once made in the home or exchanged in barter networks but today are obtained from the industrial sector. Such is the case of candles, clothing, shoes, spices and *yista*, an alkaline chewed with coca leaves which today has been replaced by baking soda. It is also the case of those foods described as *mercaderías*, which were added to the daily diet in the twentieth century and replaced local agricultural products. These include pasta, rice, cooking oil, wheat flour, wine, tea and coffee, which have replaced dried maize, animal fat, corn flour, chicha and aromatic herbs in the local cuisine.

The industrial foods are highly standardised. Within each category of product, the evaluation is homogenised. The merchants have only one brand per product, and only a few brands circulate for each one: the ones specialised in the cheaper, large-scale packaging favoured by peasants, who prefer to purchase enough to avoid going back and forth to the city for the family food supply. These are the cheapest brands available on the market, and price is the key criterion peasants use in comparing similar goods. Price is indeed the only information peasants ask about before making their choice. Many times, peasants order the commodity from the merchant, who keeps his or her stock in his vehicle, thus out of sight of potential consumers. All flour, vegetable

**Figure 3.7.** Commodities on sale at the Manka Fiesta in 2008. Photograph by the author.

oil, sugar or rice sold at fairs is seen as having the same qualities. Once acquired, they are all appreciated as signs of the successful articulation of the household economy with the wider society.

At the moment of consumption, I have never heard anyone comment on the gustative, culinary or dietetic qualities of those mercaderías. This feature contrasts with the agricultural goods, for which there is a complex scale of subspecies and qualities. Here the peasants carefully select their goods, according to criteria that attest to their fine-tuned knowledge of their diversity, scarcely discernible to the untrained eye. In any case, meals prepared with mercaderías are seen as less healthy and nutritious than those with local produce. Mercaderías can nonetheless receive the same libations and prayers as agricultural produce when included in the larder, in order to ask Pachamama that these items not be used up too quickly. This speaks to mercaderias' involvement in criar practices.

In addition to the necessities listed above, those attending the fair can also find pots and pans, clothing, furniture, radios and other objects rural families like to have. In contrast to the mercaderías produced by Argentinean industries, these goods come from Bolivia, where they have been made (as is the case of the furniture from Santa Cruz or of clothing), or are imported from China. The fair is also a place to consume products that mark the festive character of the event, such as ice cream, hot dogs, alcoholic beverages, toys or beauty products. Generally speaking, the merchants specialise in a particular product, but these specialities are not a criterion that distinguishes the merchant's identity.

In their fine-grained ethnographic accounts of Ecuadorian economies, Colloredo-Mansfeld (1999) and Weismantel (2001) both note that consuming commodities is seen as a way of becoming less Indigenous. In this southern part of the cordillera, this is not entirely true, since the possession of cars, televisions or cellular phones does not jeopardise one's identity as Indigenous campesino. However, this would be relevant about food consumption. Eating locally produced maize and sheep or llama meat is indeed viewed as a preferential vector of energy, or fuerza, which makes it possible to perform the heavy labour required by agriculture in the highlands. Liking mote is used as a stereotype to attest one's belonging to an Indigenous community.

## Food Circulation and the Creation of Subjectivities

Meat and maize are the pillars of agricultural production in the highlands and lowlands, respectively. Therefore, they crystallise their producers' membership in one of the two economic communities that complement each other in the peasants' representations of their economy: Puneños and Quebradeños. They indicate both geographical origin and main economic activity. The latter is in turn interpreted as one facet of a lifestyle characterised by a set of daily practices. Such identification between people and the fruits of their agricultural labour is verbalised by using the latter as a metonymy for the former. When I asked a cultivator whether there would be a fair at a given saint's day feast in the highlands, she predicted: 'If the fruit is going, yes [there will be a fair]. But the fruit is not going.' Likewise, a cultivator lamented when observing that herders had already left the fair that 'the meat had gone'.

In addition to incarnating collective identities, the produce composing the stalls at fairs displays the household's agricultural success. The protagonists pay particular attention to the owners of specimens with attractive qualias. Obviously, they are looking for handsome produce to purchase. But they are also curious about outstanding production in their own category. Stunning agricultural produce is seen as the objectification of the producer's quality as a hard-working peasant, master in the arts of criar – as opposed to lazy people unable to grow coveted items. The colourfulness and abundance of the stall reflect its owner's virtue. Women stand proudly behind their piles of fruits and vegetables. They liked to emphasise the quality and diversity of their harvest, although they knew I was not a potential partner for cambio. Conversely, attacks on the quality of one's produce are taken personally, as I shall show in the next chapter.

As mentioned in chapter 1, crops and herds are endowed with personhood and intentionality. I wrote earlier about the emotions and reflexivity attributed to the various organic entities that humans care for and cultivate for their own consumption. Such agency implies a dense communication between these species and the peasants who ensure their growth: through the circulation of signs and sounds between the criador and the animal or vegetal being, through the circulation of affect and finally through the circulation of fuerza – in which ancestor and telluric beings contribute. The quality of harvested goods is thus inseparable from the quality of their producer, involving skills, care and physical strength. Displayed on the stage of the fair, beautiful agricultural products therefore display their grower's diligence and generosity in the practice of criar. Generosity and diligence are highly praised virtues, instantiated in the size of the product the peasant has been able to harvest.

Lucia's speech during the Yavi Easter fair illustrates the intertwining between the appreciation of a peasant, its agricultural production

**Figure 3.8.** A cultivator gladly setting up her diversified stall at the Yavi Easter fair in 2005. Photograph by the author.

and the place where it is brought to fruition. She was from the high-land community of Suripujio, at 3,650 metres above sea level, where ecological conditions are favourable for herding. While talking, she waved the fruits of her harvest, taken from a wicker basket:

> I am from Suripujio, and I was the leader of the mourners [for the Easter procession]. But I also come to bring my produce, and we also bring a bit of meat, and we also bring craftwork. So, you watch. And that is what I sow in my place, in Suripujio. All of you, have a look at it: the broad beans that ripen in Suripujio. Are you looking at the garlic that ripens in Suripujio? Are you looking at the carrots? They grow in Suripujio. You are looking at the purple potato, the collareja potato and all the other produce that grows but I could not bring. Green potato grows; oca grows. You will say that in Suripujio nothing grows. Everything grows! And likewise, we breed [animals]. And likewise, we make craftwork. That's my word. You will know me. My name is Ramirez[17] Lucia. I always set off to the fair, *cambalaches*,[18] barters. That's my word.

The fact that her sentences switched from 'I' to 'we' speaks to her iden-tification to a broader collectivity. Her pride in abundance extended to her community of Suripujio, including the fertility of the land. Still, she ended her speech by emphasising that her name will circulate, and everyone will know her as being a fruitful producer and mobile exchange partner. This corroborates the aforementioned statement that participation in fairs contributes to the extension of prosperous subjectivities towards other ecological milieu – the irony being that the carrots and garlic she displayed were obviously tiny, giving proof of Suripujio being first and foremost a herding (and wool crafting) highland community.

In a fascinating article on ritual drinking of soju in South Korea, Harkness shows how the qualia of softness as materialised in this drink merges gustative and social appreciation. This appreciation, he con-cludes, 'links consumers to culturally valorised, highly gendered, and temporally positioned identities within contemporary Korean society' (2013: 28). In a similar vein, sensible qualities related to dimension-ality experienced in agricultural produce are associated with a value combining sensual and moral appreciations. Social values reflect the relation between the size of the items and the producer's fuerza, as well as the latter's willingness to take care of nonhuman beings living in the fields. Hence, the size of the agricultural products is not only admired for its nutritive potential: it is also appreciated as an instantiation of a peasant's virtues.

The indexicality between the strength of life embodied in agricultural produce and the strength of the body that produces it reminds me of the identification Munn made between the lightness of a canoe and the lightness of human bodies in Gawa. In her fieldwork in Oceania, Munn identifies directionality and spatiality as clusters on which the construction of qualisigns is articulated. The study of Andean value creation suggests that the dimensionality expressed in the contrasted qualities of smallness and bigness constitutes another potential cluster of value creation. Dimensionality thus serves as an axis where strength is constructed as a key qualisign in Kolla agricultural practices. I shall say more on this later. For now, I would like to stress that this is not true of industrial goods, whose quality is dissociated from the identity of their producer and from that of the person who proposes them for exchange. When instantiated in mass-produced objects, the qualia of bigness is separate from the seller's subjectivity: it is not indexed to the seller's life strength, diligence or care for other organisms. Therefore, and because mercaderías are not appreciated as singular entities and their value is homogenous for each range of product, they cannot serve as an index of subjective appreciation.

Intended to be consumed the whole year round, agricultural products procured from complementary ecological niches can also index the consumers' identity once exchanged. I have already said that human vitality is not seen as a permanent quality. Ánimo and fuerza are fairly unstable, and food ingestion plays a prime role in their fluctuation. In principle, consuming ingredients produced by a campesino in a complementary zone is a key source of strength. Colloredo-Mansfeld has shown, however, that consumption is a key moment when a nonhuman being could capture one's ánimo. In this sense, 'consuming reduces the subject's authoritative control, internally diversifies capacities, and allows an influx of external potentials and moralities' (2003: 279). Opening one's body to substances produced by others supposes accepting the danger of losing, instead of increasing one's vitality, if the value of the food was of poor quality. And this risk extends until the maize, meat or tubers brought back from the fair are used up. I have never heard of people being the victim of *brujería* (sorcery) through bartered acquisition. Still, they express their concern in terms of the nutritious qualities of the food they are purchasing: cultivators would not want to eat meat from a sick animal, while herders would not want to stock potatoes eaten by worms. Clearly, the purpose of barter is to fill the larder with the best-tasting and most nutritious agricultural produce.

Furthermore, understanding how the value of agricultural products reflects the value of people requires more than just looking at production and consumption processes: their appreciation also depends on how they are circulated. Munn brilliantly makes this point when she shows that kula heirlooms instantiate the value of acts of production, as well as acts of exchanges. Indeed, in the Massim context, Munn identifies gift-giving as a key practice in the chain of value transformation: an act that impacts the evaluation of both the subject and the object, the latter becoming an instantiation of the virtue of the person who gives it away. This perspective is highly relevant for exploring the social fabric of fairs. Indeed, we shall see that transactions in this context participate in the creation of subjective values – values that are entangled in the objects of exchange. This is a point that I will examine later. Before that, though, I need to take a closer look at the different kinds of material transfer that compose the fairs, as well as the social relationship they are enmeshed in.

## Notes

1. The original words in Spanish are 'Dulce Jesús mió / Mirad con piedad / Mi alma perdida por culpa mortal Mi dulce Jesús De mi corazón / Llagado de heridas / Solo por mi amor.'
2. This is an extract from the church archives.
3. The original expression is: *se reciben de compadres*.
4. The men's dress does not present any regional peculiarities that I was able to perceive.
5. This Quechua term designates the metre-and-a-half-long thick strings decorated with tassels on the ends and designed to be braided into the hair.
6. In the case of the Department of Santa Catalina, it has only been since the treaty was signed in 1925.
7. Peronist labour laws established a contrast between Argentinean citizens and Bolivians migrants, who were not protected by a legal framework.
8. 'Pueblos originarios / Kollas, omaguacas y ocloyas: la raíz', *Encuentro*, video, 28:52, http://encuentro.gob.ar/programas/serie/8008/548?temporada=2 (accessed 30 December 2017, my translation).
9. Omaguacas, Atacamas, Apatamas, Cochinocas, Casabindos and Chichas predominated in the pre-Incaic political configuration. These ethnonyms have now lost their relevance since inhabitants of the highlands of Jujuy have lost track of these ethic belongings, corroded as they have been by massive migrations imposed by Inca and Spanish settlers.
10. Karasik (2010: 267) noted that this movement takes precedence in the 1980s, when, at the end of the dictatorship, Indigenous populations started to trace ancestral memories.

11. Though those who organise institutional meetings display the Kolla ethnonym, a point I shall come back to in the final chapter.

12. Its strategic uses, the fact that it keeps and can be broken up, have made salt a preferred good for use as a mediator of exchange and as a reserve value, thus becoming a quasi-currency (Karasik 1984: 63; Cipoletti 1984: 515; Madrazo 1982: 150). Today, blocks of salt no longer play the central role they once did in fairs.

13. I regret that I did not pay enough attention to agrobiodiversity when doing my research. I documented criteria of selection according to phenotypes (related to colour, shape, size), but I did not record the name of the many varieties of maize circulating at fairs. Yet, the most common of the white varieties was the *capia*.

14. Those who live at an even lower altitude, in the hot region called Yunga, have access to citrus fruits, wood, chickens and pigs. The historical studies (Gonzalez, Merlino and Rabey 1986: 137; Karasik 1984) mention the presence of these products at fairs in the transborder puna until the last quarter of the twentieth century. I personally saw them only at fairs in the village of Iruya, which is located in the lowlands near the Yunga. In Argentina, the inhabitants of these tropical zones do not grow coca. It is smuggled in from La Paz either by specialised traders or by peasants living close to the border who transport bundles of coca to make their trip pay.

15. The latter is the one who harvested the outstanding piece. When kin gather to harvest a plot, the guests are welcome to return home with the erracas they have been so lucky to encounter while working.

16. Note that this is not always the case. In the many miniature fairs organised throughout the Andes, life force is epitomised by the smallness of the commodities (see Angé 2016b).

17. This is a pseudonym.

18. *Cambalache* is the Lunfardo word for barter. Lunfardo is an argot from the province of Buenos Aires mixing Italian and Spanish vocabularies.

# Modalities of Transactions at Fairs

After having described the goods and the people that come together in the fair, I now turn my attention to the interactions in which people circulate their products. Their discourses distinguish fundamental modalities of transactions, each of which is characterised by specific sociability: cambio, negocio and invitación. Cambio is aimed at procuring agricultural goods that the protagonists do not produce, or at least not in sufficient quantity. That kind of transaction of produce from complementary ecological zones has been described in other parts of the cordillera. Harris (2007) and Platt ([1982] 2007) have documented it in Bolivia, and Fonseca (1972) and Mayer (1982) in Peru. The practices of cambio in Argentinean fairs will be discussed in light of existing ethnographies of Andean direct exchanges, including literature on other figures of barter that do not focus on agricultural produce (Ferraro 2011).

I will then outline peasants' normative distinction between cambio and negocio. The latter is intended to produce quantitative profit and is associated with the monetary circulation of industrial commodities. In contrast, 'invitations' are not designed explicitly to acquire new goods. Instead, they are chiefly intended to be pleasing to the beneficiaries so as to nurture a gratifying relationship. Any eventual material interest expected by the giver must therefore remain implicit, which implies the absence of negotiation over the conditions of a possible counter-gift.

In addition to these three modes of material circulation, I will address the yapa[1] alluded to earlier – a small quantity of goods given by one of the exchange partners on top of the previously agreed equivalence. The amounts of goods concerned by yapa are minimal. It is nonetheless a practice crucial to understanding the social fabric of barter at fairs. I shall come back to this point in the next chapter. At present, I will provide an account of the etiquette of the yapa when it closes direct exchanges of agricultural produces. Although the yapa is mentioned in many works on Andean economies (see e.g. Absi 2007: 359; Burchard 1974: 232; Göbel 1998: 171; Lecoq 1987: 25; Mayer 2002: 156; Orlove 1986: 93; Seligmann 1993: 197; Weismantel 2001: 145), detailed ethnographic descriptions of this transaction are still scarce (but see Angé 2011). I hope the following account will shed light on the relevance of this furtive gesture to the understanding of Andean economics.

For each of the exchange categories cited above, I will describe the modality of the material transfer, as well as the social backdrop of the transaction. At the same time, I shall examine the normative precepts and their practical expressions.

## Cambio

### Cambio and the Precepts of the Elders

As noted in the introduction, campesinos at fairs use the word *cambio* to refer to the direct transaction of their agricultural produce. However, this word is not used as a synonym of *trueque* (barter) in the official Spanish spoken in Argentina. This linguistic distinctiveness is associated with a practical dimension: because it involves llama or sheep meat, potatoes and maize, the cambio network is restricted to the producers of these goods – the herders of the puna and quebrada cultivators.[2] With the exception of wicker baskets and clay pots, cambio items are intended to be transformed into food and ingested. Besides forming the bulk of peasants' daily diet, these are key ingredients in the preparation of meals used to feed the ancestors, both the recently deceased and older ones incarnated in the landscape such as Pachamama.[3] In principle, then, cambio items are coveted for their use value. As a herder said to me at a fair in Abra Pampa, after acknowledging the very long distance she had to travel to reach the fiesta, some hundred kilometres from her village: 'We must run because of our passion for fruits. Some [are looking] for fruits, others for meat.' Her gloss emphasises the importance of desire in barter practices mentioned in the previous chapter.

There are fixed exchange rates for pairs of agricultural products circulating in opposite directions: for example, a dried sheep is equivalent to an *arroba* (between 11 and 13 kilos) of maize; a bag of potatoes equals the same volume of corn on the cob; a clay pot equals its content in foodstuffs. This traditional scale of value significantly departs from monetary prices. It is difficult, however, to attribute a fixed price to cambio produce, for reasons similar to those mentioned by Benja-

**Figure 4.1.** According to the elders' measures, a sheep from the highland is worth two cradles of fruits from the lowland. Photograph by the author.

**Figure 4.2.** Cambio scale of value is mostly based on volume: a clay pot is worth its content in food – here, dried meat. Photograph by the author.

**Figure 4.3.** Cambio scale of value is mostly based on volume: a wicker basket is worth its content in food – here, dried fava beans. Photograph by the author.

min Orlove in his article on barter on Lake Titicaca (1986: 93). Some goods, like dried meat, are not usually exchanged for money. Llama meat is sold at the central market of La Quiaca, although not legally, since they are no authorised slaughterhouses for these animals. As for vegetables, tubers and cereals, prices vary according to the quality and species, as well as the weather conditions and the period in the agricultural year. At the beginning of my fieldwork, a kilo of the nicest maize was worth about six pesos on the market. An average lamb could be sold at about one hundred pesos at the market. Still, a lamb was worth an arroba of maize, the market price of which was about seventy pesos. In any case, during the time I spent in Argentina, the price of meat increased constantly, without having major influence on cambio equivalences.

The crucial point is that monetary calculation should not serve as a point of reference to quantify the products' value. In this sense, cambio thus differs from the system of *unay precio* (old price) applied by peasants in central Peru (Mayer 2002; see also Fonseca 1972), where agricultural items are assigned a fixed price in pesos, departing significantly from market prices.[4] Equivalencies between products from different ecological zones are then established according to this non-market money scale. Instead of being settled in monetary prices, the cambio scale of value is essentially based on volume (wooden crates, sacks, and baskets are the most common). Even when reference is made to the arroba, peasants gauge the volume of the bag serving as the container. They do not weigh the goods, unless they are suspicious that their partner might try to cheat them. The importance of volume to establishing equivalencies between agricultural produces has already been stressed in other Andean contexts (Fonseca 1972: 331; Harris 2007: 77). When no established equivalence exists, the partners may agree to swap the goods *peso a peso* (weight for weight). They usually know their produce so well that they are able to estimate the weight by hand. In any case, distrust for scales is widespread, since they are suspected to be falsified. This suspicion fits with the relationship that Fonseca establishes between the use of the scale and the logic of profits, rather than direct consumption, an observation Harris corroborated in her Bolivian fieldwork (2007: 77; see also Orlove 1986: 93).

Broad cambio equivalences seem to be stable over time and have not evolved since the mid-twentieth century. They are called *medidas de los abuelos* (lit. measures of the elders), in an allusion to their ancestral transmission. The expression does not refer to any particular ancestor but broadly alludes to forebears who have died and to elders who were able to communicate with them while they were still alive. Generally, the voice of the elders is imbued with authority because they are seen as prime communicators with the ancestors. As Telesforo told me: 'The ancestors have settled [the measures] like that. They used to talk with Pachamama.' This filiation, with no clear-cut separation between elderly people, those recently dead and remote ancestors, sketches a lineage that goes back to Pachamama. This form of transaction therefore testifies to acknowledgement of the authority of the predecessors from whom the etiquette of exchange is being transmitted.

Furthermore, applying the elders' measures in barter transactions requires shared economic intimacy between the partners. Indeed, the ability to evaluate one's own goods as compared with those from another ecological zone according to the elders' scale entails a long-lasting personal engagement that occurs under the tutelage of an initiated person. When I enquired about the value of the llama she was transporting, Griselda, who had grown up in the city of Abra Pampa, replied:

> I don't understand barter. Only a little. I don't come [to fairs]. I am just accompanying my grandmother, because she is getting old. If I try to exchange, I can't. I didn't grow up with this. My grandmother has been

coming every year since she was a kid. She knows: this must be exchanged for such an amount of that stuff. They could give me miserable
quantities, and I wouldn't even realise.

Griselda means that mastering cambio etiquette results from a long
training, which is gained by accompanying elders on this kind of venture. The subtlety of bargaining the elder's equivalencies appropriately
is related to the fact that these measures lack precision. One easily
imagines that there are no exact criteria for deciding whether a bag of
potatoes is full. Far from being inviolable, these equivalences actually
serve as 'reference points for bargaining to take place' (Mayer 2002:
144). The quality of the goods, the abundance of the harvest, the ecological zone in which the fair takes place and the nature of the social
relationship between the partners are the main parameters mentioned
in the course of the negotiation.

The approximation of the elders' scale of measure thus opens a space
of negotiation also based on shifting subjective criteria. When Pancho
met with Masimo, an acquaintance from the valley, to exchange two
lambs for fruit at the Yavi fair, he engaged the conversation by recalling previous events at which they had met. As they were chatting, the
friends started to bargain over the traditional measures of exchange.
Pointing to the quality of his lamb, Pancho launched the negotiation:
'It's not skinny. No, it isn't. How do you want to exchange?' The cultivator replied: 'I will exchange, Brother. I will make up [to the traditional
equivalences].' Pancho mentioned that he needed many apples for his
nine children waiting at home. He then dwelled on the long way he
had to go to supply fresh meat to cultivators, stressing that the fair's
location was much closer to Masimo's home. 'In one's place, as I said,
everything costs almost double', he mentioned later on. When Masimo
stuffed some extra fruits into the herder's bag, the former commented,
'To friends, one must give different treatment.' This vignette shows that
cambio equivalences are adjusted according to the personal situation
of the partners, their social relationship and the context in which the
transaction takes place. Hence, equivalencies between the goods arise
as a 'performative moment to be re-created at every transaction', according to its particularities as Jane Guyer notes in her analysis of
conversions in Atlantic Africa (2004: 155).

## The Economic Benefits of Cambio

When discussing with participants at fairs, I have been surprised to
hear peasants wrapping their transactions in altruistic tropes, arguing

that they were bringing goods to please those who cannot produce them. Some participants in the fair claimed that their presence was a favour to their counterparts from other ecological niches, arguing that they would get better value at the market. I alluded to the moral appreciation of inter-ecological exchange in the first chapter. The moral duty to engage in that kind of barter has been observed in other Andean settings. Harris has noted that, between Laymi people, 'the definition of wants is affected by social obligations to circulate their produce' (2007: 78). Mayer has also witnessed the rhetoric of inter-ecological solidarity. Peasants put it forward to justify the maintenance of an unay precio that was disadvantageous to them. In 1969, Mayer recorded some peasants' reluctance to comply with the unay precio when engaging in exchange with their partners from complementary ecological zones, arguing that it would be in their interest to sell at the market. He nonetheless concludes, 'Highlanders felt the obligation to provide meat at an unfavourable exchange rate, without taking into account the real market price' (2002: 155). The moral appreciation of interecological exchanges suggests that a sense of collective duty certainly exists in Argentina as well. However, despite such narratives, the negotiation over the conditions of exchange shows that the transactors are concerned with their own benefits. In the next paragraphs, I point to potential interest peasants may find in participating in a barter fair instead of going to the market.

As noted in the introduction, economists disregard barter for not being as efficient as monetary exchange. This perspective fuels the myth about barter being a primitive form of monetary exchange. In this vein, a key argument is that barter increases the cost of transactions, the latter resulting from the necessity to meet the double coincidence of needs. We have seen that this impediment is easily overcome in the ecological context of the Andes, where every tier needs products from the other. This is generally true for inter-ecological exchange, as noted by Heady: 'In mountainous environments, neighbouring communities at different altitudes specialise in different crops, so that the existence of demand for one's own crop and of the supply of the neighbouring crop are well known to all concerned' (2006: 266). The Andean cordillera thus offers a geographical context in which barter can be potentially convenient.

Inter-ecological exchange is expected to produce use value, since one can swap plentiful goods for others lacking on the spot. As compared to caravans, fairs provide the advantage of gathering people from different niches at a meeting point fixed in space and time. Furthermore, the transnational, multi-ethnic and inter-ecological backdrop of the fairs constitutes a complex social and natural geography that multiplies the thresholds at which gains can be made (Guyer 2004): between currency and other standards of measure, between spatiotemporal locations and between social groups.

The valuation system used at fairs differs from formal markets governed by national legislation and Creole norms. Fairs are thus efficient settings in which to exchange products without value on the formal market. One possible reason is that their monetary price is too low for their transport to be worthwhile, which is the case for wool. Alternatively, their quality may not match the market standard, in the case of, say, worm-ridden, small or old items. Within this informal economic network, one can also circulate items that infringe sanitary laws, such as meat infected with parasites or logs informally traded from Bolivia. Other goods are excluded from the formal market for not being coveted by the creole population that constitutes the bulk of potential clientele, as is the case of dried meat in the form of charqui or chalona. While herders have a rough idea of the monetary price of a chalona, they would in fact hardly be able to sell it at the urban market. The efficiency of cambio is reinforced by the instability of the national currency, which discourages its use as a store of value. Those peasants living far away from regional markets convert their pesos into goods or herds, as they are aware of the risks of inflation. The influence of money availability and stability on the development of barter systems has been documented in other historical contexts, such as the Himalayan or the postsocialist economies (Cellarius 2000; Hivon 1998; Humphrey 1985; Seabright 2000).

Thresholds between space and time also provide an opportunity to improve economic gains. Travelling is generally regarded as a chance to access exotic items whose value increases as they move away from their place of production (Harris 2000: 61), especially if they go through multiple ecological zones. When nonperishable items are purchased, they can also be stored and exchanged in times of shortage. This was Andrea's strategy when she swapped her overdried broad beans for clay pots she did not need but which she planned to exchange later in the year at Christmas, when these are widely used for preparing offerings.

Because the fair's economy is located at the crossroads of different economic networks, sharp transactors attempt to eke out a profit by juggling between measurement systems in successive transactions sometimes combining barter and sales. Generally, economic instability in Argentina and Bolivia makes monetary values highly volatile, thereby increasing the opportunity for the sharp-eyed to obtain quantitative benefits by exploiting the gap between national pesos. So, value fuzziness is further amplified by the prevalence of the elders' measures, sometimes called upon by protagonists who are looking to increase their own gain in consecutive transactions. At the time of my field-work, the market value of meat surpassed its worth in complementary products according to the elders' scale of value. Herders were keen on complaining that the traditional measures were not convenient for them, but the cultivators defended the respect of the elders' stipula-tions, even though some used it to make profit out of it. Yet, such strat-egies are denounced as infringements of the ideal etiquette of cambio.

## Value and Virtue in Cambio

Because value in cambio is not simply an estimation of material ob-jects but is also an appreciation of people's acts, I shall now examine how economic values and subjective virtue are in fact entangled (this is a point generalised in Graeber 2001; see also Lambek 2008). I men-tioned earlier the importance of use and desire in the appreciation of cambio items, which are coveted as core ingredients in human and ancestor meals. The desire manifested for a given product is also a way of acknowledging the fruitfulness of others' labour. In this vein, the elders' scale of equivalencies is deemed to gauge the importance of the effort required to produce the items exchanged. In other words, these measures establish equivalencies between the efforts provided to produce the respective agricultural produce. The fact that partners are expected to consider transport effort, by offering more goods to those coming from further away, corroborates this point. A participant in the Saint Catherine fair clearly stated this fact, as he noted: 'Harvesting also requires sacrifices. If it freezes, crops are damaged. If it snows in the countryside, lambs die of starvation. This relationship mani-fests itself between those who conduct cambios: everything is sacrifice [*sacrificio*].' In this light, encounters around the value of agricultural produce compare the yield of the sacrifice required to raise and care for their animals and vegetables.

Indeed, peasants constantly verbalise that their life in the country is *sacrificada* (made of sacrifice). This notion in fact refers to a form of self-sacrifice, since it is related to the physical efforts expended to produce and distribute agricultural goods. When unsatisfied by the counterpart obtained, partners often underscore their intense effort – as this herder did, disappointed as he was by the quantity of maize re-ceived for his meat: 'That's very few. So much suffering in the country.' This idea relates to the extreme ecological conditions faced to breed animals and grow vegetables in the cordillera – conditions that peasants oppose to urban livelihood, gratified with town amenities while being largely exempt from intense physical labour.

Still, peasants never count the time spent to produce a given item in order to define its value. They do not proceed to a calculation similar to the one in Maurice Godelier's (1969: 13–14) original study of the worth of salt bars produced by the Baruya in New Guinea. The value of labour encapsulated in agricultural produce is not a numeraire, referring to units of time. Herders instead insist that they must tend their flock every single day, comparing the relative flexibility of llamas that graze alone with sheep that need the constant vigilance of a herder. Highlanders see the labour required to grow vegetables as less intensive, since the tasks are distributed according to the cultivator's priorities, only requiring full dedication at sowing and harvest time. Lowlanders retort that criar vegetables require intense strength in the fields, while watching a herd is a resting activity.

I am not in a position to state the truth, partly because I lack data to precisely estimate the effective proportion of daytime devoted to the production of different goods but mostly because it would be impossible to gauge the intensity of the effort provided. We nonetheless see that, in cambio, labour is evaluated as an intensity of force inverted in a creative interaction with the environment. This is not a strictly economic appreciation. In his study of value transformation through kula labour, Frederick Damon contrasts the production of instrumental items that mark a spatial complementarity between the partners – like fish, vegetables or canoe – and the crafting of shells that are intended to 'producing those kula generated names' (2002: 116). The labour involved in agricultural practices considered here is devoted to producing items of use in a context of spatial complementarity, as well as producing one's renown as a good person. As I mentioned before, the size of agricultural produce is a qualia that indexes the moral value of its producer: it instantiates his or her fuerza and criar capacity. Those elders' measures stipulating equivalencies according to volumes (one bag of potatoes for a bag of maize, any content of a clay pot is equivalent, etc.), infer that peasants' objectification through work produces substances that are analogous in value. This further means that the partners' labour is posited as being of equal worth if it involves a comparable sacrificio.

Sometimes, the interweaving of subjective and objective estimations is explicitly enacted in the course of the transaction. When we went to the Abra Pampa Easter fair to exchange fruits and vegetables, Mirta argued with a herder who had refused to barter because he deemed the exchange value settled by the cultivators was overrated. Her reply clearly relates the denigration of the value of her produce to a lack of appreciation of her quality as a diligent grower: 'We are required to provide effort. For you, it doesn't cost anything. You say that we only gather [fruit] from the ground, as if God was doing everything and we nothing.' The herder retorted: 'We also suffer. Bye!' And Mirta concluded: 'Yes, see you next time. We will continue gathering what's on the ground.' In this quotation, Mirta articulates the little worth of her fruits with the suspicion that no effort is required to produce them and that she therefore is a lazy person who distributes the fruits of other's efforts, that is, God or Pachamama. The appreciation of material and subjective value clearly merges: the underappreciation of Mirta's fruits is an offence to herself and her creative capacities.

Watching women bartering sago and fish at a market in Melanesia, Marilyn Strathern too observes a commensurability between people and their products: 'The kinds of computations that turn on amount and quality – how many sago lumps for how many fish, how large a pig in return for how large a pig – signify how the person appears in the other's eyes' (1992: 179). She further argues that this subjective valuation is entangled in the comparison of the products' region of origin that barter entails. Graeber is certainly right to reply that women exchanging fish in Papua New Guinea may be comparing not their products to their region of origin, but instead the regions of origin with each other (2001: 43). In an Andean region where people's identity is entangled with the ecological niche of their residence, itself influencing their economic identity, Graeber's remark pinpoints how barter simultaneously compares the value of agricultural goods, human producers and their region of origin. Indeed, Mirta's bitterness also attests that the value with which cambio items are imbued establishes a broader comparison between the partners' ways of life. The altercation speaks to a depreciation of a whole ecological community's capacity to perform creative labour: as if valley cultivators were idle people making a living from the earth's fertility without putting in personal effort. The foundation of value in cambio is based on a comparison of a whole livelihood, where the fruitfulness of agricultural labour is entangled with the ecological conditions that make it more or less productive.

Although cambio items are alienated through exchange, the identity of the producers remains attached to the goods. This is an important point of distinction from mercaderías, a characteristic that cambio items share with gifts. Indeed, as Gell contends, 'What is not "alienated" in gift-giving is not the gift-object itself, but that which *cannot* be alienated, namely, the social identity of the donor, which still attaches to the object after it has been given away' (1992: 145; emphasis in original).

Rather than corresponding to the commodity model of value, based on separation between the qualities of persons and things (Gregory 1982; Lambek 2008; Mauss [1925] 2002), the theory of value posited by cambio partners combines both subjective and objective criteria. Objective equivalence between the goods implies subjective esteem of the partners, which is encapsulated in the following widespread formula: 'With cambio, we all end up equal.' The reference to an end, suggests that people were not necessarily equals initially. In this light, equivalence not only arises from the similarity that barter produces from material dissimilarity between agricultural products (Humphrey and Hugh-Jones 1992b: 11) but also stems from the similar subjective appreciation produced from dissimilar campesinos (Quebradeños and Puneños).

In as much as the goods circulating in cambio are entangled with their producers' subjectivity, and their ecological niche of origin, exchange equivalences assert similarity of goods, people and their environment. This suggests a divergence with the model of capitalist commodity outlined by Michael Lambek (2008), whereby exchange is a matter of choice as opposed to the realm of judgement, which compares virtues. At fairs, selecting between different agricultural products is an economic choice that is also a judgement about a person's diligence and the fertile potential of his fields – fields that are gorged with the vital power of their own ancestors. A key distinction Lambek stresses between economics and ethics is that the former establishes equivalences between commensurable objects, while values are incommensurable in the latter (2013: 144). I have pointed out that dimension is a qualisign that reflects both the economic value of agricultural produce and the virtue of its producer. The reason being that size instantiates the fuerza of a plant (or animal) and the fuerza of the peasant devoted to its production. The common criterion merging economic and moral value is thus life force: human and other species are appreciated chiefly as vectors of life flourishing.

As an act of judgement, cambio produces ethical subjectivities that are appreciated as such within the exchange community. Julia's fame as a good person is related to her capacity to grow desirable products, as well as her propensity to engage in fair barter transactions any time she is solicited. By doing so, she enacts her generosity and circulates her virtue towards other ecological niches. In this sense, cambio produces moral values in a vein quite similar to the kula performed by the Massim people in Munn's ethnography. Cambio not only produces material value by converting agricultural produce dissimilarity into similarity, but also creates and expands ethical subjectivities. This was clearly verbalised by Lucia in her speech cited in the previous chapter as she stated: 'That's my word. You will know me. My name is Ramirez Lucia. I always set off to the fair'. Against the prevailing conception of barter as being first and foremost about materiality, cambio demonstrates how economic and moral values actually merge in these transactions that are simultaneously about objects and acts.

## The Vicissitudes of Contemporary Cambio

As mentioned earlier, market prices should not influence cambio measures, or only as one among many arguments used in bargaining. Between transactions, Julia, who likes to barter potatoes at fairs, explained to me: 'We weigh, "that much . . . for that much", because it's a cambio. Potatoes are not worth as much as grapes; grapes are worth more. But we do not put prices on things. We are making cambios.' However, another system of measurement, regarded as newly adopted but nonetheless widely used, consists of comparing the products in light of their monetary value in the regional market. My neighbour Lola, who also used to exchange her potatoes at fairs, commented:

> Of course, now they usually add up how much something is worth. Before, people did not do such sums . . . Most people say, 'How much does your kilo of potatoes cost?' 'Meat costs that much.' And then they add it up. Formerly, they didn't. That's why, as I told you, they used to give 300 cobs of corn for a llama haunch, or 250. It was an exchange that was not a *negocio* [business]. It was an exchange left by our grandparents, our great-grandparents.

Lola's observations suggest that, if monetary evaluation departs from the code of cambio as established by the ancestors, it edges the transaction towards *negocio*, by which traders aim to generate a quantitative profit from start-up capital. This was how Perfecto, a Bolivian cultivator in his forties whom I used to meet at the Yavi Easter fair, explained it to me: 'Cambio enables you to fill your stomach. Negocio enables to fill your stomach and to increase your capital.' In a Marxist perspective, while cambio, as stipulated by the elders, raises qualitative benefits through the procurement of use value, business is intended to provide quantitative benefits through the accumulation of exchange value.

Although profit-making is not regarded as immoral in itself, it is deemed unfair when one of the partners engages in a cambio transaction based upon a use value that assumes self-consumption, while the other strives to appropriate exchange value from the transaction. In the latter case, the equity encapsulated in the elders' measures is sub-stituted by an asymmetry in the subsequent gain. Generally, peasants denounce matching monetary prices as a betrayal of the balanced rec-iprocity that should prevail when local products are bartered. During the 2009 Easter fair, a herder complained: 'Nowadays, they want to give us less than what we give them. They measure with money.' This departs from the ideal of equity in cambio, which should be balanced: 'The same from them, the same from us', as participants usually say.

Complaints about the spreading of a business mentality, at the ex-pense of the elders' ethical code, are embedded in a temporality that posits the latter as a remnant of an idealised past and the former as the infelicitous outcome of modern vice. Derogation from the elders' equivalences is pointed to as a key cause of the fairs' decadence. If peasants grumble about respecting old weights, they say it is because they now barter 'as if it was a business' or as though they are 'thinking in money'. This pursuit of profit is posited as a modern drift, since the elders would have respected their predecessors' etiquette of balanced reciprocity between peasants coming from different ecological niches. This nostalgic rhetoric depicts regretted bygone times when the oppo-sition of the partners' individual interests was fully contained by their complementarity.

However, the ahistorical nature of the past to which such rhetoric refers is underscored by the decontextualisation of the arguments and their internal discrepancy. For instance, young Zara asserted that, in the olden days, her mother 'used to undertake exchange journeys and she would procure all kinds of things. Now, it is not like that anymore.' However, she did not identify which fairs her mother attended, nor the amount of meat she took. At the same time, Simona complained in a symmetrical narrative: 'Now they [herders] ask more, and they bring leaner lamb.' It is thus bewildering to hear herders and cultivators ac-cusing each other of disrespecting the elders' equivalences and over-valuing their own goods at the expense of their partner. Let us listen to Joaquim's complaints:

> We want to respect the old equivalences, but those who have the meat do not want to. They always want us to increase the quantity. For in-stance, for a sheep, we used to give one of those white bags almost full, but not that much. But now, they want us to give it filled up, with some extra fruits on top.

And herders retort likewise.

Paradoxically, such laments are verbalised by those who perpetuate the condemned practices. Cultivators deplore that herders sell their meat at the market instead of swapping it for lowland products. For this reason, the latter are accused of favouring business at the expense of old solidarities. But cultivators do not proclaim as openly their own intention to resell the meat from the bartered sheep. On the other hand, when they complain about the poor quantities of maize obtained at fairs, herders do not specify that they have offloaded old or sick animals with no market value. As attested by these few examples, at fairs, not all narratives about idealised vanishing reciprocities suppose the mixed feelings of 'loss, lack and longing' (Pickering and Keightley 2006: 921) presented in the literature as specific of nostalgia.

For example, during the 2010 Yavi Easter fair, cultivators were lamenting the absence of herders, who were particularly few in number. I could hear Perfecto, a leader in the community of Chosconty, conferring with Lucio, a counterpart from the highlands. He was announcing that the cultivators were planning to give up the fair as well. He dramatically concluded that the fair and its barter were vanishing. Lucio argued that herders did not want to barter their meat anymore because they could get a better price for it in the daily market. Perfecto advocated the rehabilitation of the elders' equivalences, alluding to former merry-making and abundance. Lucio agreed, and concluded diplomatically that he would raise his neighbours' awareness of the matter. And yet, he knew that part of the bartered meat would be reinvested in profit-making transactions. He also knew that Perfecto himself refused to apply the elders' equivalences to some of his most appreciated fruits, which were set aside for sale.

Even if all the speakers do not enact the lamented social order, these nostalgic narratives are nonetheless interesting in that they delineate an ideal type of cambio, contrasting with how it is in fact practised. Such lamentations thereby perpetuate vanishing norms and representations as a past 'available' (Schudson 1995) for framing social interactions. Through these nostalgic narratives, fair transactions manifest a moral continuity with an ancestral past, even when practices shirk the very ideology with which filiation is claimed. I will further analyse these tropes in the next chapter in order to tease out the social performativity of these lamentations about a vanishing idealised cambio.

## Negocio

### Merchants' Transactions

In many fairs, transactions involving manufactured goods are overwhelming in terms of the volume of goods in circulation. However,

direct exchange still constitutes the cornerstone in the way the participants conceive of the fairs. When I asked a herder whether some of
his goods were on sale, he replied: 'We have nothing to [exchange for]
money. We brought [things] for cambio, because it's a fiesta.' Sales are
realised for the most part by travelling merchants selling industrial
foodstuffs and the other manufactured goods mentioned in the preceding chapter. The products are bought wholesale and then retailed
at fairs in view of making a monetary profit. The peso is the yardstick
for defining the terms of such exchange. The merchants, who position themselves as spokespeople for the market, set the value of the
goods. Prices fluctuate wildly, since they increase with the rising inflation characteristic of Argentina's economy. Because inflation does not
affect the value of all agricultural goods equally, the peasants' buying
power also fluctuates, which is felt to be unfair and is denounced as
such.

Contrary to the elders' measures, which are relatively stable while
leaving room for negotiation, the exchange equivalences used in selling fluctuate with inflation and are not negotiable. It is necessarily the
seller who imposes the terms of the transfer, and bargaining is not a
frequent practice in this case. When the announced price seems too
high, the potential buyer simply walks away without a word. This contributes to the contraction of the interaction: a few strictly utilitarian
words are enough to carry out the transaction. These furtive and verbally abbreviated exchanges contrast with the dialogue that envelops
negotiation of cambio, ready at each moment to cross over from the
strictly economic framework into a warm-hearted conversation. In
this way, the circulation of industrial goods is accompanied by a minimal verbal exchange, attesting to the fragility of the social relation
between the partners. Furthermore, at fairs, the peasants do not generally show a preference for a particular merchant, thus eliminating
from this place of exchange the casero relationship that can develop in
the urban market setting.

Because they are looking for monetary income, merchants do not
usually engage in barter. Some may nonetheless accept direct transactions, mostly to offload unsold goods during the last days of the fair.
But they do not regularly consume Andean tubers, maize, sheep or
llama meat. Therefore, they would only accept a few native potatoes or
some cobs to be served occasionally as a side dish to a meal composed
mainly of beef and wheat, which are the core ingredients of the Argentinean Creole diet. At the Manka Fiesta in 2007, a seller of plastic con-
tainers coming from Salta mentioned the absence of desire for local
produce as a justification for not conducting cambio: 'The campesinos

do barter. Plastic items are for sale. Exchange? With what? The fact is that [barter] is useful depending on to one's needs. You exchange according to your needs. It is not question of exchanging for the sake of exchanging.' This intervention corroborates Humphrey and Hugh-Jones's (1992b) insistence on reciprocal desire for what is owned by the other party as a distinctive dimension of barter.

However, other merchants do specialise in direct exchanges, as is the case of large-scale traders, who arrive with trucks from cities such as Buenos Aires, Rosario and Cordoba to exchange manufactured foods for local wool or clay pots. These ventures generate a double profit for the dealer: the first stems from retailing manufactured items at fairs, and the second from selling Andean rural produce in southern cities. In this context as well, merchants position themselves as representatives of the market: they settle non-negotiable equivalences at which they will accept to exchange their commodities for local produce, explaining that their scale of value hinges upon prices on the national market. There is usually an agreement between those who offer similar goods, so peasants have no control over the price of their products. Such transactions are comparable to the transactions Fonseca describes in Peru as 'barter performed as a form of "negocio"' (1972: 332, my translation), which takes precedence in historical exchanges between Indians and mestizos. The former would provide grains and tubers, while the latter would supply basic commodities.

While Fonseca insists on categorising these transactions together with inter-ecological complementarities, this does not seem relevant to understanding material circulation at fairs. This kind of trade is perceived locally as different from cambio, to the extent that those involved do not recognise it as barter, or, when they do, they explicitly distinguish it from peasant exchanges. For example, when I enquired about his transactions, a man exchanging industrial items for wool answered: 'Here we are not bartering. If you want to see barter, go to that sector, over there, where the peasants are.' Among the Jujeñan Creole population, Indigenous barter used to be depicted as an archaic mode of exchange, peculiar to the peasant economy from which merchants generally strive to distinguish themselves. With the new appraisal of Indigenous people and pre-Columbian cultures, as well as the dramatic crisis of the ultra-liberal government in 2001, a romantic appreciation of barter has slowly arisen, in which it is associated with a benevolent economy of small community versus the destructive capitalism of modern society. This perspective prevailed in another kind of barter network, driven by an impoverished middle class and involving millions of Argentineans during the 2001 crisis

(Ould-Ahmed 2010; Pearson 2003; Saiag 2013). Moreover, nonmonetary exchange is also a pervasive practice within diverse social contexts of commerce and manufacturing in Jujuy. Thus, barter is actually not an exclusively Indigenous practice; it comes to be seen as such through a social construction.

### Peasants' Business

Peasants also engage in monetary exchanges. Some of them buy goods from neighbours who do not want to travel to the fair, although they have a surplus of production that they want to get rid of. Others stop in the city where they purchase mercaderías at a good price to resell at the fair. Agricultural produces may also be used in such business transactions. Coca leaves are profitable because their trade is prohibited in Argentina, while it is legal in Bolivia. But some peddlers buy tomatoes, mangoes or any other produce appreciated by their exchange partners but not produced within the peasant economy. Fabiana, who every year attended the fair in Yavi although her daughters urged her to stay at home because of her advanced age, only cultivated potatoes in small quantities. She nonetheless strived to compose a well-stocked and diversified stall, completing her harvest with produce bought in the city. She knew that business very well, since she had a stand at the market. She told me that it was important to her to display an array of goods, a gratifying practice she lamented her daughters did not appreciate.

In any case, the vast majority of the peasants in fairs set aside part of their goods to sell. Herders usually keep the best pieces of fresh meat for that purpose, while the dried meat is used for barter. For their part, the growers prepare crates of their best produce. 'I already separated. This [maize], the biggest, is to sell. It all comes from the same plant, those are just smaller', Simona explained, as she commented on the organisation of her stall at the Yavi fair. The price of these goods is defined by conditions on the formal market. When they get to the site of the exchange, the peasants who are not informed ask their colleagues for information, which is all the more necessary because the price of some fruits fluctuates widely according to weather conditions, the advancing season and the distance travelled from the place of production. 'How much do you give pears for?' Andrea asks her sister-in-law, while a neighbour set up farther away comes up to join the discussion. Each fruit is thus discussed until what is regarded as the optimum price is agreed on. The main point is that they should not value their produce at more than the formal market rate in Argentina (usually higher than the price at which the cultivators sell their fruits on the Bolivian market), in which case they run the risk of going unsold. Beyond this constraint, the peasants propose and impose the price of their goods.

The agreed price serves as a starting point for the exchange and then evolves with the supply and demand at that fair. On the last day, the remaining fruits are sold off at cut rates to spare the growers having to take back the same products and pay for their transport a second time. In addition, the monetary value of goods is sometimes adjusted to the partner in the transaction. Visitors from far away customarily pay more than those who live in the surrounding villages, who, in any event, are already well informed of the values of local agricultural products on the urban market. In this case, otherness in itself justifies the appropriation of a material profit that would be judged immoral between relatives or allies. I came to understand this when Lola scolded a cultivator for having sold me a wicker basket for an exorbitant price: 'She lives here. It's here that she lives. She's my neighbour. You can't make her a price for tourists.' It was not so much that he had overvalued his item that he was reproached, but rather that he had treated me like a tourist, whereas I lived in the village where the fair was being held.

Tourists, and gringos in general, thus constitute a group one is allowed to cheat. They represent the ultimate degree of otherness with whom no figure of long-lasting reciprocity is expected. As mentioned before, the practice of negocio is not reprehensible per se. It is disapproved when the merchant accumulates profits at the expense of his clients, and even more so when they are linked by a personalised social relationship. Strategies of negocio are particularly condemned when peasants exchange the produce of their labour. When describing the benefits of cambio, I suggested that some actors were engaging in inter-ecological exchange with the intention of generating profits instead of looking for use value. These practices are also seen as negocios, in contrast to the normative model of cambio. A common practice consists of acquiring products that are meant for further profitable transactions. At the time of my fieldwork, cultivators commonly made a stop at the urban market to sell the meat obtained through barter.

Another strategy consists in accumulating more food that one will eat, in order to exchange it at a more profitable rate in further fiestas. A Bolivian cultivator, who had bartered ten sheep at the fair in Yavi, told me he was satisfied, as he had gathered enough meat to feed his family until October, when the Manka Fiesta takes place and he could obtain meat again. The following year, when I had become friends with his wife and comadre of the couple, I learned that this meat was in fact intended to be dried and further exchanged at the San Santiago celebration taking place in July in the Bolivian lowlands. No one other than my comadre mentioned this practice, although it is common in the communities of Sococha valley. When I enquired, cultivators would instead affirm that the meat gathered would feed their family.

In their ethnographies of barter in central Peru, Mayer and Fonseca mention similar chains of transactions. Mayer describes peasants engaging in inter-ecological barter to obtain potatoes, which they afterwards sell at the weekly market in order to 'make a profit in money' (2002: 151). While Mayer counts such strategies of negocio – through agricultural produce barter – as morally neutral and embedded in the inter-ecological solidarity, this is not the case in Argentinean fairs, where the aura of secrecy suggests that these practices are not morally acceptable. These negocios are well known to herders, who feel betrayed by their valley counterparts. Some have even stopped bringing meat to fairs, arguing that cultivators are making a business out of what should be a cambio.

## Largesse

### Invitation to Human and Nonhuman Guests

The transactional field of the fair includes gifts, whose principal expression is the 'invitation'. The most obvious form of this oblative transfer consists in inviting allies to taste the result of one's domestic production. This is a frequent practice, so on the first day of the fair, I would systematically receive samples of different harvests as I struck up conversations with people I had met previously. Such samples are presents handed out without expectation of an equivalent counter-gift. I did sometimes bring to fairs foods intended to please my companions. But it was by no means systematic, and I was greeted with fruit invitations even when I had brought nothing to reciprocate. These gifts are reserved for kin and allies from another village. Since they tend to produce the same things, neighbours do not usually make each other gifts of their goods. Another type of invitation, this time prevalent among relatives and allies from similar territories, consists in sharing cooked food. Some offer the holders of neighbouring stalls cooked foodstuffs ready to eat, which they have brought from home; others invite friends, relatives and compadres to share a festive meal. Barbecues are improvised beside the stalls, and beverages and food circulate among the guests, clearly delighted to be meeting again.

While a spontaneous flow of words between partners necessarily accompanies this transfer of food, the dialogue never addresses the modality of the counter-gift. Because it does not explicitly expect a material counterpart, the invitation shows itself to be disinterested. Of course, reciprocation is expected, but implicitly, and it is never strictly measured. When circulation in the opposite direction is not immediate, as is often the case, the length of time elapsed is also left to the initiative of the guest. In fact, reception of the counter-gift, which is never guaranteed by an economic or legal contract, is ultimately uncertain: unlike the cambio, which is returned by obligation, the invitation will be returned according to the recipient's *voluntad* (will). As the reception of a counterpart is not a condition of the initial transfer, the resulting uncertainty enables the giver to think of their gesture as an unconditional favour (Bourdieu 1980: 179; Descola 2005: 429). The moral obligation to return the invitation is typically oblative, then, and is distinct from the legal obligation to provide a counterpart in the case of an exchange, be it barter or selling (Testart 2001: 720).

In the context of the fair, invitations are made within the circle of friends and kin. Invitations are not issued within the household. As I mentioned in the first chapter, the sharing of cooked food is the very basis of the household, so commensality in this setting does not qualify as an invitation. The offer of food in the case of collective consumption can extend to complementary economic producers in so far as they are closely related, usually through compadrazgo. Kin from other ecological zones can also receive invitations in the form of uncooked food. These goods nurture the bond that is challenged by physical separation. During the Iruya fair, I witnessed the reunion of two comadres. As they talked, one of them held out a small sack of sweet potatoes, blaming bad harvests for her meagre present. Thus, when the partners do not share the same economic activity, compadrazgo telescopes two circuits: their encounter may give rise to invitations of raw products, as occurs with remote complementary peasants, as well as to invitations of cooked food, as in the case of very close similar peasants.

Invitation not only reaffirms and nurtures existing social ties between close people but is also used to establish social relations between yet unknown people who want to engage in exchange. The strategy of using the gift to create a social context for further exchanges between culturally distant people became clear when I went with my friend Maria to the Manka Fiesta. A well-off architect from the vicinity of Salta, with no indigenous stock, she brought for exchange quantities of walnuts that she had harvested on her estate and wanted to get rid of. When we arrived at Genoveva's stall, the latter greeted me and asked who my companion was. The following question was about the goods Maria was carrying in her bag. After Maria replied 'walnuts', they exchanged greetings. Maria asked Genoveva if she wanted to buy some. 'Let's have a look', Genoveva replied. Handing over three dried apples, she commented: 'In order to become friends. How much are your walnuts?' Then the negotiation over the price started. This example is striking in that the partner was a white woman, suggesting that instrumental exchange between strangers are facilitated by previous circulation of gifts. Yet, invitation might also happen between Andean peasants who recognise themselves as potential cambio partners but fear that the transaction will fail. When a herder announced she was going to come back later to conclude a transaction, Genoveva handed her some dried fruits, insisting, 'You're gonna come, aren't you?' Like other forms of gifts, invitations can be used to create a moral obligation to further reciprocate.

Nonhuman beings are also invited to share food and drink. When settling in, some stall keepers dig a hole, into which they pour some of their meal, coca leaves or alcohol to feed Pachamama. Most of them simply sprinkle some beverage on the ground, an action that will be repeated any time they share a drink. 'It's to show your respect to Pacha – to thank her. Otherwise, she will stop giving us our products. We must give her everything we eat', explained a cultivator after having poured a few drops of her chicha on the ground in between two exchanges.

People agree that the elders used to make major offerings to Mother Earth in order to ensure their venture would be fruitful. They even impute a degradation of their transactions to the transgression of these prescriptions. 'This is the reason why we can't exchange anymore. We are punished. Before, people used to burn incense, make libations when undertaking a trip for barter or business. That's why we do badly', concluded Sylberia, who was about to leave the fair in La Quiaca with part of the meat she had brought. In any case, these glosses illustrate that the success of economic transactions is considered to be under the sway of nonhuman agencies. Even though they do not perform these offerings with the same diligence as they used to, peasants' invitations to Pachamama before any consumption attests to her intervention as an active protagonist of the transactions that take place at fairs and a vital contributor to the success of exchanges.

Pleasing the Earth with material gifts is meant to ensure that the value transformation fostered by the movement of people and their goods will be favourable to the traveller. With these offerings, peasants ask permission to journey across unfamiliar spaces and circulate agricultural produce that has been grown in collaboration with Pachamama. Ødegaard has pointed out, 'how different places are associated with different kinds of, or possibilities for, prosperity and therefore how movement in space can be seen to influence not only people's well-being but also their prosperity' (2011: 345). Yet, mobility can also provoke calamities, since physical displacement is a potential danger for both people and their goods' integrity. Displacements are relatively safer than in times of caravans, when traders used to sleep under the star, braving the dangers of potential attacks by human enemies, animals, or other telluric powers' threat of climatic calamities. Nowadays, travellers mostly fear car accidents, rivers' spate in the rainy season, or confiscation by national police or sanitary force. Hence, if lacking divine protection, the products' value could be absorbed by telluric powers or by inimical human beings, instead of being enhanced through circulation and exchange. This explains the necessity of pleasing the Earth at different thresholds of the venture, such as departure from home, arrival on the site of exchange and storage of newly acquired products.

### Yapa: Rounding Out Exchanges with a Gift

In the Argentinean cordillera, yapa is associated chiefly with barter.[5] Only when the conditions of the exchange have been settled can a yapa be appended to the transaction as a sign of generosity materialising mutual contentment: 'When there is a yapa, it means that the exchange was good: satisfaction on both sides', Griselda glossed as she was initiating me into the etiquette of cambio. In principle, any good can be offered as yapa. In practice, people customarily use goods they have produced themselves.

Cultivators can offer a few cobs of corn, fruits or potatoes, while herders can give a small piece of charqui or a sheep's head or foot. These extra goods are extracted from the piles of produce intended for barter, and, most of the time, they are of the same nature as those that have just been exchanged. When a handful of maize is added to the agreed arroba, a bunch of grapes to the full basket or a few nuts on top of the dozen, the yapa is materially indistinguishable from the items bartered. When extra goods are given silently, the treat is barely perceptible. Yet, when spontaneously outbidding a previously agreed equivalence, the partners usually accompany their gesture with a stereotyped utterance that points out their generous intention: 'With yapa and everything' or 'Here goes, very well weighed.' Some even dare to explicitly ask for a yapa at the end of the transaction. 'Increase me [the equivalence] with something!' they will say after concluding barter.

If yapa is translated in Spanish by *aumento* (augmentation), the two terms are not equivalent: yapa is a special case of augmentation, independent of the negotiation of the terms of exchange. Lucio, who helps his wife, Julia, cultivate and exchange her potatoes, patiently explained this difference to me:

> Let's say I exchange [cambio] five kilos of potatoes for five kilos of corn, for instance. You yourself don't want the five kilos of potatoes. You want two kilos of potatoes and three kilos of onions. You say, 'Augment me some more onions'. That's not a yapa. That's balancing out [*igualar*] the cambio I am making. Now if, in addition to these three kilos, I give you another three onions or a kilo of potatoes, then that would be a yapa.

An augmentation can thus be requested or proposed in the course of the interaction. It will be recognised as a yapa only if it increases a previously established equivalence. Otherwise, the augmentation is not a yapa; it is *lo justo* (lit. what's fair), as Lucio said, making the distinction. Failing recognition as a yapa, the added goods are considered an integral part of the quantity of foods required to reach a fair cambio. When one of the partners launches into a series of strategic glosses meant to suggest that it would be unfair not to be granted a yapa, if obtained such a yapa is denatured and becomes akin to bargaining designed to establish the equivalence of the cambio. Hence, there are some tangential figures in which the yapa is confused with other figures of augmentation, such as bargaining. These are exceptions, however, and to define yapa as being 'a part of Andean bargaining' (Mayer 2002: 156) does not seem pertinent. As Lola stressed, for a partner to receive a yapa, 'it is enough . . . that you have the friendship to give it to him, because there would be no need to do it since you have already concluded the cambio.' Coming back to the distinction established by Alain Testart (2001: 720), the yapa is a type of augmentation motivated by a moral and not a legal duty; it comes under the heading of gift, whereas the other figures of augmentation are part of exchange.

In sum, unlike the other types of augmentation that precede the material transfer and establish its terms, the yapa results from an exchange but does not condition it. This point is a fundamental distinctive feature of the yapa.[6] Through the yapa, the transferred goods change owners without the giver being able legitimately to demand a counter-gift. The yapa shares this characteristic with the invitation, although the latter does not result from a previous exchange. Nevertheless, when the intention is not explicitly expressed, the yapa can be confused with the establishment of the terms of the cambio or with the invitation. In addition, each of the parties can interpret it differently. Lastly, as Lucio summed it up, 'it all depends on the nature of the intention.'

While a commercial technique is effectively involved, since the donator expects the yapa will bring forth further transactions, yapa still entails an act of generosity and is ideally presented as the initiation or expression of a long-term social relation, eventually valued in the same manner as economic collaboration. Far from being guided solely by the desire for profit, this gesture is 'apparently free and disinterested but nevertheless constrained and self-interested' (Mauss [1925] 2002: 4). Little additions that conclude exchanges are thus forms of gift. In this light, they share similarities with the *pura kiana* (complements), an Indian version of the yapa, analysed by Gell under the category of gift-giving. Describing the gifts granted by Indian traders, Gell asserts that they contribute to creating hierarchical relations by placing 'the buyer in the position of the recipient of the trader's largesse' (1982: 486). While pura kiana reinforce hierarchical relations between social categories, these gifts in the Andes are intended to ensure the complicity of partners belonging to the same social class. Yapa also differs from pura kiana, whose efficacy depends on the anonymity of the Indian market. This dependency shows that the social performativity of the top-ups proposed by traders differs with the cultural setting in which they occur. As well as expressing an interpersonal relation, yapa materialises the existence of a social context familiar to both parties. I shall come back to this later.

## Overlapping Different Kinds of Transfers in Practices

In this chapter, I have distinguished modalities of transactions identified as cambio, negocio, invitation and yapa. However, one should not conclude that there is always a clear-cut distinction between these transactional forms. In his typology of forms of exchange in the Trobriand Islands, Malinowski noted that 'there are so many transitions and gradations . . . that it is impossible to draw any fixed line between trade on the one hand, and exchange of gifts on the other' ([1922] 2002: 135). The fabric of transactions at fairs supports this important point, and I will address this conceptual conundrum in the final chapter. For now, though, I would like to stress the practical and linguistic fuzziness between the categories of transfer verbalised by these Andean peasants. Some prestations lie in between these categories without fitting into one or another. I have just mentioned the case of some transactions in which the goods given as yapa and those bartered as cambio are inseparable. Such confusion also characterises mutual invitations between compadres living in complementary ecological zones. As etiquette prescribes that the receiver reciprocates the invitation according to the elders' measures, the final movement of goods may seem similar to those cambio taking place between known partners.

Another example of transactional confusion is provided by the cultivators who stop at the market on their way home in order to sell part of the meat they have obtained through direct exchanges following the elders' prescriptions. What originally seemed to be a cambio, then, becomes a commodity exchange in which one of the parties is not interested in the use value of the goods but is instead intent on creating an exchange value from the transaction. Others engage chains of transactions whereby barter is used to produce a quantitative benefit, an example being cultivators who keep meat bartered at the Yavi meeting to realise further profitable exchange at the San Santiago fair. However, at the time of the transaction, the cultivator may not yet know whether the coveted meat will become part of his own larder or whether it will be sold directly at the market or dried and exchanged as charqui later on. When I met my comadre at the Manka Fiesta in 2010, I asked her how her transactions in San Santiago had gone. I learned that she could not go because her husband was travelling at this time, and she could not leave the house unattended. However, when bartering meat in Yavi a few months earlier, she had mentioned her intention to bring it for San Santiago. I wondered whether the meat had gone bad. 'We must eat', she replied. 'We are eating a lot.' Finally, the meat has thus been used for domestic consumption in fitting with the cambio etiquette. Therefore, at the moment of the transfer, it is not always possible to determine whether it is a proper cambio or a business transaction. Furthermore, what appears as a cambio to one of the partners can be conducted as negocio by the other. Humphrey and Hugh-Jones point out such discrepancy in the appreciation of the transaction as a common situation in barter practices (1992b: 2).

The practical porosity between the different transactions is expressed linguistically by expressions that mix the registers of sale, gift and barter. 'To pay in potatoes', 'to give price', 'to sell fruits for money or meat' and 'to exchange [cambiar] for money'[7] are the hybrid expressions peasants use in glossing their exchanges. Barter tranfers can be expressed in oblative terms as in the common formula dar un buen cambio (give a good cambio). While a monetary exchange can take on the verbal appearance of barter in expressions such as 'Your baskets, do you sell them for money or for fava beans as well?'[8] as the elderly

Andrea asked a potential exchange partner. Nevertheless, the providers do not fail to make it clear when necessary that these transactions are not equivalent. 'Not sell! You said barter [*cambiar*]', a grower rectified, fearing that she would be asked for money to obtain the sheep her partner had promised her.

Beyond the practical overlap between the different transactions, peasants make a clear distinction between monetary exchanges and cambio, which they see as the legitimate figure of barter between peasants. This is an essentially practical difference indicating whether money is used as a medium of exchange by one of the partners. Peasants are further concerned with the economic logic lying behind the transaction, and here is where the distinction between cambio and negocio is fundamental. Cambio and negocio are recurring notions in the Spanish version of Mayer's article on barter. In his first analysis, these are overlapping categories: he mentions peasants doing '"negocios" de trueque' (business of barter) to describe inter-ecological exchange following the unay precio (1982: 90). The two categories delineate another moral economy in the Argentinean puna. This is made very clear in nostalgic narratives pointing out that the direct exchanges of agricultural produce should be intended for domestic consumption, not to produce further material profits, which is the realm of negocio.

Harris also observes circuits of exchanges combining barter and money, where profits are quantified by at least one of the parties (1989: 243). She explains that townspeople obtain livestock and agricultural produce at favourable rates by exchanging them for commodities such as coca, alcohol or cloth (2007: 76). She contrasts these transactions with barter of self-produced items between ecological tiers. While the terms *cambio* and *negocio* are absent from her ethnography, the two logics of exchange they refer to seem pertinent to understanding Laymi modalities of barter. The broader relevance of these categories becomes clear when translated into Marxist terms. As used by fair protagonists, cambio and negocio are two logics of transaction, based on a distinction between transactions intended to increase a starting capital (money – commodity – money') and those transactions intended to purchase a product different from what one already owns (commodity – money – commodity'). The latter are anchored in a mode of 'production designed for mere replacement', to borrow Damon's formula (2002: 115).

Such transactional form based on use value, corresponds to cambio, in so far as money is not used as medium of exchange (commodity – commodity'). Harris documents the case of barter between peasants in which people earlier buy products to then engage in barter and thereby obtain agricultural products from those who refuse cash (2007: 76). But she does not give enough precisions as to the modalities of the transactions to be able to analyse them further. Such monetary trade guided by consumption desire would seem to correspond to the category of *comercio* used by people in Ferraro's Ecuadorian fieldwork, who distinguishes it from negocio, for it is not intended for making a quantitative profit (2011: 178). This is a fascinating distinction, but not one that is used in the Argentinean region. Conversely, barter can be used in a chain of transactions intended to produce a quantitative profits. Throughout the chain, economic values are gauged in light of the market prices that will at the end determine the profit generated in the transactions. In the Argentinean cordillera, such practices are denounced as an infringement of the moral principles of cambio.

The broad definition of barter as an exchange of goods that does not involve the material use of money (Heady 2006: 262) is thus not able to account for the peculiarities of cambio. The material absence of money is of course an important aspect, if one accepts that barter items are desired for their consumption value, while money is almost always coveted for its exchange value. Still, to grasp the peculiarities of cambio, it is essential to make it clear that money does not intervene, even as a scale of measure. The eviction of a monetary scale brings forth another pattern of value in which the goods are directly compared to one another. In the same vein, Harris notes that monetary evaluations are avoided in inter-ecological barter of use value, and equivalencies correspond instead to 'concrete qualities of what is changing hands' (2007: 77). However, she states elsewhere that there seems to be no systematic difference between barter and monetary transaction (1989: 243). Ferraro comes to a similar conclusion through her analysis of trueque, which, she argues, is neither trade nor barter. Fonseca also ignores the theoretical relevance of the scale of value the partners put forward, in his attempt to think together exchanges intended for direct consumption and 'forms of appropriation of agricultural produce with purpose of profit' (1972: 318).

While I acknowledge that the material use of money is not always a crucial feature in capturing local economic configurations, my study of fairs shows that its use as a yardstick is an essential dimension for understanding Andean exchange systems. Indeed, exclusion of the peso as the main reference for establishing equivalences gives way to another value pattern, which supposes that the partners are 'socially understood' (Humphrey 1985). The final part of this work is devoted to the social effects of cambio.

# Notes

1. This derivation from the Aymara verb *yapaña*, meaning to increase, is also in use in the Quechua and Spanish spoken throughout the cordillera.
2. Maize, grown at sea level elsewhere in the country, is another product that people in the cordillera do not appreciate at all. Maize culture there is large scale, using genetically modified varieties, and production is aimed at the massive urban market. I have not seen such cobs at fairs.
3. During a festival in Cusi Cusi, I met a herder who was planning to travel to Yavi, some 100 kilometres away; she wanted to purchase maize from an acquaintance in order to make the best tistincha (a meal of meat and corn) for the celebration of San Santiago.
4. At that time, twenty pairs of ears of dried maize was worth ten cents at unay precio, instead of seventy-five cents for each ear at the market (2002: 154).
5. Yapa can be offered at the closing of sales, mostly in informal trade. Here I will not address this figure of the yapa, which I have examined elsewhere (Angé 2011).
6. In Indian markets, Gell also observed the independence between the small extra quantity offered and the conclusion of the sale: 'This could be mistaken for bargaining over the quantity of goods offered at a fixed price, but it is important to stress that the sale is in no way dependent on the size of the "extra" amount, having been concluded before anything additional is offered' (1982: 486).
7. The original expressions: 'pagar en papas', 'dar precio', 'vender fruta por plata o carne' and 'cambiar por plata'.
8. The original expression: 'Tus canastos, ¿por la plata vendes, o por habas también?'

# CHAPTER 5

# Barter and the Making of Society

While, in the previous chapter, I considered an array of transactions in order to provide a general panorama of exchange at fairs, I shall now concentrate on barter. This is not only related to the concerns of the book. It is important to bear in mind that, although sales might be prominent in terms of the amount of goods involved, cambio is seen as the stereotypical form of exchange at fairs. 'Barter for the fiesta' is a refrain that speaks to barter's status as a constitutive ingredient of the fair and the broader celebration.

In the preceding chapter, I stressed that cambio at fairs participates in the physical reproduction of peasants and in the creation of virtuous subjectivities. I would now like to show how cambio participates in the weaving of new forms of sociality. To examine the social performativity of inter-ecological transactions in the context of fairs, I shall begin by looking at the relational setting of cambio and the effect of the material circulation on relations between the protagonists. We saw in the previous chapter that Puneños' and Quebradeños' identities are constructed in relation to one another, in a relationship of complementarity. Enacting their interdependence, cambio at fairs also outlines their participation in an encompassing social entity. Furthermore, the interactional analysis of cambio will bring out the importance of mutual satisfaction fostered by exchange. Joy triggered by the transaction enlivens the fiesta, thus positing barter as a constitutive ingredient of the celebration. Viewed in this light, we understand that these exchanges are not only aimed at the acquisition of use value, but are also meant to produce cosmological values by securing the stability of the relationship between peasants and the ambivalent power of their saints and ancestors.

Lastly, I address another instance where fairs participate in the production and reproduction of social fabrics: the process of the formal heritagisation of fairs, which involves a complex interplay between cambio participants' cultural intimacy and the composition of a national society. As a whole, this final chapter highlights the fundamental differences between ritualised transactions performed in the context of fairs – spontaneous or institutional – and those exchanges occurring in ordinary context.

## Social Performativity of Cambio

### From Stranger to Kin: The Potentialities of Yapa

Dense relationships are considered to provide an ideal social background for engaging in cambio. To establish such a frame of interaction, partners tend to repeat successful transactions and weave social ties via material and linguistic exchanges. In so doing, strangers become *conocidos* (acquaintances) who, in the course of further meetings, can become *amigos* (friends) or even *compadres*. All three are regarded as preferential economic partners. From one stage to the next, the weight of the social relationship increases and, accordingly, so do the economic obligations and expectations. In contrast with market transactions embedded in relations of casero, cambio relationships deploy under the more intimate sign of friendship – and kinship.

When they meet, regular partners greet each other warmly. They engage in personal conversation, into which economic exchange is blended. They ask about each other and compare ecological, political or cultural features of their villages. In addition to linguistic communication, complicity is expressed with smiles, laughter, handshakes and embraces. The convivial framework is also signified through material circulation. Aware of their respective desires and habits, the closest partners set aside their best produce for the event. A cultivator who had concluded only a few cambio at the Yavi Easter fair pointed to such moral obligations: 'The point is that sometimes you have to wait for your conocidos. For instance, you bring something for him [the conocido] and when he arrives you give him.' To ensure the durability of the relationship, conditions of exchange should be agreed upon without stinting, 'according to each other's need', as people say. In the course of the interaction, one partner may also invite the other to taste ready-to-eat items, thereby emphasising both the generosity and the strength of the relationship. And, at the end of the transaction, generosity is enacted through the yapa.

Many cambios take place between unknown partners. However, they mobilise a common language made of recurring formulas that contribute to establish a social framework of trust favourable to the transaction. In order to illustrate how these transactions unfold concretely, here is an extended extract of a typical cambio between two women who do not know each other yet. At the beginning of the interaction, a herder from Chalguamayoc, who just arrived at the fair after having wept over Christ the whole night, was standing near her packed meat. Two cultivators approached, asking for exchange. Her preference went to a young fruit producer from Chosconty, who promised beautiful grapes:

Grower: Are you going to exchange [*cambiar*] the small lamb with me? I will give you an assortment; I will give you a basket of grapes on top of it.

Herder: Nice grapes?

Grower: Of course.

Herder: Sometime they bring, not that good . . . underneath.

Grower: Why would it be so? It's a cost for you; for us as well it's a cost bringing [the fruit].[1] A small lamb, exchange with me [*cambiame*].

Herder: But, what do you have?

Grower: I have fruits. Peaches, grapes, apples, pears, quinces.

Herder: No.

Grower: Prickly pear?

Herder: Prickly pear! [She starts unpacking her lamb, commenting on her meat.] Beautiful, tender [*lindo, tiernito*].

Grower: Look. That one [the lamb], exchange with me.

Herder: But, you will give me a good deal, won't you.[2]

Grower: Of course. [She starts touching the lamb as well, for the first time her challenging face is illuminated with a smile.]

Herder: Let's exchange.

Grower: Let's go, let's go.

Herder: But you have baskets of grapes, don't you?

Grower: Of course. I'll give you a basket of grapes on the one hand and an assortment on the other. [She leaves with the lamb.]

Herder: Wait for me! Wait for me!

Grower: I am right here.

Herder: Where?

Grower: Right there, where the man is sitting. There I am. I am not going to cheat on you [*engañar*]. [She reaches her stall, kept by her husband while she prospected for meat.] . . . As an *amiga*, I will give you [the fruit]. I will increase [the equivalence] with apples.

Herder: No, no, no.

Grower: What? Are you not going to eat apples? Here, completely full. Take it, take it. [She hands her the basket of grapes.]

Herder (about the grapes): It's very good, large.

Grower's husband: Grapes are also expensive.

Herder: Have you added up?

Grower: I will add up, I will add up. . . . I will increase with pears.

Herder: With pears increase [the equivalence] for me. . . .

Grower: Here goes. How is it that I must give you abundantly? Here goes, have a look. I gave you the yapa. Have a look.

Grower's husband: From which place are you bringing [meat]?

Herder: Oh, I come from that corner of the hill.

Grower's husband: We come from far away as well, further. You must take the truck in that direction. Back on that side, they don't let us cross [the national border].

Grower: I will give you pomegranate on top. Here goes. Have you seen? Here goes, with a good yapa – as for a friend.

This interaction clearly shows how a rich social setting is composed by exceeding the elders' measure and verbally relating the excess with a tie of *amiga*. Looking at these two women, I was struck to notice how a rough discussion turned into a warm dialogue once the cambio was agreed. Lévi-Strauss noted that his Amerindian interlocutors classified strangers as either 'bad' or 'good' ([1947] 2002: 71), the former being those who are doomed to war and suffering and the latter those who are gratified with hospitality. This moral judgement delineates the circle of exchange partners, circumscribed to the good strangers. To understand cambio, we need a dynamic perspective, showing how successful exchanges participate in the transformation of unknown, potentially harmful, strangers into benevolent persons, thereby knitting new alliances through material circulation.

The dialogue indicates the vital role that yapa plays in the setting of the cambio social framework. On the one hand, the few items generously thrown in can materialise a pre-existing social relation and the resulting moral obligations. In this case, the transfer is the economic expression of the relationship between friends or compadres entertained by the partners, and in virtue of which they are duty-bound to agree to exchange. In this sense, it grafts a pre-existing social relation onto the material transaction. On the other hand, as it marks the transaction with a sense of largesse that characterises material circulation between 'cherished' people, it can also weave a relationship between still-unknown partners. In both cases, the yapa comes to counteract the fragility of the social ties that bind barter partners, who, in principle, are quits when their transactions have been concluded.

At fairs, yapa formulates a promise of long-lasting collaboration: satisfied partners will be eager to find each other at further encounters

**Figure 5.1.** A Bolivian cultivator greeting an Argentinean herder after a good cambio, crowned with a yapa. Photograph by the author.

and to repeat their successful transaction. When he added extra fruits to a previously agreed equivalence for a cambio he conducted at the Yavi Easter fair, Perfecto explained to me: 'Yes, we always give more. It's to become friends for next year. You see? I increase [the equivalence] so that next year, he will bring more meat and we will know each other.' Seen in this light, yapa paves the way for a stranger to become an acquaintance, who might go on to become a friend or a compadre.

Although it may be materially insignificant, the social effect of yapa is crucial in that it alludes to the ideal relational framework for cambio transactions and holds out the possibility of creation of compadrazgo. While an exception at present, this relational figure still perfuses the social framework underlying exchanges. In fact, if friendship is now only ratified in exceptional cases by the establishment of kinship,[3] the protagonists continue to direct their actions towards the stability typical of compadrazgo. 'Some yes, obviously, some yes. When friendship grows, they become [compadres] too. But now no longer, rarely', Joaquim observed at the Yavi fair, thus showing that, when friendship grows, it may shift towards this model, even though it only rarely complies in full.[4] At any event, when social affinities are knitted, interactions between cambio partners exceed economic opportunities. Then, herders and cultivators invite each other for a barbecue at their home, participate in their respective agricultural activities or join the saint patron celebration in their community.

Although peasants barter with their kin and strive to establish friendship or even kinship with their partners, many transactions occur with unknown others. 'Sometimes, yes, you know the partner. Then, you arrive, you deliver and that's done. Better. If not, [you can barter with] anybody,' replied Griselda when I enquired about her grandmother's partners. In any case, yapa contributes to the mutual personalisation of the partners and ensures them a favourable social framework in which to carry out their transactions. By giving and receiving yapa, they express their mutual wish to repeat the exchange. Of course, the yapa does not create an obligation; there is therefore no certainty that the partners will in fact meet again. By expressing the wish to make this economic collaboration part of a long-lasting relationship, this gift projects the present exchange towards a future time of greater social complicity. When examining the circulation of food in Massim inter-island hospitality, Munn points out that 'food is the basic non-verbal persuasive medium' (1986: 60) for generating agreement with others. Through the act of giving, she further explains, the donor extends the space of control beyond himself by making himself present in the mind of the other. In the same vein, giving extra food before concluding the transaction is indented to extend intersubjective spatiotemporality, by remaining present in the mind of a partner from another ecological tier. When giving a yapa, the donor expects their generosity to be remembered at the next fair, thus inducing the partner to engage in further transactions. Yapa is a furtive act in the present, but it is expected to create potentialities in the future.

Clearly, cambio features the ambiguity fundamental to the Maussian notion of gift, which is both generous and interested. This dimension is put forward when cambio entails a final yapa. In surpassing the equivalencies agreed for a cambio, the yapa fits the principle of increment that has been identified as a feature of competitive gift exchange (Strathern and Stewart 2006: 241): it triggers an imbalance calling forth further exchanges. Concluding cambio with a yapa thus opens the space for the manifestation of trust and the creation of a social tie.

### From Complementarity to Duality: Types of Cheating

While the social bonds that convey care and generosity are considered the normative framework, even between preferential partners, kindness alternates with harsh defence of personal interest. Interactions usually include bitter dialogues that are sometimes tinged with humour or irony. Agonistic interactions are commonplace, and the transaction can occur *in extremis* or be aborted. Such was the case of abuelo Telesforo, who felt insulted by the lack of consideration for the value of his meat and argued that it would have a better fate if he ate it himself. 'Why should I stay here begging? They're just pretending to be nice', he muttered, quickly packing up the haunch of the llama he had slaughtered that very morning for an unknown valley cultivator. When set in a difficult negotiation, the yapa itself can take on an agonistic colouring and then turn into a drastic bargaining session. 'I'm not giving you yapa. And if you're not content, I'll give it [the meat they were about to exchange] back', a young cultivator threatened at the fair in Yavi. If the term is still used, it refers here no longer to a little something added spontaneously but instead to a demand that conditions the success of the transaction, thus denaturing the very principle of yapa and the generosity behind it. Harsh negotiation over equivalencies is commonplace. Such interactions alternating between defiance and benevolence are observed in other Andean contexts as well, where sharp bargain does not exclude solidarity and enduring social ties (Ferraro 2011: 173; Fonseca 1972: 329; Mayer 2002: 156).

In addition to quantitative measures, another frequent bone of contention is the quality of the goods. Doubts are sometimes voiced that challenge the partner by calling into question his capacity to produce goods of value. This might be a well-founded accusation or simply a way of depreciating the products in order to impose advantageous terms of exchange, as in the case of the following transaction, whose favourable outcome attests that the maize was appreciated despite the criticisms voiced:

Grower: You want peeled corn?

Herder: An arroba, a chalona.

[The grower opens her sack to show the quality of her husked maize.]

Herder: It's ugly.

Grower: What do you mean, ugly?

Herder: It's not going to cook.

Grower: What do you mean it's not going to cook! It's peeled with ashes and not with lime.

Herder: It smells. It's not washed.

Grower: I let it soak a whole night. [The grower holds out her maize.] Here. Too much, good weight.

[The herder gives her chalona. They part without saying goodbye.]

Other forms of slander might also suggest or explicitly denounce the partner's deceitfulness. Although described as friendly gatherings, fairs are also convenient places for *engaño* (cheating). A common trick consists of filling a bag with defective items, then covering them with some good pieces. Others give short measures. Such was the case of one cultivator who had asked Hilda if she could put a chalona aside for him while he went for his maize flour:

Cultivator, presenting his flour: Here, for the chalona.

Hilda, without using a scale: This isn't a full arroba. As if this small quantity was an arroba!

Cultivator: Let's exchange, madam, come on.

Hilda: There's not even ten kilos.

Cultivator: But for this [meat], madam, it's fine. There are also legs; it's all mixed up.

Hilda: No, no, no. Bring a full [arroba] or leave [the meat] here. Someone else will bring [maize]. There is one kilo missing for an arroba.

Cultivator: Madam, I take it.

Hilda: No, you must complete [the arroba].

Cultivator: But these are only small bones.

Hilda: This is all meat. Or is this not meat perhaps? This, empty it here and bring the missing kilo. Come on. Don't cry.

Pretending to apply cambio etiquette while targeting profitable nego-cio is also seen as a form of cheating. As Hilda exemplified during the Santa Catalina fair: 'They [those bartering maize] cheat a lot. They buy and resell at twice the price; they do not work like we do. Be-fore, it wasn't like that: they used to tend their fields and we our flock. Foodstuff for foodstuff. Now, it's a business.' While it is hard to gauge the actual extend of fraud, I was nonetheless struck by the pervasive accusation of cheating in the rhetoric of agonistic moments during interactions. Even if displaying distrust towards people and disdain for their goods, practices of engaño do not prevent the possibility of further exchanges. Cheating, be it supposed or real, does not call into doubt the necessary complementarity between herders and cultivators. When bringing the missing kilo, the cultivator in the aforementioned exchange with Hilda offered some ready-to-eat roasted corn and pro-posed another exchange. The interest manifested by Hilda attested that her partner's cunning had not excluded the possibility of further transactions.

Moreover, not even friends are necessarily immune from abuse; it is more by assuring recourse in the event of dissatisfaction that this social relationship protects people. Faced with a complaint, the friend will always manage to invent some excuse so as not to lose face, but he will not be able to avoid acknowledging his responsibility and dealing with the ensuing unpleasantness. Thus, after having joyfully covered her friend Cristina's eyes with her hand and being recognised only by the sound of her voice, Silvia did not wait any longer to formu-late her complaint: 'You tricked me. The apples are sour. Sour and full of worms. The two crates are still there. The children haven't even touched them. They didn't like [them]. You have to admit it.' Arguing that the darkness was responsible for this mishap, Cristina obtained forgiveness by promising to hand over two new crates of fruit at the next harvest. While the possibility of engaño haunts every transaction, even those conducted between the closest friends, its recurrence would put their complicity at risk. Those who deceive their partners regularly will suffer a bad reputation and be shunned in the future. This will, in the words of Munn, provoke negative value transformation: they will lose their possibility to persuade faraway partners to engage in endur-ing complicities.

As the extracts above attest, the terms of cambio are defined through a codified confrontation of stereotyped formulas by which two socio-economic communities are reified: herders from the puna and cultiva-tors from the quebrada. When economic communities coincide with national identities, the confrontation between cultivators and herders tracks that between Bolivians and Argentineans, fostering the utterance of the stigmas in use in this cross-border region. Depending on the partners, the nature of their relationship and the quality of their goods, each cambio therefore manifests a particular swing between duality and complementarity among peasants from different Andean ecological niches. This condensing of generosity and harsh bargaining, or even cheating, within a single interaction challenges Salhins's (1972) mapping of social distances and types of reciprocities. Salhins famously establishes a correlation between figures of reciprocity and the quality of the social relationship between the partners. Building on exchange categories identified by Malinowski in the Trobriand, Salhins outlines a continuum of reciprocities (from generalised, to balanced and negative) anchored on degrees of social cohesion.

Instead of constituting disjointed spheres of exchange like Salhins' circle of reciprocities, the intertwining of generosity and confrontation socially shapes cambio interactions. This intertwining stands in sharp contrast to the interactions underlying large-scale traders' direct exchanges, which unambiguously match Salhins' negative mode of reciprocity.[5] This exploration of cambio interactions suggests that generosity and strict defence of personal interest do not necessarily constitute disjoined spheres of transactions each relating to particular social relationships, as Salhins asserted. This fact supports Harris's findings, as she concludes that Salhins's mapping of social relationship upon economic exchange is of little value for understanding Laymi transactions: 'While there is an analogy that close kin should show uncalculating generosity to one another, the reality is otherwise' (2007: 81). In the context of fairs, the concentration of largesse and appropriation within one interaction, as manifested by cambio, crystallises an economic intimacy shared by the partners.

### Use Value and the Social Fabric of Barter

As suggested by the ethnographic account above, production and consumption practices set material limitations on the potential circle of cambio partners. People taking part in cambio must share the same daily and ritual dietary habits, and produce its ingredients. Such a network includes peasants who cultivate plots in one of the complementary ecological niches of the cordillera. It excludes merchants, whose capacity to participate in cambio is further restricted by the goods they are looking for. They do not regularly consume the agricultural foodstuffs to which cambio relates. They instead need monetary income to fuel their business and meet their living costs in town. In contrast to cambio, which supposes that partners produce and eat similar items, merchant sales do not require shared labour and food practices. Therefore, the simultaneous substitution of products from Andean niches through cambio enacts an economic community made up of two mutually dependent groups of peasants with identical food habits. This sameness is performed through the specific interaction underlying cambio, which takes the form of a codified encounter between two complementary groups sharing economic intimacy.

Furthermore, the acceptance of the measures that the ancestors put in place with little regard for market prices superposes on this economic entity an ethnic community based on shared kinship with such ancestors. When they respect the scale of value they have settled upon, the partners legitimise the authority of these ascendants and thereby assert the continuity of their lineage. Conversely, those who depart from the elders' measures in favour of market prices are accused of eroding old reciprocities between herders and cultivators. Puneños and Quebradeños sometimes explicitly acknowledge the existence of a common filiation. We can see this in the case of two women unknown to each other who, during a cambio, came to question the qualities of their respective lands, separated by some one hundred kilometres. When they introduced their surname into the conversation, however, they inferred a shared genealogy. 'My grandmother was Abracaite. Therefore, all Abracaite are my *parientes* [kin]. Here, almost all of us are kin', one of them concluded. It is noteworthy that inferring kinship from a shared family name is unusual. Many patronyms are in fact widespread across the Andes and all Hispanic America, but their bearers do not acknowledge a shared kinship. Hinged upon the institution of compadrazgo between cherished partners, this 'imagined community' gathers cambio partakers into the circle of relatives, whatever the specific tie by which they may be linked.

Along with an acceptance of the elders' authority, the nature of the products involved in cambio participates in the constitution of this community conceived in the idiom of kinship. The mutual transfer of part of the domestic produce implies that the partners will fill their larders with identical foodstuffs and eventually cook with identical ingredients. In the case of food, the mingling of subject and object inherent in consumption practices is particularly intense. Through cambio, the partners feed one another with ingredients that are the objectification of bodily labour in their fields, while their ingestion in the form of meals rests on previous transactions between lowland and highland people. As flesh is made of food, and dietary habits shape people's identities, cambio items participate in making subjectivities, both symbolically and biologically. Cambio transactions reveal a process of community-making through consumption that does not require people to use up and ingest all together, as described by Colloredo-Mansfeld in Ecuadorian fiestas. Rather, in this case, people's gathering produces use value through their exchanges. Apart from sharing meals during the fairs, consumption operates mainly as a 'generative moment for community' (2003: 273) after households have once again dispersed on the mountainous slopes.

In the Andes, where people are aware that eating the same food produces similar bodies and people, daily ingestion of the same ingredients is further conceived as the point at which kinship is created. Rather than strictly resulting from sex, parenthood is seen as a processual construction in which blood filiation is important but not necessary, or sufficient. As Weismantel put it, following Indian ideas about motherhood, 'feeding, rather than insemination or birth, is the act that determines who a child's parents are, and so gives it a social identity' (2001: 256, see also 1995). In fact, this is not specific to the Andean context, as attested by Janet Carsten's important study on the role of feeding in the creation of kinship ties in South East Asia. From her field research in a Malay fishing community, she identifies rice as a key ingredient in the fabric of kinship: 'The consumption of rice meals cooked in the hearth not only strengthens existing ties of kinship between household members, it can actually create such ties with those who have recently come to share residence' (2012: 40).

As I indicated in chapter 1, in this Argentinean region, members of a household, which is the fundamental unit of kinship, are acknowledged as those who 'share the pot' (*compartir la hoya*). Commensality also plays a key role in the establishment of compadrazgo, to the extent that the ritual prescribed when I became Genoveva's comadre (her son's godmother) comprised a meal shared at her home with our husbands and children. For the first time in several years on the puna, a host worried about being able to cook a full meal that would fit my vegetarian diet. Ødegaard (2010: 109) has also noted the importance of food consumption for fuelling compadrazgo relationships in her Peruvian fieldwork. The vital role of eating likewise in creating relatedness stresses the practical and embodied dimensions of this figure of kinship, wrongly described in the literature as 'fictive' or 'spiritual'.

Significantly, the food circulating at fairs includes the ancestors in the circle of commensals, as they will be fed with these ingredients when offered meals. This is made clear in the case of the Manka Fiesta, which takes place a week before All Saints' Day. On this occasion, llama fat, dried fruits, *cayote* (black-seed squash) and onion flowers circulate between herders and cultivators so that they can prepare the offerings made to the dead and the ancestors.[6] The cultural intimacy with which that kind of interaction is imbued can be seen in the following inter-action at the Manka Fiesta. A Bolivian cultivator looking at a piece of meat from an Argentinean herder asked whether it was llama meat and whether the meat was fresh. The herder confirmed, suggesting the cul-tivator have a closer look. The cultivator smelled and tasted a tiny piece of raw meat. To conclude the transaction, she proposed flowers for the souls. She also offered cayote and dried grapes, which are used to pre-pare the *empanadillas* (sweet filled buns) featured in all offerings for the deceased. But the herder asked for maize to prepare her kalapurca, which is Pachamama and other ancestors' favourite. They came to an agreement and proceed to the exchange. The cultivator told me that she was pleased by the transaction because she needed llama fat to bake *turquitos,* small breads in the shape of humans and other beings such as birds or stars, which are offered to the souls. 'With the fat of beef', she added, 'the result is not nice. With that [llama fat, the turquitos] are nicely browned.' By swapping the produce of their respective labour, the partners mutually contributed to the nurturing of their ancestors. Telesforo explicitly stated the resulting relationships among feeding, kinship and ancestral filiation when he explained that Pachamama is people's mother because she feeds them as women feed their children.

The speech by Perfecto, given in representation of cultivators from an adjacent Bolivian valley for introducing the Yavi Easter fair, bril-liantly emphasises how the encounter of people with their agricultural produce delineates a collective belonging tracing a descent from com-mon ancestors:

> I am here representing the producers from the south of Bolivia. It's a tradition, year after year, we make the effort from one place to another, and even the transfer to Yavi to . . . in order to fraternise [and do] what our ancestors did: barter, cambio and sale of the produce that all year we bring to fruition in order to go and offer it. From that time to this time, I see that the fiesta is becoming a bit smaller. And that may discourage us from coming. But we continue making the sacrifice to come and look for affective relationships [*cariño*], always, and the fraternity that links us, Bolivia and Argentina. The only thing that makes the difference is a simple line that distinguishes whether we are Bolivians or Argentineans, but looking at the traditional customs, we are the same. As someone said, Bolivia and Argentina have always been united, and what ties us together are our things: that is the fiesta, Easter in Yavi.

Perfecto stresses a sense of belonging that cross-cuts national borders and ecological tiers. His words speak to the recognition of shared ancestors, despite the forced population displacements that have been recurrent in the history of the puna population. To sum up, then, Puneños and Quebradeños are conceived of as suitable cambio partners in virtue of a 'sameness' that stems from the nature of what they produce, eat and exchange – in contrast to merchants and visitors, who are not the same. When making offerings of food and drink, and when applying the elders' measures, people extend this kin network towards the ancestors incarnated in the landscape. Interestingly, the collectivity thereby delineated, is not named by a given ethnonym.

If cambio weaves complicities that are expressed in the idiom of kinship, this mode of relatedness nonetheless does not rest on the territorial and the linguistic unity that essentialist approaches have seen as objective criteria for the crystallisation of ethnicity, along with descent and shared cultural practices.[7] Cambio delineates a deterritorialised form of ethnicity in the sense that it is based not on a fixed area on the map but on the articulation between lowlands and highlands. According to where the fair takes place, these correspond to different microzones: the Talina valley and the central puna at Santa Catalina's fair, the Sococha valley and the puna of Yavi at Easter, the Iruya valley or the puna of Abra Pampa for the celebration of the Virgen del Rosario. Note that these many subregions gather yearly in the main encounter of the Manka Fiesta.[8] The sense of sameness is not based on language either: while most Bolivian cultivators natively speak Quechua, Spanish is the language of exchange, with distinctive pronunciation by Argentineans and Bolivians. Campesinos' Spanish nonetheless feature a shared transactional vocabulary. This is exemplified by the very use of the term *cambio*, which as noted above is not used in the same way by Argentinean Creoles. Yapa provides another example, as well as the rhetoric and formulas used to negotiate the value of the agricultural produce.

Studies on barter acknowledging its social dimension notice forms of complicity intended to ensure minimal trust between partners in the absence of an overarching institution that would maintain peace (Graeber 2011: 30; Hart 1986: 648; Heady 2006: 268). Heady refers to the highlander/lowlander relationship as the typical case of trade between potentially agonistic groups, whereby the gift-like dimension of barter is used to avoid potential adversity. 'The transactions have a gift-like element', he says, 'because they could not take place without the existence of the secure social relationship which the gift-like aspects of the transaction help to ensure' (2006: 268). This perspective positing social ties as instrumental means for barter does not account for complicities in the cambio network, though. The social relationship in cambio exceeds the minimal trust required for strangers to negotiate their personal interest. Barter at the fiesta nurtures social relationships that are appreciated for themselves. Once I asked a herder why she continued participating in the fair when she was not satisfied with the rates of exchange. She replied: 'Here, we meet with friends, kin who have come from remote areas. We are in harmony.'

In this light, I propose looking at cambio as a figure of 'reproductive barter'. Gell used the notion of 'reproductive gift' to refer to 'prestations explicitly linked to phases in the relations between affinally linked groups' (1992: 143). I am extending his concept to barter transactions, but I am also using it in a more general sense that is not restricted to marriage, child or death prestations. By 'reproductive', I mean that partners nurture each other and thereby create a broader social community. Instrumental transactions securing a full diet to peasants from complementary ecological zones are further articulated upon a realm of transactions intended to foster cosmological reproduction. I will develop this argument later. Before, I will examine how nostalgic tropes about vanishing cambio paradoxically assert the elders' authority and shared ancestry.

### The Vanishing of Virtuous Barter: The Social Performativity of Nostalgia

During their negotiations, the protagonists regularly allude to the equity that would have characterised their elders' transactions. More broadly, they regret the decline of the reciprocal exchanges materialising the ideal complementarity that is reputed to have formerly bound highland and lowland people together. Other lamentations hint at the spread of negocio strategies between peasants. As I mentioned earlier, because it diverges from the ancestors' measures-related fairness, barter performed in a logic of business is collectively denounced as inequitable. Those regrets also recount the dissemination of cambio's agonistic drift. While this barter network is reputed to have formerly been completely embedded in a dense social fabric that mitigated dissension, the protagonists depict the contemporary experience of cambio as overrun by its antagonistic facet. According to the protagonists of the fairs, the elders were keener to engage in compadrazgo and to respect the social and economic commitments that go with it.

As Perfecto told me with regret: 'Before, people had more conscience. They used to give the [old] measure, to make sure that you would leave satisfied. Nowadays they don't. Everyone defends their own interest.' Old Telesforo concluded: 'We can't trust anymore. Like that, barter is useless.' Apart from having corrupted economic transactions, this social crumbling impinges on the endless parties they say formerly went with economic exchanges. As Lola remembered: 'In the past, fairs used to be different. People were not looking to barter so quickly.' Later she continued, recalling that, when breeders and cultivators used to dance and exchange extensively, both 'had everything. Nothing lacked.' These discourses present the dense network embracing the dwellers of complementary ecological niches as a condition of both social balance and economic profusion.

Broadly speaking, these lamentations allude to the crumbling of the economic solidarity they say formerly united herders and cultivators. When taking the form of a negocio, the current cambio is deemed to reflect the duality between herders and cultivators, at the expense of the complementarity that fostered fertility and abundance in the past. In this light, those longings for an idealised past actually lament the erosion of the balanced reciprocity that draws the boundaries of what Harris famously called the 'ethnic economy' (2000). Thus, at fairs, structural nostalgia points back to a 'time out of time' when prescriptions framed interactions, guaranteeing both the economic and the social reproduction of Andean communities. Such observations lead some protagonists to conclude that 'manhood is vanishing'.

In the previous chapter I explained that many nostalgic speakers are obviously not intent on strictly putting the ancestral etiquette into practice. Sometimes, these narrations in praise of the elders' economic code can be successfully summoned for winning an ongoing negotiation. For instance, these formulas can induce the partner to agree upon a balance that disregards market values, even if it is not exactly in line with the elders' criteria. Such formulas can also convince the partner to provide a yapa. If the partners do not intend to actualise the vanishing transactional ethic, the social relationship brought forth by commemoration explains the economic efficiency of theses formulas. Developing a phenomenological approach to social memory, Casey pointed out that commemoration deals 'with overcoming the separation from which otherwise unaffiliated individuals suffer' (2011: 185). During the fair, the co-evocation of the ancestors' economic order gathers the partners within a shared collective, or what Casey called a 'horizontal participatory communitas', smoothing out the 'separation' inherent in the Andean barter system, which rests on the meeting between peasants coming from disparate ecological and economic communities.

This horizontal community lies perpendicular to the 'vertical community' established with the named predecessors. The collective emphasis on the ancestors' economic behaviour assumes the existence of a common descent, which justifies that this behaviour should be regarded as exemplary. This imagined genealogy implicitly draws the ethnic boundaries within which members should be granted special treatment, which materialises their economic solidarity. In this case, nostalgic narratives do not ensure continuity of individual identity as much as they 'forge a shared (if illusory) sense of group identity, cohesion, and long-term continuities' (Bissell 2005: 226). This reminder of a genealogy asserts a shared group identity, which impels the partners to materialise their solidarity by granting preferential equivalences. In doing so, they withdraw from the national market and seem to periodically re-establish the ideal trust and reciprocity that the modern economy is said to have corroded.

Nostalgic utterances concerning a vanishing economic order shed light on the social performativity of cambio. The discrepancy between the nostalgic discursive register and speakers' actions that refute their intention to re-establish the missed social order attests that, at fairs, the ancestors' code of ethics is not expected to be rigorously implemented. Rather, the efficiency of its commemoration rests upon acknowledging a shared social belonging, thus impelling favourable economic treatments. By performing the solidarity induced by the outlined lineage, fairs' protagonists approve the elders' precepts and their current relevance, even when overall practices deviate from them. These formulas allow the partners to engage with the present situation with reverence to the elders, while at the same time infringing on the ancestors' morality of exchange. Some participants make subtle use of this discursive stratagem by emphasising considerations regarding the social and cosmological orders in an attempt to secure personal benefit in the immediate transaction. Clearly, such allusions to a past order aim at overcoming current struggles and at gaining the speaker a favourable outcome. That nostalgia serves present purposes has been widely addressed (Bissell 2005; Davis 1979; Herzfeld 2005; Pickering and Keightley 2006). Here I have indicated how the economic and social performativity of longings are entangled in the fact that nostalgia tends to essentialise ethnic belonging by delineating an idealised image of collective cohesion (Bryant 2014) and unconditional reciprocities (Herzfeld 2005).

## Barter in Ritual Economics

### *Extending Subjectivities beyond the Mundane World*

I have shown that cambio produces social values by establishing a new kind of relationship between the partners or by nurturing an existing relationship. Plentiful cambio nurtures favourable relationships with Catholic and telluric beings too. As such transactions please these ambivalent beings, generous barter also produces cosmological values. In as much as they are essential to human vitality and to economic prosperity, benevolent cosmological ties in turn yield further production of economic values. Anticipation of material reward is made explicit by the common assertion that pleased deified agencies support those who provide their exchange partners with abundant counterparts. 'Then God will help me as well', glossed Isabela when I expressed my admiration at her generosity in bargaining equivalencies. This means that economic benefits are expected not only during the fair itself. Having contributed to the fiesta by performing mutually gratifying transactions should also benefit future economic endeavours.

The link between material circulation and the creation of cosmological values is made very clear in the myth relating the emergence of the Manka Fiesta, which, as I said, means 'clay pots party' in a mix of Spanish and Quechua. This main gathering in the Argentinean Andes is, significantly enough, the only spontaneous one out of step with the ecclesiastical calendar. This narrative puts the Manka Fiesta's origin back thousands of years ago, when a 'splendid and young', 'cheerful [*alegre*] and entertaining' woman settled 'at the crossroads of the paths going from north to south, and from east to west'. She was carrying an abundance of goods such as blankets, ponchos, hats, musical instruments and clay pots of all sizes and shapes. When travellers would pass by, she would suggest they take a rest, drink some maize beer or chew some coca leaves; she would tell endless tales or sing folk songs. She would also propose her goods in exchange for what they were carrying 'without setting prices, because money didn't matter for her' (Tolaba 2010: 43, my translations).

Thanks to the unexpected presence of the Manka Warmi (Pot Woman, in Quechua), passers-by continued their journey *felices* (happy). They gradually started to converge on that place at the time of her mysterious appearance three time a year. One day, she did not turn up at the October gathering. While waiting for her, travellers shared food and drink, told stories, sang folk songs and enjoyed times of happiness and entertainment. They eventually decided to exchange each other's products without waiting for the woman to arrive. When they realised that she was not coming any more, the grateful travellers decided to perpetuate an annual meeting to pay tribute to this beautiful woman whose largesse had been exceptional.

As stressed by the myth, the Manka Fiesta is intended to praise a supernatural being and her exemplary behaviour – namely, the handing out of food and drink, speeches and dances together with instrumental exchanges. Portrayed with seductive attributes such as long black braids, large shining eyes, colourful dress or mastery of knitting, and by abundant goods to be swapped and shared, this woman epitomises fertility. According to the narrative, this fiesta celebrates a supernatural being distinguished by outstanding fruitfulness. By extension, the case of the Manka Fiesta suggests that spatial and temporal condensation of economic exchanges can constitute a tribute to fertile entities. Here incarnated in the mythical Manka Warmi, this fertile power is encapsulated in other contexts in deified beings like the Virgin Mary and the array of saints celebrated during Andean festivals.

When composing a fiesta, cambios are analogous to the different kinds of immaterial offerings Anne-Marie Losonczy observed in her Colombian fieldwork. She identifies them as the most typical and pleasing human interactions, like speech, musical performance or dance, which act as counter-gifts for the fertile breath received from the celebrated entity (1997: 259). Since these counter-gifts are expected to foster new prestations, they trigger a two-way circulation by which human beings please deified entities through their exchanges and expect that in turn their exchanges will profit from these deities' support. Munn's insight on the convincing power of the gift is also relevant in the case of gifts circulating beyond the human realm to the space-time of deities. Importantly, we see that not only gifts are performed as offerings meant to trigger further prosperity. In this Andean region, other kinds of transactions, like barter, can have the same effect, as long as they are conducted with generosity.[9]

During the fiesta, this interaction is obvious when religious processions pass through the stalls to bless the transactions and, at the same time, to *entretener* (entertain) and *alegrar* (cheer) the saint with the fair's hustle and bustle. The intensity of noise is used to gauge the success of a fair. *Silencio esta* (it's silent) is a formula used to lament poor participation, which indicates that cambio are expected to involve effervescence, expressed by the sound of human voices. This expression stands in contrast to the stereotype of barter as silent trade and to other descriptions of such transactions unfolding in a 'quiet and subdued place' (Barnes and Barnes 1989: 406). Indeed, the mythical story of the fairs' origins insists on the importance of alegría as both a precondition and an outcome of the barter performed to please the Manka Warmi.

Such appreciation of joyful cambio by deified entities, involves them in the cambio sphere of transaction. Once pleased, these ambivalent beings are in turn expected to endow people with increased life force

**Figure 5.2.** Worshippers pleasing the Virgin with the hustle and bustle of the Santa Catalina fair while the Virgin blesses the fair in hope for fruitful exchanges. Photograph by the author.

and prosperity. Barter is thus addressed to them in an attempt to prompt them to reciprocate by endowing the generous partners with good fortune in further economic endeavours. In this light, cambio is appreciated as a practice that opens intersubjective space-time with the realms of deities and ancestors. Cambio's potential to extend the partners' spatiotemporality towards this realm requires practising the etiquette ancestors used to apply themselves, which is a way of actualising the ancestors' presence through living behaviours. It translates into a series of norms and prescriptions – presented in the next section – that should be respected in order for the ancestors to be pleased.

### Ritual Prescriptions

As noted in the introduction, the notion of ritual exchange has been used with diverging acceptation in Andean ethnographies. Some scholars use an interactional approach to emphasise features that are inherent in the social interaction underpinning material transfer. What they call 'ritual kinship' is a common case. In this view, any kind of material transfer between such kin is seen as ritualised, whether it takes the shape of barter, gift or commodity (Burchard 1974: 227; Lecoq 1987: 24; Molinié 1975: 52; Rivière 1979: 153). Relationships between peasants from different ecological niches entail another type of interaction that has been interpreted as ritualised. Murra describes these as 'relations of ritual barter and seasonal exchange' (1985: 16). Platt, for his part, identifies a ritual type of haggling, whereby the equivalence between the commodities establishes a symmetrical relationship between the partners (1988: 404). Those scholars who see ritualisation as stemming from a communication with spiritual entities provide yet another illustration of this interactional perspective. In this line, Patrice Lecoq (1987) interprets Bolivian shepherds' trading journey to the valley as an initiatory ritual calling forth intimate contact with supernatural beings invoked through prayers and offerings. Without actually qualifying them as ritual, Harris relates similar operations: 'Night and morning they chew coca and make offerings to the guardian spirits of the mountains (kumpriras), not only to safeguard their journey, but also to ask help in obtaining all the valley produce they require' (2000: 112).

Others take a transactional approach considering that particular types of transfers are being intrinsically ritualised. In this vein, Mayer identifies as ceremonial all transactions of goods or services underpinning communal and domestic celebrations. These prestations are those fitting one of the three local figures of reciprocity he recorded in his Peruvian fieldwork (*yanapaña*, *ayni* and *mink'a*), and which he explicitly distinguishes from barter. 'Barter', he asserts, 'represents a sphere of exchange separate from that of reciprocity as well as buying and selling' (2002: 143).[10]

Mayer's stance departs from another group of scholars who adopt a contextual approach. The latter consists in relating ritualisation to a delimited space-time without specifying the modalities of exchange that are performed in this context. Poole speaks of ritualised trade (1982: 101) to emphasise the synchronisation between religious, agricultural and commercial activities. She defines an economic-religious regional complex as the 'integration and articulation of sanctuaries and celebrations with territories and economic processes' (1982: 79). In addition to their economic and religious dimensions, these ceremonies span geographic regions corresponding to colonial and pre-Columbian sociopolitical entities. Also drawing on cases from the Peruvian province of Cuzco, Glynn Custred observes a 'close relationship of political, social, economic, and ritual interactions within definable regions' (1980: 205). When celebrating the Holy Cross, peasants from a given territory gather in urban centres according to the weekly market in which they participate. Both authors agree on the vital role of religious centres in structuring economic exchanges and outlining sociopolitical territories.

Historian Brooke Larson combines the contextual, transactional and interactional approaches in two different articles. In the first one, she apprehends rural markets as highly ritualised spaces for displaying goods, kinship and political relations (1995: 36). However, she does not detail further the interactional features of these markets as compared with other places of exchange that would not be ritualised. In the second article, coauthored with Rosario Leon, she takes a transactional stance distinguishing between commodity exchange and barter, positing the latter as 'ritualized exchanges through kinship ties that bound clusters of valley peoples to their original highland ayllus' (1995: 235). The criteria for barter being classified as ritualised in this case thus relates to the social mode of interaction.

This brief overview of Andean scholarship suggests that the ritual quality of a transaction is a matter of the author's appreciation, and his analytical perspective. In this section, I would like to question the relevance of these approaches to understand exchanges at fairs, by addressing cambio partakers' conception of ritual exchange. Although the word does exist in Spanish, I have never heard any peasant distinguish a set of practices as a 'ritual'. They instead differentiate ordinary acts with fiesta, or *celebración* (celebration). I have mentioned above that the term fiesta is used as a synonym for fair. For barter to be entangled in the fiesta, a series of norms are prescribed.

In Argentinean fairs, for barter practices to be taken as part of a saint or ancestor's celebration, they should align with precepts specifying decent dress. The traditional outfit that I have described, featuring a colourful skirt, a white shirt, a hat and braided hair with tullmas, is convenient for women; while hat and poncho are the key attire suited for men. Temporalities of exchanges and their articulation with other festivities are also normatively framed. Exemplifying temporality, Hilda's complaint highlights how the timing of exchange should be respected as part of the saint's celebration: 'They [cultivators] all come earlier, and there is nothing left for us [herders]. One must arrive on the eve of the fiesta in order to be leaving on the day of the celebration. [Otherwise] we are not accompanying the Virgin.'

Still more important are the prescriptions regarding the kinds of goods, their quality and their equivalences. The relationship between the fair and the celebration is made clear by the connection peasants establish between inter-ecological reciprocities and cosmological balance. While generous exchanges between peasants are expected to appease the bad temper of Catholic and telluric beings, failing to provide fair equivalences could provoke their deception and subsequent retaliation. At the Santa Catalina fair, Hilda told her partner off as he was trying to give less maize than was stipulated in the elders' measure: 'Why is this ten kilos when you must give me twelve? Come on, come on. Don't cry. God Tata will get upset and he will thunder.' The Quechua name Tata refers to a paternal authoritative ancestor with a sacred connotation. With this formula Hilda hints at the convergence between ancestors, Catholic figures and earthly forces. This confrontation therefore indicates that ancestors, here in the guise of Tata, are pleased as long as their measures are respected. As Joaquim explained to me, when a protagonist does not respect their equivalences, 'he doesn't think that the fair could die. He is just thinking of himself. Profits . . . and the other, busted! And when he becomes aware that the other is busted, he doesn't come to the fair anymore. If people do not come, the fiesta disappears. That's the way it is.' Following Joaquim's words, respect for the elders' code of exchange therefore conditions the contribution of material circulation to the celebration. This point does not seem to be specific to the regenerative potential of material circulation between highland and lowland communities which has been observed in other Andean settings as well (Harris 2000; Ødegaard 2010).

So, for material transfers to enliven the fiesta, individual interest must be contained by altruistic considerations. If they apply fair equivalences, partners give rise to mutual alegría, which peasants regard as a key ingredient for pleasing telluric beings (see chapter 1). On the other hand, I mentioned that undertaking an economic activity in a bad mood exposes one to cosmological retaliation, as Mother Earth is said to capture ungrateful people's souls and absorb their bodies' life forces. So, participants are expected to go to the fair happily. An elder made this explicit as he was reprimanding a group of teenagers in a truck driving back home after a fair for not respecting the elders' etiquette: 'You must go to the festival *tatayalegre*.[11] Joyfully, singing', he said after lamenting that they were not wearing the traditional ponchos and hats suitable for performing religious activities. Along with cheerfulness, faith is also acknowledged as a key feature of participants' emotional engagement in the fair. Lamenting that 'now people come [to fairs] with the sole interest of trade, not for faith anymore', Hilda pointed out, a contrario, that participants should come motivated by both economic and religious concerns. The mingling of profit and devotion transpires in the prayers performed before travelling to the fair. Old Marea mentioned in Yavi that she would not sleep on the fair's eve, as she 'prays until sunrise'.[12] Hence, the participants' state of mind in the fair should combine cheerfulness and devotion with economic interest.

Thus, at the same time as being personally engaged, economic interactions at fairs are socially prescribed, thereby fitting a fundamental criteria of ritual actions (Humphrey and Laidlaw 1994; see also Bell 1997; Turner 1995). In their important book, Caroline Humphrey and James Laidlaw stress that a ritual act differs from an ordinary one in that 'it severs the link, present in everyday activity, between the "intentional meaning of the agent" and the identity of the act which he or she performs' (1994: 3). Likewise the identity of cambios performed during the fiesta does not strictly depend on the intentions and thoughts of the actors at the very moment of the transaction. Whatever their intention when bartering, feasting, dancing or walking with the procession, participants are celebrating the saint together. But, when they greet a barter partner, display an abundance of agricultural products, bargain equivalences, grab a sheep, pack corn or present a yapa, this supra-intention is disjoined from their action of the moment. Practices of fiesta thus seem to fit with what anthropologists means by ritual.

Now, I am not contending that every barter is engaged with the intention of celebrating the saint. I propose, then, to regard fairs as a space-time where ritualisation of interaction is expected, even if not always fulfilled. While the partners do not apply these rules strictly, they all have in mind a kind of 'archetypal action' (Humphrey and Laidlaw 1994) that appears to them as the ideal transaction. These archetypes are made very clear in nostalgic discourses about the elders' precepts that I discussed in the preceding chapter. Such an approach accounts for the stance of reverence and devotion adopted by most protagonists, who nevertheless acknowledge their economic interest. Such an intimate involvement in instrumental transactions, additionally structured by an objectified code, is what distinguishes transactions at the fiesta from those performed in daily contexts. Coming back to the three approaches to ritual exchanges that I have identified in Andean scholarship, the examination of cambio suggests that ritualisation is chiefly related to an interactional code, involving human and nonhuman beings.

Strathern and Stewart point out that, when appended to economic exchange, the qualification 'ceremonial' refers to the 'formalised and customary practice of display and communication that take place on these occasions' (2006: 230). It is my contention that ceremonial exchange is a notion that covers exchanges that share the fundamental feature of other kinds of ritual acts. This is a point that is not considered in many anthropological studies, where the concept of ceremonial exchange is loosely used, with no regard to whether the transaction under discussion fulfils local perceptions (or anthropologists' definition) of a ritual act. Furthermore, most of the time, ceremonial exchange appears as synonymous with the Maussian gift, which does not fit with this ethnography of cambio. Other modes of transaction, like barter, fit with the local peculiarities of ritual acts, positing these transactions as an integral component of a broader fiesta. Berndt (1951) categorises these exchanges as composing ceremonial economics. The ethnography of cambio thus furthers an old claim formulated by Berndt, that 'ceremonial economics' does not entail any exchange carried out at the margin of a ceremony. This concept instead covers transactions that make up the very celebration. I am more inclined, however, to use the term 'ritual economics' to stress the fact that these practices fit with the feature of ritual actions.

### Alegría as Value and Virtue

I would like now to further explore the affective dimension of cambios at the fair in order to better understand the process of value transformation at stake in these ritual exchanges. Paradoxically, participating in the fair is described as a self-sacrifice and an enduring source of happiness. The elder Marea glossed on her venture: 'Delighted – as I am praying. Well, that is it. I get prepared, I make meat. Here is the offal, the meat I make to bring here. That's all, that's my *felicidad* [happiness].' I pointed out that the participants must join the fair joyfully and that alegría is posited as a key ingredient for any celebration of telluric beings. Yet cheerfulness is not just a precondition of ritual economics: material circulation at fairs is posited as a source of joy creation itself. Cambio is expected to trigger a shared contentment. Indeed, a successful cambio is one in which 'both partners leave each other *contento* [joyful, happy]'. Therefore, cambios are expected to produce a mutual satisfaction, which in turn enhances the celebration. As long as the elders' measures are seen as a reference for establishing mutually gratifying transactions, the satisfaction procured by material circulation is shared with the elders and ancestors to whom respect is addressed by perpetuating their norms and scales of value.

These practices are very much in tune with Émile Durkheim's analysis of ritual effervescence emerging from the participants' collective performance of a shared ethic, thereby generating an exhilarating sense of togetherness. As resumed by Robbins: 'We experience effervescent happiness when we feel we are joined together with others in sharing the same representations and evaluations of a situation and are therefore acting in concert in relation to it' (2015: 221). Robbins furthers his argument by explaining that this moment of ritual effervescence produces ideals that create shared values. Lambek corroborates his point when stating that rituals contribute to assert and formalise criteria for appreciating the values of acts, as shared by all the participants (2013: 154). Through their circulation at the fiesta, meat and maize come to encapsulate peasants' collective value, epitomising a shared appreciation of agricultural labour and fuerza, across the puna and quebrada. More precisely, collective estimation of fuerza is encapsulated in beautiful products, appreciated as they are according to their size. Thus, when ritually addressed to deities, joyful cambios of plentiful harvest assert dimensionality as a collectively acknowledged axis of value transformation.

I have observed a similar pattern of value unfolding in miniature fairs, although there smallness was appreciated as a central qualia, triggering collective effervescence. I have developed this argument drawing on an ethnography of the celebration of Saint Anne through the exchange of small objects in Humahuaca (Angé 2016b, 2018). Miniature practices are observed throughout the Andes and Mesoamerica (Angé and Pitrou 2016), and I did participate in such rituals with my neighbours Lola and Mariel when I was living in Yavi. Every 8 December, people from this transborder region meet to worship the Virgin Mary in the sanctuary of Aguas Chicas, situated on the Bolivian side of the border. After the church rituals, the devotees go on to buy an array of commodities representing, in miniature, their economic ambitions for the forthcoming year. Small replicas of restaurants, and other businesses, houses, cars, computers, bills, herd or babies, are sold in a market of miniatures surrounding the church. Every household then settles down with their closest kin and compadres to share a festive meal. They spend the afternoon in a joyful atmosphere building miniature houses with pebbles gathered locally.

It is beyond the scope of this book to develop an ethnography of this specific ritual. The point I would like to stress here is that tiny offerings compose another range of ritual establishing dimensionality as an axis of value transformation, and positing alegria as a core ingredient of the ritual economics. When exploring the qualias of agricultural products, I pointed out an indexicality between the life force embodied in their size and the strength of the body that produces them. In miniature fairs, I highlighted an opposite indexation wherein the smallness of handmade miniatures reflects the virtue of the producing subject (Angé 2016b). In both cases, dimensionality, expressed in the contrasted qualities of smallness and bigness, constitutes another potential cluster of value creation, in addition to the directionality and spatiality identified by Munn (1986). Importantly, dimensionality serves as an axis, where fuerza is constructed as a key qualisign in this peasant society. Hence, by performing plentiful transactions propitious to the emergence of joy, the fair extends virtuous subjectivities in space and time while simultaneously asserting the collective criteria indexing virtue.

Still, in fiesta economics, effervescence is not only a side effect of the shared experience of a collective value, as a Durkheimian perspective would have it. The appreciation of joy as a ritual ingredient outlines a nonascetic ethics, where collective moral values are raised by the visceral experience of sensual delights, related to feasting, dancing and music. Lambek observes something similar in a Malagasy ritual, where consumption of pastries is a key ingredient. He concludes that 'food is valuable in itself (and its sensory qualities not without significance) but the primary value lies elsewhere, in mutual acknowledgement as kin, fellow citizens, or simply fellow human beings' (2013: 154). As an exchange based on mutual regards that create similarity out of difference, cambio indeed constitutes a powerful interaction that acknowledges others as fellow human beings. It is important to note, however, that sensory qualities and the creation of kin relationships are enmeshed: because they appreciate a common diet, also shared with their ancestors, Quebradeños and Puneños look upon each other as fellow people, despite their alterity. In this way, material circulation at fairs shows how the creation of moral values is entangled in joyful sensory experience.

Observing the amount of food dilapidated during Malagasy rituals, Lambek notes that some rituals transform economic values into virtue: 'They do this', he adds, 'by means of the money and labor that goes into their performance' (2008: 148). Barter ritualised as patron saint celebration also transfigures economic values into virtue but in a somehow different way. The material value of the crops is not consumed through the ritual so as to produce moral values. Instead, crops use value increases, since peasants obtain food that they are unable to produce themselves. Peasants nonetheless insist that participating in the fiesta is a gesture of sacrificio. In cambio, the sacrifice to the celebrated entity is not made of dilapidated food, it is a self-sacrifice of vital impetus, manifested with alegría.

The fact that joy stirred up by material circulation and sensual pleasures is addressed as a tribute to saints and telluric beings, so as to

temper their ambivalent mood, delineates a conception of human happiness in which its hedonic dimension is enmeshed with cosmological reproduction. Using Robbins's (2015) insight on the temporality
of happiness, we see here an articulation between the long and the
short terms of it: the latter referring to instantaneous intense feelings
of happiness, while the former point to lifelong achievement of what
one considers a good life. Robbins identifies creative work and sex as
key practices by which humans construct long-term goods, with mo-
mentary pleasure. The morality and temporality of alegría at fairs suggest that, in this Andean society, material circulation is another key
practice humans use to compose a flourishing life, in particular when
it entails ritual economics.

In the next section, I shall address another kind of ritualisation of
barter, unfolding in what I have proposed to call institutional fairs. We
shall see that the process of value transformation through material
circulation in this context brings forth other virtues.

## Barter in the Nation-State

### Barter as Cultural Heritage: Practical Arrangements

Not only are peasants concerned about the perpetuation of fairs. Development technicians and city council officers also manifest nostalgia
for pristine Indigenous economies of solidarity – a nostalgia that they
enact through a process of official heritagisation. The impact of this
process depends on the event, its accessibility and the local influence
of public institutions. When municipal authorities formally declare
fairs part of the local heritage, their entire temporal and spatial structure may be reshaped. Furthermore, as mentioned in chapter 2, it has
become common for rural development programmes in the Argentinean puna to organise their own fairs. They do so to both achieve local
development targets and promote the institution. During the first two
years of my fieldwork, I worked as a volunteer in a local NGO promoting the commercialisation of peasants' production. In this context, I
had the opportunity to help organise several fairs. I also participated in
other institutional fairs, where I accompanied my neighbours in Yavi.
Here I present some practical changes I had observed in the different
gatherings I attended. Of course, each fair features a peculiar combination of these rearrangements.

To improve order, hygiene and safety norms, fairs that once took
place on the outskirts of the city have been moved to the centre, where
institutional fairs usually occur. There, fences delineate their boundar-

ies, and thresholds are indicated by posters and flags announcing the event, advertising funding institutions or vaunting Kolla 'cultural idiosyncrasies', to use an expression favoured by the organisers. During mayor meetings, information desks, police, public toilets or first-aid points surround the entrance. Inside, protagonists are told where to set up, depending on the nature of their goods, and maps are made available to visitors. Along with the geographical displacement from the periphery to the centre of the city, flyers, invitation letters and institutional flags are also meant to entice potential visitors.

Opening and closing ceremonies are performed, where Indigenous leaders and state and NGO officers extol Kolla cultural richness. Picturesque stages can be installed for this purpose. Personalities are honoured by hoisting national and Indigenous flags, while the public bow their heads reverently at the sound of the national hymn. At the annual fair of a governmental institution, I saw members parading in costumes whose colours and designs symbolised their Andean culture. Participants clustered according to their communal belonging, and each community waved a handmade flag symbolising the productive

**Figure 5.3.** A peasant bowing his head at the hoisting of three flags (for Indigenous people, the nation and the ministry of agroindustry) during the inauguration of an institutional fair in 2009. Photograph by the author.

highlights of its ecological niche. Patronal celebrations in which spontaneous fairs are embedded also involve civil ceremonies, speeches by state officials, parades of pupils and teachers and the raising of flags. However, these activities take place in the centre of the village, usually in front of the city council, while the fair unfolds on the outskirts.

Opening ceremonies may also include a collective challa, where all participants are summoned to pour into a hole dug in the ground alcohol, coca leaves and cigarettes provided by the organisers. Meals are normally poured in as well, although only assiduous organisers include cooked food among the ritual ingredients. This ritual, during which foodstuffs are offered to telluric figures so as to foster fruitful transactions, introduces visitors to telluric beings worshipped by local people. All day long, participants can listen to music and watch folklore shows being performed on the central stage, all aimed at entertaining the public. In between folk songs, speakers list the gamut of products available, as well as the names of the remote villages from which peasants have brought them. Such mapping delineates a territory of communities networked through economic transactions. They simultaneously appear as geographically remote and integrated in the national landscape. In this sense, the heritagisation of fairs provides peasants with a sense of place, not only in its physical dimensions but also as a position in the national society (Smith 2006: 75).

While peasants are told where and when they can proceed with their transactions, the organisers also tend to practically reshape the economic interactions. Some decide to forbid exchanges before the opening ceremony. To make sure the rule is respected during an NGO meeting, a team of organisers decided that all goods would be sequestered in a room until the start of the fair. As they explained to the participants, this was to ensure that the stalls would be plentifully supplied and that a large variety of local products would be exposed in order to impress visitors with the luxurious rural production. Particularly in the case of institutional fairs, barter is circumscribed within a specific sector, where peasants are comfortably installed under a sunshade and near the toilets and other services so that they enjoy the afternoon. However, the peasants' contentment depends mainly on the quality and quantity of the products available for exchange. Aware of this, organisers invite particular economic communities or urge that a certain amount of their goods is on offer, in order to make sure the participants will be able to barter what they have brought and appreciate their venture.

Craftspeople are also encouraged to bring the product of their talents. At most fairs, a special sector is devoted to the exhibition and

**Figure 5.4.** Peasants displaying their 'Indigenous identity' admired by the provincial secretary of agricultural production at an institutional fair in 2009. Photograph by the author.

sale of fabrics and knitwear featuring Andean patterns. However, some fairs also attract merchants trading pieces that are sold throughout the cordillera as Indigenous handicraft but in fact come from large-scale industrial production. In all events, these products circulate exclusively through sales involving tourists and visitors, since peasants are not interested in such acquisitions. Another subtle yet significant move one can observe is the separation between private and public life that has been acknowledged as a feature of a modern capitalist economy – a separation that Weismantel contrasted with the social life of Andean markets, where cholas perform typical household activities such as washing dishes, dressing their hair or resting (2001: 75). Depending on the event, the installations of toilets, canteens or dormitories separate economic interactions from those related to what then is constituted as intimate physical care.

At some fairs, contests are organised that congratulate exemplary peasants and display the fruits of their outstanding talents, encouraging peasants to display their items beautifully. There is a sharp contrast between the decorated and tidy stalls of participants who are targeting a prize, and the messy jute and plastic bags of those who are more concerned with exchanging their goods. Tables raise the products off the ground, which the organisers see as dirty and unhygienic. This contrasts with the perspective of the peasants, who do not see the soil as necessarily contaminating, since it is where agricultural products come from. Stalls are also decorated with objects devoid of exchange or use value. According to the ecological provenance of the stall keeper, flowers, weaving, colourful maize cobs or hats surround foodstuffs. The purpose is essentially a semantic one: to underscore the economic identity of the producer as a rural peasant from a particular ecological niche. Agricultural products are thereby linked with their terroirs and, as such, deserve to be appreciated as singular delicacies rather than ordinary foodstuffs. To make local products available for appreciation by strangers, the produce carries labels with information about the species and origin. Such arrangements of agricultural diversity are part of the categorisation and listing practices that Harrison has identified as constitutive of official heritage management (2013: 27).

When fairs are organised by development institutions, they target goals different from those of spontaneous fairs. An organiser who was quite critical of his own interventions confessed that the meeting was intended for promoting the convening institution. On the one hand, it provided a setting in which to display the achievement of ongoing programmes. On the other, the attendance displayed the scope of the institution both internally, according to the number of peasants, and externally, according to the political personalities and press attending the event. That the organisers insist that they would like the peasants to 'appropriate' (*apropriarse*) the fair attests that they are not yet experienced as an endogenous initiative.

Even if they refuse to organise institutional fairs, locals nonetheless take inspiration from them to invent new traditions at their own gatherings. The influence of the former on the latter is tangible indeed. One reason is that Indigenous leaders in development programmes have been enrolled in the council's politics and therefore participate in the organisation of the fairs that take place in their jurisdiction. During my stay in the puna, I saw fairs integrating elements that were once typical of institutional events. The influence of heritage partakers is tangible when fairs that used to spring up with no major previous organisation gradually involve the hoisting of flags, contests, folklore shows, or sanitary services. The Manka Fiesta and the Yavi Easter fair both underwent significant changes: the former, under the influence of local development promotors who had been in charge of organising the fair of their development institution while simultaneously working for the municipality – the latter following the council of La Quiaca's designation of the Manka Fiesta as cultural heritage and its subsequent intervention to 'safeguard' the event. At this point, the fair that used to take place at the edge of the city was brought into its centre. The entrance was clearly designated by a poster reading: 'Manka Fiesta' 08 – Pots Party – Living culture of the Coya people – Municipality of La Quiaca . . . supporting our culture' (my translation).

Hence, I use the distinction between institutional and spontaneous events as a heuristic tool to help disentangle a more nuanced reality. While the events organised by development programmes are clearly different in nature, there is an array of fairs that used to emerge as part of religious celebration and are now institutionalised by town councils.

### The Morality of the Indigenous Peoples' Barter

I will now address the moral displacement of barter that goes along with the physical relocation described above. Apart from material display, heritage practitioners and rural development technicians produce singular representations of peasants' transactions. When organising the meeting, they explicitly combat what they identify as the commercialisation of fairs. As I have said, they fear that monetary transactions are replacing barter and that peasants' products are taking a back seat to traders' industrial items. When defending their cause, organisers circulate a particular interpretation of barter, which they imbue with a sense of ethnic solidarity. Organisers posit barter as a transaction that reflects a communal economy of peasants, who are encouraged to conduct generous transactions and to disregard personal interest. During one fair convened by an NGO, I heard a staff member explaining to the participants: 'The purpose is to share all we have, not to compete. We are all brothers. We know that the people who are here today will be here next year as well.' This emphasises a perspective in which non-monetary exchange is associated with domestic production and the benevolence of an economy of solidarity. A tourism and culture secretary in Humahuaca valley told me: 'It's absolutely wonderful to participate in a barter fair, it's so nice to experience it. I mean, there, there is no money in between, but only the value of solidarity. And that's part of our cultural heritage.' In public discourses, barter is shown from the romanticised perspective of generous solidarity associated with an Indigenous sense of community.

Accordingly, barter etiquette is opposed to selling. Being alleged to be mercenary, the latter is blamed for the cultural and social erosion of Indigenous culture. At the annual meeting of the aforementioned NGO, the conveners explicitly banned monetary transactions between peasants in order to counterbalance the detected tendency to the commercialisation of fairs. The participation of traders retailing industrial items is also prohibited. Such an appraisal contrasts with the critique of Indigenous barter as backwards and irrational, which still prevails among the Jujeñan Creole middle class. An older woman who claimed to be of Italian descent said miserably in one of the few fairs happening in the valley: 'They have to travel so loaded down with their products. They spend the night outside, suffering the cold and sleeping on the ground. All these pains to purchase a few potatoes.' Her perspective coincides with the image of a wretched Indian being incapable of carrying on a profitable business that was forged during the late nineteenth century according to the then-emerging liberal positivist discourse (Harris 1995; Larson 1995). Clearly, this stereotype is refuted by the vibrant, large-scale commerce managed by Indigenous and cholo peoples since early colonial times (for contemporary data, see also Colloredo-Mansfeld 1999; Ødegaard 2010; Tassi 2010).

In these perspectives, barter and monetary transactions are distinctively associated with a specific value, be it one with a positive or a negative valence. This association contrasts with peasants' point of view on barter and economic exchanges more generally. Their appreciation of a transaction depends on how equivalents are defined. As we saw in the preceding chapters, peasants distinguish between benevolent and abusive barter. Those transactions reflecting the elders' moral economy are indeed praised with one accord, though they are not entirely driven by communal generosity. They are imbued with an ambivalent principle of complementary opposition between lowland and highland peasants. Instead of displaying a homogenous community of Kolla peasants, that kind of interaction also stresses divergent identities according to agricultural activities, ecological zones of residence and nationality. Since it features friendly transactions as well, shifting rivalry should be regarded as an expression of alternating and competing moieties, which, in many Andean societies, is semantically linked with notions of fertility and abundance (Harris 2000: 49; see also Gelles 1995; Platt 1995). In contrast, peasants reject barter leading to an asymmetric allotment. Direct exchanges of agricultural products established according to inflated market prices are viewed badly. Equally condemned are the barter transactions engaged in with urban traders who provide industrial foodstuffs in exchange for peasants' wool and clay pots. Peasants accept these barters because they do not have a better option, but they regard them as unfair and abusive.

With regard to monetary exchanges, I have stressed that peasants' perspectives are ambivalent as well. Money is not regarded as a pernicious medium of exchange in itself. Its moral worth shifts according to the social and economic context of its circulation. It is imbued with the highest value when entangled in gifts or offerings. Bank notes are indeed part of the ritual ingredients for feeding Pachamama, along with food, coca leaves and alcohol (for Bolivian and Peruvian data, see also Harris 2000; Sallnow 1989). And money figures among the most appreciated gifts for rite-of-passage celebrations such as baptism, first haircut or marriage. Money may also be said to pervert the social and cosmological balance if it is involved in personalised transactions in which one of the partners accumulates profits at the expense of another. If peasants sometimes speak ill of money, they actively seek it, lament its lack and cherish it when obtained. At fairs, peasants do not actually criticise the use of money as a medium of exchange. What they most regret is its intrusion as the primary scale of value, even for the transfer of local produce that should be measured according to the elders' equivalences. As Lucio commented in 2008: 'Before, we used to weigh with quantities; the point was to exchange products that one had plenty of for an unavailable one. Profits did not matter. The logic was different. Now everything is evaluated through money and nothing else matters.' Because it diverges from ancestral measures equated with fairness, peasants' barter performed according to market prices is collectively denounced as inequitable.

In the process of heritage making, a new idea of a purely generous and abundant Andean barter has been constructed, which does not match previous local perspectives, be they Kolla or Creole. The image of benevolent barter that emerges is not appreciated for its instrumental efficacy. By asserting that barter needs to be safeguarded as a remnant of past Indigenous economies rather than for economic benefits, fair conveners transform it into a *lieu de mémoire,* in Pierre Nora's sense – that is, a site 'where memory crystallizes and secretes itself at . . . a turning point where consciousness of a break with the past is bound up with the sense that memory has been torn' (1989: 7). As a memory site, cambio is projected back towards the past, and its present manifestation only appears as the felicitous remnant of failed transmission of ancestral economics. When convening barter fairs as part of their heritage programmes, Creoles and gringos, who only intervene as outsiders in spontaneous fairs, are displayed as actors of the perpetuation of Kolla ethnicity.

## Value Transformation in Institutional Fairs

Cambio's template of value transformation, based on the use value of agricultural produce from different ecological niches, is relevant for analysing barter at institutional fairs: participants' purpose is to obtain fundamental foodstuffs to complement their daily and ritual diet. The value of agricultural produce is entangled in their producer's virtue as a diligent and careful peasant. Through material circulation, complicities emerge resulting in the creation of new social relationships with faraway people, which extend human subjectivities in space and time. This being said, there are significant differences between the processes of value creation in the different kinds of meetings, which I will point out in this section.

Generally, participation in institutional fairs is seen as more profitable in terms of use value for two main reasons. On the one hand, participants receive free transport, food and accommodation, all costs they are used to supporting when attending a fair on their own initiative. On the other hand, some institutional fairs are renowned as settings for particularly fruitful barters. In some cases, the organisers are in charge of monitoring the products to be brought by peasants. In establishing a balanced quantity of the different products, they want to make sure that the participants will be able to barter what they have brought so that they find their participation worthwhile. In any case, institutional fairs gather the population targeted by their development programmes, that is, herders from the puna and cultivators from the southern Humahuaca valley (and not from the northern Talina and Sococha valleys situated in Bolivia, which are usually represented). Argentinean cultivators are seen as providing bigger fruits and maize, although many of these are also produced with the help of chemicals and pesticides. Puneños usually do not access their harvests, which are mainly destined for the urban markets in the provincial capital. Cultivators from the Argentinean quebrada agree to supply institutional fairs as a mark of their engagement in the institution, while many of them have dropped out of the barter networks that were still alive in the past century (see also Göbel 1998: 173). It is noteworthy that, as beneficiaries of development programmes, they are under pressure from the providing institution, and failing to contribute to its annual fair may jeopardise opportunities to be accepted in future projects. Here lies another motivation to take part in the event.

Besides enabling material benefits, institutional fairs also compose a field of interactions where agricultural circulation serves as backdrop for spatiotemporal extension of subjectivities. Some regular participants have gained an established reputation as good partners across the institutional network. The fame of Julia, whom I described above as a potato cultivator widely renowned as a generous exchange partner, encompasses the institutional fair network. Yet, the spatiotemporal extension of a virtuous subject in this case is not based primarily on the conduct of plentiful cambios or the display of exceptional strength encapsulated in a harvest's qualia.

I have mentioned that such fairs are intended to display the achievement of development programmes. Contests, parades and stalls provide opportunities to distinguish the peasants who have successfully assimilated the skills, norms and strategies transmitted the whole year round. By the end of the meeting, all participants are acquainted with those who have applied new sanitary norms to their herd, engaged in the preparation of pickled dishes or produced colourful wool with local plants. Those who win several contests subsequently become distinguished as exemplary peasants. They epitomise the process of subjective transformation targeted by development programmes intended to offer the tools for peasants to *superarse* (surpass oneself) and *crecer* (grow). The case of a woman, renown for excelling in the preparation of pâté after being trained in the context of a development programme, speaks to these fairs' potential to extend subjectivities in space and time. These are exceptions, however, since the conveners themselves acknowledge that transmission of skills during their workshop is not a real success.

Another value transformation is produced during fairs and is not a matter of exception: the acknowledgement of the status of *promotors*, who are local people co-opted onto development institutions. Some peasants take an active part in development projects, looking for material or social rewards, or convinced by technicians' discourses, which incite them to struggle for the political defence of Indigenous rights. If they actively take part in an institution's projects, their role is recognised by being awarded the status of promotor and a small wage that distinguishes them from the *socios*, who are ordinary members of the institution.

When running a workshop, rewarding the winner of a contest, chairing opening ceremonies, driving a jeep or enunciating tropes of rural development, promoters display their status and make sure everyone acknowledges that they are not simple socios. The daughter of herders who had grown up in a rural community had been very successful in carrying out her duties of promotor. She was satisfied that she had become renowned for this: 'Without the association, I would have been another shepherdess for my family – a housewife and nothing else. If

I am someone, it's thank to this.' Clearly, fairs provided a scene to display her achievement to the public at large. She never failed to bring agricultural produce, as well as craftwork she produced before she took on organisational duties. Yet, it was when she was driving a jeep with the institution's logo or giving opening speeches or interviews to the press that she clearly distinguished herself from her neighbours.

## Barter and the Construction of a Multicultural Society

To conclude this section on institutional fairs, I would like to examine how they participate in the reproduction of a social order. The above description suggests that barter transaction can contribute to knitting another kind of ethnic configuration when used by heritage stakeholders as part of a complex process of cultural and political integration of Indigenous people in the Argentinean nation-state. The formal heritagisation of fairs rests on a twofold movement of appropriation and estrangement of cultural symbols, as a reflection of a multiculturalist endeavour that simultaneously brings out ethnic minorities and adjusts them to fundamental national values. This ambivalent process of exoticisation reflects the broader paradox of building Indigenous citizenship. In the Andes, the complex status of Indigenous people within the national apparatus has been noted in contexts as diverse as education programmes (Garcia 2005) and markets (Seligmann 1993) in Peru, and beauty pageants in Ecuador (Wroblewski 2014) – an ambiguity that Maria Elena Garcia captures, noting that 'a particular notion of Indigenous identity is hitched to a supposedly universal category of citizen' (2005: 165). Fairs count among the concrete settings where Indigenous people negotiate the paradox of their aspiration to be acknowledged as full citizens while maintaining their cultural intimacy. I thus see them as fascinating scenes in which to explore how constitutionally established multiculturalism is implemented and negotiated on the local stage, and the role of fairs in this process: a fundamental question in the broader context of Latin American nations' multicultural turn (Wroblewski 2014).

In the contemporary Argentinean cultural context, the revitalisation of fairs is intended to extol the cultural treasures of Indigenous people on the national scene. Practices that had been disdained as marks of primitiveness until the end of the twentieth century are now extolled as expressions of cultural diversity. This is the case of traditional clothing, the worship of Mother Earth, llama herding or barter. Working on paintings and decorations, Fred Myers has pointed out that the incorporation of Indigenous elements into national aesthetics establishes new systems of value in which the peripheral position of Indigenous people is supplanted by a multiculturalist formulation: 'Here the ability of the nation to embrace qualitatively different modes of cultural life – a symbolic transformation – get[s] registered as a measure of its strength and vitality' (2002: 46). Even if an intention of cultural appraisal is manifested in the organisation of fairs, we cannot conclude, as Myers does, that Kolla people are recognised as having comparable status with non-Indigenous citizens.

The very pattern of values according to which Kolla heritage is appreciated is established by people who do not enact it, even though some of them may claim indigenousness. This is also the case of cambio. At the same time, Indigenous resources are denigrated by the supposed necessity of exogenous institutions' interventions. Through these fairs, the organisers select the elements deemed emblematic of an ancestral Kolla culture and worthy to be counted as part of Argentinean heritage; they also select the features they expect to be reshaped so as to fit the national imaginary of 'Indigenous people'. While participating in these activities, peasants are told which behaviours and skills they should assimilate, veil or deploy in order to become proper Argentinean citizens in a symbolic and juridical sense.

To fit the image of indigenousness configured by the government under the new national constitution, Kolla peasants are also expected to produce local foodstuffs and handicrafts fitting the desires of urban populations. Although these arts are recognised as being their area of expertise, they are convened to workshop on natural dying, knitting and weaving. They are taught how to produce and commercialise meat or preserve it, according to the ministry hygiene criteria.[13] And they should praise their pre-Columbian Andean cultural past by venerating Pachamama, cooking local foods, singing Indigenous songs or, indeed, bartering. In adopting the expected behaviour during parades, contests or transactions, socios therefore implicitly endorse the social identity they are expected to bear in the context of institutional fairs and, more broadly, in regional development policies. During ceremonies, parades, economic exchanges and workshops, socios are also confined within the roles and attitudes relevant to their status: namely, proud members of Andean Indigenous communities, integrated within a nation-state where their ethnic identity is associated with their rural economy.

This is a point shared with Quebradeños and Puneños who relate their sense of ethnicity to their relation to the land, and to Pachamama. However, it is important to bear in mind that the image of the Kolla displayed through parades, contests and folklore spectacles does not match the realities of the Kolla people under the contemporary republic. Of the seventy-five thousand registered Kolla people in 2001, more than 30 per cent live in the city. Urban livelihoods, marked by economic and political discrimination, are obfuscated by the image the Argentinean has of the Kolla people as llama herders. National integration is declined as rural development, denying trajectories that are not yet accepted as legitimate for Indigenous people.[14]

Creating civic value and social cohesion is an explicit purpose of the organisers. An engineer who lamented that people in the puna did not know each other explained to me that the fair was intended as a 'meeting point' to break down peasants' daily solitude. By convening the fair, his intention was 'to open up a space for meeting and realise: "Well, we love each other, we are all the same. We don't recognise each other? Well, that's the place where we can get to know each other."' The mode of sociability the organisers promoted was verbalised as *compañeros*, a term referring to the idea of comradeship with a political connotation. The social ties the fair is expected to weave are thus tainted with the idea of composing a strong civil society articulated on development programmes. This is a key aspiration of development technicians who constantly encourage peasants to 'become protagonist of their citizenship'[15] – a motto that feels somehow ironic given these peasants' political exclusion from public affairs on the regional and national scene.

In these fairs, we also observe the feature of ritual acts pointed out by Humphrey and Laidlaw, that is, a divergence between the intentional meaning of the exchange partners and the identity of their interactions (1994: 3). However, this ritual of exchange is of a different nature: while the meta-objective in spontaneous fairs was to celebrate a powerful deity, the meta-objective in institutional fairs is to celebrate the convening institution and reproduce the social order that it is advocating – a social order entangled in the nation-state view on Indigenous people. Hence, as used here, the qualification of 'institutional' also alludes to the Bourdieusian concept of 'rite of institution' (2001), which stresses the capacity of rites to consecrate participants' social identity and thereby reaffirm the social order.[16] This is the social order targeted by rural development programmes whereby white technicians train Indigenous people to become exemplary citizens, as epitomised in the status of the promotor. Such an order matches the public discourse of the state, as well as international institutions funding the local NGOs.

This order does not correspond to that displayed during spontaneous events, where the opposition between lowlanders and highlanders is played out along with their belonging to a wider transnational cultural entity and where the relationship with Creoles is more overtly antagonistic. While the geographical zone represented in institutional fairs depends on the institution's zone of intervention, it usually involves the puna and the Humahuaca valley, while old complicities between the puna and the Sococha and Tarija valleys, now part of the Bolivian nation, are severed. The ethnic group delineated by institutional fairs corresponds to a fixed territory on the national map, extending in the Argentinean Andes of Jujuy and stopping at the Bolivian border. Despite the display of unity at fairs, the shared ethnic identity between the Argentinean puna and quebrada is nonetheless polemical, as attested by the later acknowledgement of the Omaguacas as a distinct group of Indigenous people living in the Humahuaca valley. This separation, however, was not discernible at fairs during my fieldwork. In any case, the social entity reproduced at fairs is the Kolla people acknowledged by the government, that is a politicised ethnic group. This is an innovation in this region where ethnicity was not a lever for political struggle until the state acknowledged the existence of Indigenous people (see Karasik 2005: 23).

Peasants enrolled in institutions promoting fairs are aware of the organisers' appreciation. I was surprised to hear a herder answer when I enquired about his motivation to participate in an institutional fair: 'We are Indians, so we must barter', he replied, using the verb *cambiar*. Yet, we should not conclude that peasants parade in fairs like puppets of governmental and nongovernmental instances. Rather, they use institutional fairs to articulate the official construction of indigenousness with their own sense of ethnicity so as to make the most of the new opportunities raised by contemporary tropes of national multiculturalism.

### Nostalgia for Indigenous People's Barter

In this section, I would like to carry further the analysis of the social performativity of institutional fairs by examining nostalgic tropes for lost economic order as they unfold in these meetings. The discrepancies between peasants' longings, as analysed in the previous chapters, and lamentations by the organisers of institutional fairs is instructive to understand how barter is used to display an image of multicultural nationalism, veiling economic and political tensions opposing Indigenous people to the state. We have seen that peasants and heritage stakeholders share nostalgia for ancestral reciprocities that would have been corroded by modern lucre. This does not mean that they share identical consideration of the past. Enlightening in this regard is David Berliner's distinction between an endonostalgia 'for the past one has lived personally' and a vicarious 'nostalgia for the past not experienced personally' (2012: 781). Indeed, peasants' endonostalgia for the elders' precepts contrasts with the institutional exonostalgia for pristine Indigenous communities at the core of the policies that construct peasants' barter as a national intangible heritage. We shall see that different conceptions of heritage are related to each kind of glorification of the past.

These nostalgic stances also differ regarding their pragmatic expressions. Svetlanna Boym (2001) draws another important distinction between what she termed a restorative and a reflective nostalgia: 'Restorative nostalgia stresses nóstos (home) and attempts a transhistorical reconstruction of the lost home. Reflective nostalgia thrives in álgos, the longing itself, and delays the homecoming – wistfully, ironically, desperately.' In light of Boym's terms, peasants' endonostalgia is reflective, and sometimes instrumental, while heritage stakeholders' exonostalgia entails restorative intentions. We have seen that peasants' nostalgic glosses do not necessarily call for the actualisation of regretted practices, since they are emitted by the very ones who undermine the social order whose dissolution they regret.

Such reflective longings contrast with those of actors engaged in the process of heritagisation, who take practical steps to constitute a place for exchange in which peasants may update and perpetuate the generous reciprocity whose decline they lament. When exonostalgia appears in its restorative form, it delineates a cultural boundary through interventions motivated by future-directed ambitions. In institutionalised encounters, technicians and politicians without any personal experience of communal reciprocity incite peasants to continue this practice and rescue the traditions. In holding this discourse, technicians – be they Creole or white – representing public institutions appear as a clearly distinct social group from Indigenous peasants, despite the ethnic porosity characteristic of this Argentinean province's social fabric. Hence, when they portray an original Kolla culture epitomised by inter-ecological nonmonetary transactions, these nostalgic discourses and practices contribute to the essentialisation of ethnic belonging.

Rebecca Bryant has elucidated this social performativity of nostalgia. In an article on the identity stakes involved in nostalgic glosses in Cyprus, she asserts that nostalgia 'portrays to us some (imagined) essence that has been irretrievably lost . . . and this is why . . . nostalgia emerges most at times of liminality and identity confusion'. In the Argentinean Andes, the contemporary nostalgic discourse typical of institutions involved in heritage creation reverses the creolisation process that has been accelerated by urban emigration and the cultural assimilation of native people to 'white Argentina'. Like the discourse of Cypriots reminiscing about the time when the island's inhabitants lived together in peace, reported by Bryant, the nostalgia of those involved in heritagisation in the Argentinean Andes expresses a 'longing for essentialism' (2014: 156) – that is, a longing for an imagined past when Kolla formed a coherent social entity articulated on local communities cemented by a strong sense of solidarity among its members. The essence that technicians portray to themselves is a pristine pre-Hispanic community that would be the roots of a now-multifaceted Argentinean culture. It is thus an essentialism whereby Andean peasants are posited as essentially different and at the same time part of a shared nation. As they circulate their agricultural products, Kolla people are displayed as a homogenous ethnic group, despite the complexity of this categorisation, cross-cutting cultural identifications according to nationalities, ecological residences and economic activities. During such reshaped fairs, the circulation of agricultural products has become a feature that emphasises a romanticised Kolla otherness, thereby widening cultural distances and exaggerating ethnic partition.

I have noted that the fabric of cultural heritage paradoxically involves shaping fairs according to a new etiquette. While barter is displayed as a typically Indigenous practice, other aspects are indeed transformed to meet observers' expectations. This means that peasants' barter should not appear as an agonistic or bare economy. As one can imagine, organisers' narratives have not succeeded in reshaping the practice of barter, for peasants continue to exchange in their own fashion. What is actually being transformed is how barter is displayed, within fairs that are much more in tune with national norms, and with a new stance on the way Indigenous people should behave in the context of their national integration.

## Notes

1. The original expression is: 'A vos también te cuesta, a nosotros también nos cuesta traer'.
2. The original expression is: 'Pero me vas a dar bien no mas'.
3. The mandatory replacement of the Christianname by the term compadre or comadre is the most obvious aspect.
4. It is noteworthy that ties of compadrazgo are exceptionally established between merchants who regularly come to the fair and peasants who are faithful customers. For instance, this kind of relationship can arise between those trading in wool and clay pottery. However, unlike the horizontal relationship between peasant compadres, the relationship of ritual kinship established with merchants is vertical. This figure of asymmetrical

compadrazgo is a constant in interethnic relations in several Andean societies (Molinié 1975: 52; Ødegaard 2010; Orlove 1974: 304).

5. Those partners related by compadrazgo provide an exception to this antagonistic mode of transaction. I will not go into this specific relationship in any more detail because it is rather unusual between comerciantes and campesinos.

6. Harris relates similar rituals in Bolivia (2000: 35–46).

7. Observing the subtle manifestation of ethnic sense of belonging in the Argentinean puna and quebrada, a subtlety that she relates to the politics of designation and ethnonym construction, Karasik suggests in her unpublished PhD dissertation that we not restrict ethnicity to the existence of a bounded ethnic group. She affirms that 'matrixes of ethnic structuration are not restricted to discursive tropes or situations, they are rather threaded along with other processes of social structuration' (2005: 27, my translation), such as economic forms of exchange and production.

8. The Yavi Easter fair used to provide another meeting point. However, the fair has lost some of its influence in the past century. Easter celebration in Abra Pampa emerged as another important fair, reaching a rate of attendance similar to the Manka Fiesta. Still, the fact that the Yavi fair continues attracting people precludes considering the Abra Pampa fair as an all-encompassing event comparable to the Manka Fiesta.

9. In an article on the ritual circulation of miniatures, I argue that commodity exchange can also be addressed to deified beings (Angé 2018).

10. It is surprising that he writes elsewhere that barter is a 'relationship of long-term partnership based on reciprocity' (2002: 159).

11. *Tatayalegre* is a mix of Tata and the Spanish word *alegre*, which means cheerful.

12. The Spanish words are *amanecer rezando*.

13. In this regard, the use of sanitary norms provides state officials with powerful legal tools within the cultural politics of the marketplace (Seligman 1993: 193).

14. When delineating a cartography of Indigenous policies in Argentina, Claudia Briones notes a 'severe suspicion as to the authenticity of Indigenous intellectuals, whose education and political capacities distinguish them from the image of the "authentic Indigenous", as passive and incompetent, submissive and easily satisfied with policies of minimal assistance' (2005: 35, my translation).

15. The original expression is: 'ser protagonista de su ciudadania'.

16. Even if the structure of the instigating organisation stamps the deployment of institutional fairs, some activities during the event simultaneously awake an extraordinary cordiality that ostensibly smooths out the expression of social hierarchy. I have analysed this ambiguous social dynamic elsewhere (Angé 2016a).

# Conclusion

As I hope this book has made clear, our understanding of economic life would be furthered by acknowledging barter as 'a mode of exchange in its own right' (Humphrey and Hugh-Jones 1992b: 7). As a corollary, I disagree with Heady when he advises that 'it might not be a very good idea to construct a distinct subdiscipline of barter studies' (2006: 270). I am convinced that fine-grained ethnographies of barter would enrich anthropological theory on key issues such as material circulation, value creation and the reproduction of society. Anthropologists' disregard for barter, based on the premise that it is a mere variation of commodity exchange, is equivocal. Throughout this book, I have pointed out several characteristics of cambio that fit those generally associated with gift-giving: the goods in circulation are entangled with the identity of their producers and are inalienable in this restricted sense (Gell 1992: 145). Cambio is an act used to extend subjective spactime and to reproduce the sociocosmological order. However, cambio transactions do not fit other core characteristics of gift-giving: the defense of self-interest is made very explicit, and the acquisition of use value is a key motivation of the transactions. This confirms that barter shares features with both gift-giving and commodity exchange, depending on the sociocultural setting in which the transaction takes place (Humphrey and Hugh-Jones 1992b: 2).

This is where the specificity of cambio can be grasped: barter is the direct exchange of use value with no reference to a third object. The importance of use distinguishes it from the gift, while the nonmonetary regime of value distinguishes it from commodity exchange. Therefore, I want to underscore that an understanding of barter requires a shift of focus, from its relationship to money to one that addresses the nature and principles of the new model of value posited by the partners. This conclusion departs from existing scholarship on Andean exchange that argues that the use of money is not crucial for distinguishing between different forms of exchange, thereby calling into question the usefulness of the concept of barter. While I agree that the material use of money tells little about the social setting of the exchange and its morality, I nonetheless insist that the elimination of market prices as a core scale of measure leaves a space for another regime of appreciation, based on use value for both partners. This particularity makes barter a distinctive category of exchange, distinct from gifts and commodities. Of course, direct exchanges agreed according to market prices are commonly referred to as barter. Although such transactions might be important in terms of the volume of goods they engage, I see them as a particular kind of direct transaction that constitutes an exception in the light of the variety of scales of value barter partners from across the world draw on to set up equivalencies between goods of different nature. I believe that when a direct exchange strictly based on market prices is not intended for consumption, but instead for creating exchange value, it is a 'surrogate form of monetary exchange' (Humphrey and Hugh-Jones 1992b: 2), best described using the concept of commodity. In barter, monetary prices can only influence the equivalences, along with other criteria related to the quality of the goods – and the people – at stake.

Another argument advanced in this book is that the examination of the barter regime of value sheds light on its social fabric. From her investigation of trueque, Ferraro concludes that 'monetary translation of the qualitative into the quantitative does not necessarily flatten social relations' (2011: 179). Harris observes that Laymi cultivators 'accept cash, they say, as a favour for their suni kin for whom this form of transaction is more convenient' (2007: 78). I have also noted that monetary exchange can enact social relationships between kin if the commodity exchange is wrapped in largesse. I nonetheless argue that monetary translation is more likely to widen the social distance between the partners, if it is strictly used to stick to values on the formal market.[1] Guyer's study of monetary transactions in Atlantic Africa is insightful on this point. She states that, 'transactions become performances when more than several variables (or scales) are at issue' (2004: 97). When market prices are used as the single criteria, the multiple value scales are reduced to a 'particular systemic logic' under the hold of an external authority (2004:155). Then the monetary scale smooths out the social performativity that plays out when there is a leeway about where the equivalence stands for each transaction. This leeway is manifest in a barter pattern of value such as the elder's measures, whereby objective and subjective criteria intertwine.

In cambio, the model of value is focussed on goods produced and consumed by peasants in complementary ecological niches. The ethnographic examination has shown that material value and subjective virtue are entangled in this value pattern. Indeed, cambio products are appreciated as food as well as tokens of their producer's qualities as a careful and valiant peasant. Partners allude to the sacrifice involved in producing their goods, and bringing them to the fair, as a core criterion to negotiate cambio equivalences. When the partners consume bartered food, it composes their subjectivity both physically and symbolically. Eating agricultural produce provides the fuerza necessary to behave as a virtuous criador. The moral value of people and the economic value of their produce are thus enmeshed in the vital strength they encapsulate. This vitality is indexed by agricultural produce's dimensionality: large maize grains, potatoes or pieces of meat are acknowledged as beautiful items produced with diligent labor. Looking at the qualities on which cambio's items are evaluated tells us that smallness and bigness compose an axis along which value transformation operates. Inspired by Munn, this approach explains how barter practices trigger value conversions that extend subjectivities in space and time.

This approach also supports recent theories positing value as an appreciation of acts (Graeber 2001; Lambek 2008, 2013; Otto and Willerslev 2013). The evaluation of meat, potatoes or maize in cambio not only appreciates previous acts of criar performed in the fields. Cambio does more than reflect the actors' pre-existing qualities. Cambio is a virtuous act in itself, thereby pointing to barter's potential to create moral value. Like the gifts examined by Munn (1986), cambio is a morally charged transaction that contributes to the extension of virtuous subjectivities in space and time. It engages peasants from distant ecological tiers, thereby offering the opportunity to become renowned as a generous partner, and fruitful peasant, beyond one's closest kin and neighbours.

Food-giving potential as a token of value has been regarded as limited because of food's short lifetime. Weiner argues that 'food is the most ineffectual inalienable possession because its biological function is to release energy rather than store it. Therefore, in its use to humans, food changes, deteriorates, or perishes' (1992: 38). Likewise, Munn notes food restrictions as a vector of value transformation, as compared to the increased impact of kula valuables (1986: 10). She infers that the durability of an object impacts the potential of spatiotemporal extension created by its circulation. Here we see how food is used to create enduring intersubjective space-time, even though edible matter is designed to disintegrate relatively quickly. Its digestion process through eating composes human bodies and subjectivities that are more stable than food. Furthermore, in an economy based on ecological dependencies, food encapsulates mutual appreciations that remain beyond the transformation of its materiality. Meat, potatoes and maize materialise interecological esteem throughout time. While food has been interpreted as lower-level value goods (Bohannan 1955: 62; Damon 2002: 120; Munn 1986: 10), agricultural products in the Andean highland contribute to the recognition of virtuous subjects, as prestigious valuables do in other societies.

In addition to creating subjective value, the practice of cambio speaks to barter's potential to produce collective values as well. The qualities of agricultural produce index the value of their producers. Yet, the analysis of negotiation dialogues has shown that people are themselves identified with a broader economic community: herders from the highlands or cultivators from the lowlands. Reciprocated transfers of their harvests delineate an economic community comprising two complementary entities, namely, the Quebradeños and the Puneños. At the same time, acknowledging exchange prescriptions that are seen as inherited from ancestors hints at a sense of shared genealogy. The application of the elders' model of value supposes that they are regarded as a source of authority whose legitimacy is respected by both partners. The latter thus enact the existence of a descent from common ancestors, thereby appending an ethnic community to the economic one.

Engaging in cambio is therefore a way of performing a common affiliation and stating ethnic boundaries that have become blurred through the violent policies of displacement and assimilation perpetuated under the Spanish Crown and the Argentinean Republic. Hence, when conducting cambio at spontaneous fairs, protagonists experience an implicit belonging that encompasses the ecological communities that are usually verbalised. This sense of belonging also cross-cuts nationalities, since the Argentinean state recognises only Kolla under its jurisdiction, while cambio involves Bolivian and Argentinean producers. In this sense, the modality of barter operates as a marker of ethnic identity shared by peasants who otherwise verbalise regimes of identity that highlight their otherness (Puneños versus Quebradeños, cultivators versus herders, Argentineans versus Bolivians).

The study of cambio in northern Argentina suggests that barter is not only the enactment of an increased economic and cultural intimacy; in fact, it produces new kinds of relationships. At the interindividual level, it transforms strangers into friends and, sometimes, compadres. At the collective level, it creates a sense of kinship through the unification of food consumption among the participants, including the ancestors fed with identical ingredients. In his study of exchange in Melanesia, Gell concludes that 'under the "sign" of barter, social relationships come into existence which are no longer pre-empted by the morality of reproduction and its service obligation' (1992: 166). The practices of exchange discussed in this book outline a different morality, in which barter is enmeshed in social reproduction. Cambio is a reproductive barter both physiologically, since the partners' bodies are experienced as shared substance, and symbolically, since they are conceived of as descendants of the same ancestors. This social efficacy corroborates the aforementioned significance of use value in the appraisal of bartered items. Cambio produces affinity, in as much as the food obtained is consumed. Stressing consumption value to grasp the peculiarities of barter, I join Colloredo-Mansfeld's (1999, 2003) call for an examination of consumption practices on par with distribution, on which economic anthropologists' attention has been traditionally focussed.

The exploration of Andean barter further shows that its reproductive potential embraces fields and entities that go beyond human sociabilities. Considering the ancestors' involvement in fairs indicates that the performativity of barter can encompass the reproduction of cosmological relationships as well. The cosmological dimension of cambio is rooted in a morality of profit, which is associated with a positive valence as long as the transaction procures mutual satisfaction. Human contentment is in turn expected to cheer the nonhuman entities as well. The circulation of goods under barter that instantiates the elders' prescriptions participates in the production of sociocosmological values. In this sense, these transactions highlight an intriguing articulation between the two transactional spheres identified by Parry and Bloch. From their analysis of monetary exchange in an array of ethnographic settings, they distinguish two interconnected but separate economic realms: 'on the one hand transactions concerned with the reproduction of the long-term social or cosmic order; on the other, a "sphere" of short-term transactions concerned with the arena of individual competition' (1989b: 24). When transactors subject their material ambitions to restrictions stipulated by the ancestors, cambio participates in both the individual and the cosmological reproductions. This entanglement with both levels of reproduction refutes the mainstream analysis of barter associating it with the lower sphere of individual profits, without regard for the social relationship underlying the transaction.

In this light, I have suggested that Andean fairs constitute a mise en scène of barter exchanges, both agonistic and generous, which are deemed to cheer nonhuman beings from which the protagonists expect fertilising power. Scrutinising these interactions, I have shown that they are constitutive of the fiesta, and therefore I propose to apprehend cambio at fairs as a ritual exchange. However, I urge increased conceptual rigour when using this concept, which remains an unclear category as it is currently used in the literature. The analytical framework Humphrey and Laidlaw (1994) have elaborated to examine religious rites is highly relevant to point out the distinctive features of barter performed as part of a fiesta. Accordingly, I propose using the notion of ritual exchange in the sense that the transactors mix intimate engagement and external stipulation, thereby achieving a meta-objective that encompasses immediate material appropriation in order to contribute to social reproduction. In the cambio code of exchange, the ancestors formulate these stipulations, whose application is intended to please both humans and nonhumans.

While Andean literature dwells mainly on offerings to telluric agencies by means of food nurturing, this book underscores the importance of immaterial offerings, here in the guise of joy prompted by material circulation. The sacrificial dimension of cambio mentioned by the protagonists of the fiesta does not only entail the effort required for the production and circulation of the products. At fairs, as in other Andean rituals, sacrifice is also instantiated in the alegría being addressed to the patron saint. In the fiesta, alegría is a vital impetus devoted to cheering up nonhumans, instead of being invested in agricultural or other kinds of labour. This is how I understand the words of peasants when they posit cambio as a figure of self-sacrifice that enlivens the celebration of the saint. Berndt has pointed out the importance of the affective dimension of an exchange as an indice of its ritualisation. He opposes ceremonial transactions to those 'taken so much for granted by the people themselves, that no excitement nor emotional tension is manifested collectively by the group' (1951: 159). In contrast to Yunxiang Yan (2006), who sees in emotionality a key difference between gift and commodities, I join Berndt in thinking that the affective dimension characterises ritual economics, which is not restricted to gift-giving. I nonetheless join Yan's plea to carry further our anthropological reflexion on the emotionality of exchanges (2006: 259).

Lambek's insights on sacrifice are helpful in understanding the value transformation at stake in the case of ritual cambios, as he observes that self-sacrifice collates economic choices with social, ethical or political values. This alignment situates the value of objects in accordance with subjective value manifested in acts. Lambek identifies sacrifice as the archetypal virtuous act producing metavalue through the affirmation of judgement – instead of choice manifested in commodity exchange. In this Andean case, the metavalue is the life force, fuerza, extracted from 'the sacrificed life of the country' to be injected in the fiesta. Hence, the practice of cambio corroborates the idea Lambek puts forward that life is the absolute metavalue (2008: 149).

However, a cosmological dimension is not a necessary feature of ritual exchange. The sacrifice might be guided by other metavalues, as exemplified by the case of institutional fairs, whereby barter is used to produce civic values that create a sense of cohesion within the national society. While exploring the participation of cambio in social regeneration, I have also described the practical and representational reshaping of barter in a process of formal heritagisation. Heritage practitioners and development technicians cherish barter as a performance of the solidarity encapsulated in their idea of pristine Indigenous economies. Puneños and Quebradeños cherish cambio for showing reverence towards the ancestors incarnated in the landscape. Development technicians ignore barter's potential to produce cosmological value, as well as use value, focussed as they are on its civic value.

Such divergences do not preclude cooperation between organisers and peasants in revitalising barter fairs. The latter's concern to transmit the ancestors' moral economy in the context of increased participation in a capitalist economy meets the former's concern to preserve Indigenous exotic practices. Yet, spontaneous and institutional events produce different figures of ritualised exchange, embedded in different metavalues. In the new fairs, practices of bartering extend subjectivities that are appreciated in the light of civic values, somehow severed from agricultural produce's qualia. They also delineate different regimes of ethnicity. While self-sacrifice at spontaneous fairs is addressed to shared saints and ancestors, it is here devoted to the cohesion of an Indigenous people, in the sense stipulated in the national constitution. In any case, the social group in question is restricted to Argentineans, leaving aside the Bolivian cultivators, who are key actors of the sociability created in spontaneous fairs.

This ethnographic exploration of cambio invites us to extend the Maussian notion of *prestation social total* (total prestation) to barter transaction. With this concept, Mauss ([1925] 2002) hinted at three

characteristics of gift-giving in primitive societies: first, that the participants represent collectivities; second, that core institutions of the society are at stake; and third, that these acts are simultaneously free and
socially prescribed. Mayer (1982: 95) concludes his article on Peruvian
exchanges by suggesting that those interecological transactions that
are not intended for earning money exemplify Mauss's point that, in
traditional societies, exchanges take place between individuals standing for their communities. In the introduction to their volume, Humphrey and Hugh-Jones propose another reason why barter should be
considered, along with the gift, a total prestation: because 'people are
identified with the products of their way of life and vice-versa' (1992b:
10). This assertion implies a definition of barter in which the coveted
produce shapes the partners' livelihood through its production and use.

If we consider the aforementioned characteristics conjointly, we
see that archetypal cambio at fairs indeed fits the idea of prestation
sociale totale. First, the partners stand for boader socio-ecological
communities. Second, these transactions engage the core institutions
of this society, involving social, political, religious and ethical dimensions. Third, they are conducted through individual will, but they are

**Figure 6.1.** Offering to Pachamama at the central market of Villazón, suggesting
that ritual economics also entail commodity exchanges. Photograph by the author.

nonetheless constrained by moral prescriptions. Those ritual barters whereby possible economic benefits are sacrificed in the application of collective values are thus total prestations. But this should not be considered an intrinsic characteristic of barter, as implied by Humphrey and Hugh-Jones. Likewise, I am not inclined to consider that any gift is a total prestation, while ritual gift-giving certainly is.

Although this book has left the question of the ritualisation of commodity exchange largely untouched, other ethnographies on the creation of cosmological values in Andean markets attest that some commodity exchanges are also entailed in ritual economics (Angé 2016b, 2018; Ødegaard 2011; Tassi 2010). More broadly, the existing literature that challenges the polarisation between instrumental exchanges and sociocosmological reproduction suggests the need to develop analytical perspectives able to grasp, in an array of cultural settings, the particularities of instrumental exchanges nonetheless framed by social or religious concerns.

The systems of exchange such as those studied by Clifford Geertz (2003) in Morocco, Lars Højer (2012: 14) in Mongolia, Humphrey (1992: 134) in Nepal, Gell (1982) in India or Webb Keane (1997: 36) in Indonesia are some examples among the many utilitarian transactions that are personally engaged in and governed by a formal code, the respect of which ensures that they partake of sociocosmological reproduction. Challenging classical oppositions coming out of Western ideas of ritual and instrumental actions, this ethnography of Andean barter fairs concludes that ritual economics should not refer to only one kind of transaction, namely, the gift. By the same token, no transaction is by essence ritualised, not even gift-giving. Instead, the Andean data suggest that ritualisation should be regarded as a transversal feature for distinguishing between different kinds of oblative and instrumental exchanges, including gift, barter and commodity exchange.

## Note

1. This is not the case of interecological barter whereby equivalencies are set up in monetary terms that remain stable over time, severed from the prices on the local market. This form of barter, involving money as a scale of value, without turning into commodity exchange, is encapsulated in the unay precio documented by Mayer (2002: 153; see also Fonseca 1972: 328). In this case, money is used as the currency, but the market does not influence the goods equivalencies, which are appreciated for their use value and negotiated according to personal criteria.

# References

Absi, P. 2007. 'Il ne faut pas mélanger les fortunes: Travail, genre et revenus chez les commerçantes de Potosi', in V. Hernandez, P. Ould-Ahmed, J. Papail and P. Phélinas (eds), *Turbulences monétaires: L'Amérique Latine dans une perspective comparée*. Paris: L'Harmattan, pp. 355–393.

Albeck, M. 1992. 'El ambiente como generador de hipótesis como dinámica sociocultural prehispánica en la Quebrada de Humahuaca', *Cuadernos de la Facultad de Humanidades* 3: 95–106.

———. 2007. 'El intermedio tardío: Interacciones económicas y políticas en la Puna de Jujuy', in A. Callegari, B. Ventura, V. Williams and H. Yacobaccio (eds), *Sociedades precolombinas surandinas: Temporalidad, interacción y dinámica cultural del NOA en el ámbito de los Andes centro-sur*. Buenos Aires: El autor, pp. 125–145.

Alberti, G., and E. Mayer (eds). 1974. *Reciprocidad e intercambio en los Andes peruanos*. Lima: Instituto de Estudios Peruanos.

Allen, C. 1988. *The Hold Life Has: Coca and Cultural Identity in an Andean Community*. Washington, D.C.: Smithsonian Institution Press.

———. 2016. 'The Living Ones: Miniatures and Animation in the Andes', *Journal of Anthropological Research* 72(4): 416–441.

Angé, O. 2011. 'Yapa: Dons, échanges et complicités dans les Andes méridionales', *Social Anthropology* 19(3): 239–253.

———. 2016a. 'Barter Fairs, Ethnic Configuration and National Multiculturalism in the Argentinean Andes', *Ethnos: Journal of Anthropology* 81(4): 648–666.

———. 2016b. 'Materializing Virtues: Crafted Miniatures as Moral Examples in the Argentinean Andes', *Journal of Anthropological Research* 72(4): 483–503.

———. 2018. 'Reproductive Commodities: Work, Joy, and Creativity in Argentinean Miniature Fairs', *Ethnos: Journal of Anthropological Research*. DOI: 10.1080/00141844.2018.1458042.

Angé, O., and P. Pitrou, 2016. 'Miniatures in Mesoamerica and the Andes: Theories of Life, Values and Relatedness', *Journal of Anthropological Research* 72(4): 408–415.

Appadurai, A. 1986. 'Introduction: Commodities and the Politics of Value', in A. Appadurai (ed.), *The Social Life of Things.* Cambridge: Cambridge University Press, pp. 3–63.

Assadourian Sempat, C. 1982. *El sistema de la economía colonial: Mercado interno, regiones y espacio económico.* Lima: Instituto de Estudios Peruanos.

———. 1995. 'Exchange in the Ethnic Territories between 1530 and 1567: The Visitas of Huanuco and Chucuito', in Larson et al. 1995, pp. 101–134.

Banks, M. 1996. *Ethnicity: Anthropological Constructions.* London: Routledge.

Barnes, R. H., and R. Barnes. 1989. 'Barter and Money in an Indonesian Village Economy', *Man* 24(3): 399–418.

Barnett, H. G. 1938. 'The Nature of the Potlatch', *American Anthropologist* 40(3): 349–358.

Bell, C. 1997. *Ritual: Perspectives and Dimensions.* Oxford: Oxford University Press.

Belli, E., and R. Slavutsky (eds). 2005. *Patrimonio en el Noroeste argentino. Otras historias.* Jujuy, Argentina: Instituto Interdisciplinario de Tilcara.

Berliner, D. 2012. 'Multiple Nostalgias; The Fabric of Heritage in Luang Prabang (Lao PDR)', *Journal of the Royal Anthropological Institute* 18(4): 769–786.

Berndt, R. M. 1951. 'Ceremonial Exchange in Western Arnhem Land', *Southwestern Journal of Anthropology* 7(2): 156–176.

Bissell, W. C. 2005. 'Engaging Colonial Nostalgia', *Cultural Anthropology* 20(2): 215–248.

Bohannan, P. 1955. 'Some Principles of Exchange and Investment among the Tiv', *American Anthropologist* 57(1): 60–70.

Bourdieu, P. 1980. *Le sens pratique.* Paris: Éditions de Minuit.

Boym, S. 2001. 'Nostalgia', in *Atlas of Transformation.* Adopted and elaborated from *The Future of Nostalgia.* New York: Basic Books. http://monument totransformation.org/atlas-of-transformation/html/n/nostalgia/nostalgia-svetlana-boym.html.

Braudel, F. 1979. *Civilisation matérielle, économie et capitalisme (XVe–XVIIIe siècles).* Paris: Armand Collin.

Briones, C. 2005. 'Formaciones de alteridad: Contextos globales, procesos nacionales y provinciales', in C. Briones (ed.), *Cartografías argentinas: Politicas indigenas y formaciones provinciales de alteridad.* Buenos Aires: Antropofagia, pp. 9–39.

Bryant, R. 2014. 'Nostalgia and the Discovery of Loss: Essentializing the Turkish Cypriot Past', in O. Angé and D. Berliner (eds), *Anthropology and Nostalgia.* Oxford: Berghahn Books, pp. 155–177.

Bugallo, L. 2009. 'Quipildores: Marcas del Rayo en el espacio de la puna Jujeña', *Cuadernos FHyCS-UNJu* 36: 177–202.

Burchard, R. 1974. 'Coca y trueque de alimentos', in Alberti and Mayer 1974, pp. 209–251.

Carrier, J. (ed.). 2006. *A Handbook of Economic Anthropology.* Cheltenham: Edward Elgar Publishing.

Carsten, J. 2012. *After Kinship.* Cambridge: University of Cambridge Press.

Casey, E. 2011. 'From Remembering: A Phenomenological Study', in J. Olick, V. Vinitzky Seroussi and D. Levy (eds), *The Collective Memory Reader.* Oxford: Oxford University Press, pp. 184–187.

Cellarius, B. A. 2000. '"You Can Buy Almost Anything with Potatoes": An Examination of Barter during Economic Crisis in Bulgaria', *Ethnology* 39(1): 73–92.

Chapman, A. 1980. 'Barter as a Universal Mode of Exchange', *L'Homme* 20(3): 33–83.

Chumley, L. H., and N. Harkness. 2013. 'Introduction: Qualia', *Anthropological Theory* 13(1–2): 3–11.

Cipoletti, M. S. 1984. 'Llamas y mulas, trueque y venta: El testimonio de un arriero puneño', *Revista Andina* 2(12): 513–538.

Colloredo-Mansfeld, R. 1999. *The Native Leisure Class: Consumption and Cultural Creativity in the Andes*. Chicago: University of Chicago Press.

———. 2003. 'Consuming Andean Television', *Journal of Material Culture* 8(3): 273–284.

Conti, V. 1988. 'Estructura de la Feria de la Tablada de Jujuy: Su articulación dentro del espacio económico regional (1850–1900)', in *Anuario de las segundas jornadas de Promoción en Investigación histórica* 1. La Plata: Universidad Nacional de la Plata, pp. 74–85.

———. 1989. 'Articulación económica en los Andes centromeridionales (siglo XIX)', *Anuario de estudios americanos* 46: 423–453.

Conti, V., and E. Langer. 1991. 'Circuitos comerciales tradicionales y cambio económico en los Andes Centromeridionales (1830–1930)', *Desarrollo económico* 31(12): 91–111.

Custred, G. 1980. 'The Place of Ritual in Andean Rural Society', in B. Orlove and G. Custred (eds), *Land and Power in Latin America*. New York: Holmes & Meier Publishers, pp. 195–209.

Damon, F. 2002. 'Kula Valuables: The Problem of Value and the Production of Names', *L'Homme* 162: 107–136.

Davis, F. 1979. *Yearning for Yesterday: A Sociology of Nostalgia*. New York: Free Press.

Descola, P. 2005. *Par delà nature et culture*. Paris: Gallimard.

Dodd, N. 2014. *The Social Life of Money*. Princeton, N.J.: Princeton University Press.

Ferraro, E. 2011. 'Trueque: An Ethnographic Account of Barter, Trade and Money in Andean Ecuador', *Journal of Latin American and Caribbean Anthropology* 16(1): 168–184.

Firth, R. 1939. *Primitive Polynesian Economy*. London: Routledge.

Fonseca Martel, C. 1972. 'La economia "vertical" y la economia de mercado en las comunidades alteñas del Peru', in Murra 1972b, pp. 315–338.

Garcia, E. 2005. *Making Indigenous Citizens: Identities, Education and Multicultural Development in Peru*. Stanford, CA: Stanford University Press.

Geertz, C. 2003. *Le souk de Séfrou: Sur l'économie du bazar*. Paris: Editions Bouchène.

Gell, A. 1982. 'The Market Wheel: Symbolic Aspects of an Indian Tribal Market', *Man* 17(3): 470–491.

———. 1992. 'Inter-Tribal Commodity Barter and Reproductive Gift Exchange in Old Melanesia', in Humphrey and Hugh-Jones 1992a, pp. 142–168.

Gelles, P. H. 1995. 'Equilibrium and Extraction: Dual Organization in the Andes', *American Ethnologist* 22(4): 710–42.

Göbel, B. 1998. 'Risk, Uncertainty, and Economic Exchange in a Pastoral Community of the Andean Highlands (Huancar, N.W. Argentina)', in T. Schweizer and D. White (eds), *Kinship, Networks, and Exchange*. Cambridge: Cambridge University Press, pp. 158–177.

———. 2003. '"La plata no aumenta, la hacienda si": Continuidades y cambios en la economía pastoril de Susques (Puna de Atacama)', in A. Benedetti (ed.), *Puna de Atacama: Sociedad, economía y frontera*. Buenos Aires: Alción Editora, pp. 199–242.

Godelier, M. 1969. 'La "monnaie de sel" des Baruya de Nouvelle-Guinée', *L'Homme* 9(2): 5–37.

———. 1996. *L'énigme du don*. Paris: Fayard.

Gonzalez, D., R. Merlino and M. Rabey. 1986. 'Trueque, articulación económica y racionalidad campesina en el sur de los Andes Centrales', *Revista Andina* 4(1): 131–160.

Gose, P. 1986. 'Sacrifice and the Commodity Form in the Andes', *Man* 21(2): 296–310.

Graeber, D. 2001. *Toward an Anthropological Theory of Value: The False Coin of Our Own Dreams*. New York: Palgrave.

———. 2011. *Debt: The First 5,000 Years*. Brooklyn, N.Y.: Melville House.

Gregory, C. A. 1982. *Gift and Commodities*. Cambridge, M.A.: Academic Press.

Gudeman, S. 1975. 'Spiritual Relationships and Selecting a Godparent', *Man* 10(2): 221–237.

———. 2001. *The Anthropology of Economy: Community, Market and Culture*. Oxford: Blackwell.

———. 2012. 'Vital Energy: The Current of Relation', *Social Analysis* 56(1): 57–73.

Gudeman, S., and C. Hann. 2015. 'Introduction: Ritual, Economy, and the Institutions of the Base', in S. Gudeman and C. Hann (eds), *Economy and Ritual: Studies of Postsocialist Transformations*. New York: Berghahn Books, pp. 1–30.

Guyer, J. I. 2004. *Marginal Gains: Monetary Transactions in Atlantic Africa*. Chicago: University of Chicago Press.

Harkness, N. 2013. 'Softer *Soju* in South Korea', *Anthropological Theory* 13(1–2): 12–30.

Harris, O. 1989. 'The Earth and the State: The Sources and Meanings of Money in Northern Potosi, Bolivia', in Parry and Bloch 1989a, pp. 232–268.

———. 1995. 'Ethnic Identity and Market Relations: Indians and Mestizos in the Andes', in Larson et al. 1995, pp. 351–390.

———. 2000. *To Make the Earth Bear Fruit: Ethnographic Essays on Fertility, Work and Gender in Highland Bolivia*. London: Institute of Latin American Studies.

———. 2007. 'Labour and Produce in an Ethnic Economy', in Lehmann (1982) 2007a, pp. 70–96.

Harrison, R. 2013. *Heritage: Critical Approaches*. New York: Routledge.

Hart, K. 1986. 'Heads or Tails? Two Sides of the Coin', *Man* 21(4): 637–656.

Heady, P. 2006. 'Barter', in Carrier 2006, pp. 262–274.

Herzfeld, M. 2005. *Cultural Intimacy: Social Poetics in the Nation-State*. New York: Routledge.

Hivon, M. 1998. '"Payer en liquide": L'utilisation de la vodka dans les échanges en Russie rurale", *Ethnologie française* 28(4): 515–524.

Højer, L. 2012. 'The Spirit of Business: Pawnshop in Ulaanbaatar', *Social Anthropology* 20(1): 34–49.

Horowitz, A. 2010. 'Revisiting Barter under the CISG', *Journal of Law and Commerce* 29(1): 99–115.

Humphrey, C. 1985. 'Barter and Economic Disintegration', *Man* 20(1): 48–72.

———. 1992. 'Fair Dealing, Just Rewards: The Ethics of Barter in North-East Nepal', in Humphrey and Hugh-Jones 1992a, pp. 1–20.

———. 2000. 'An Anthropological View of Barter in Russia', in Seabright 2000, pp. 71–92.

Humphrey, C., and S. Hugh-Jones (eds). 1992a. *Barter, Exchange and Value: An Anthropological Approach*. Cambridge: Cambridge University Press.

———. 1992b. 'Introduction: Barter, Exchange and Value', in Humphrey and Hugh-Jones 1992a, pp. 107–141.

Humphrey, C., and J. A. Laidlaw. 1994. *Archetypal Actions: A Theory of Ritual as a Mode of Action and the Case of the Yain Puja*. Oxford: Clarendon Press.

Karasik, G. 1984. 'Intercambio tradicional en la puna juvenal', *Runa* 24: 51–91.

———. 2005. 'Etnicidad, cultura y clase sociales: Procesos de formación histórica de la conciencia colectiva en Jujuy 1985–2003', Ph.D. dissertation. Tucumán, Argentina: Universidad Nacional de Tucumán.

———. 2006. 'Cultura popular e identidad', in A. Teruel and M. Lagos (eds), *Jujuy en la historia: De la colonia al siglo XX*. Jujuy, Argentina: Editorial de la Universidad Nacional de Jujuy, pp. 467–489.

———. 2010. 'Subalternada y ancestralidad colla: Transformaciones emblemáticas y nuevas articulaciones de lo indígena en Jujuy', in G. Gordillo and S. Hirsch (eds), *Movilizaciones indígenas e identidades en disputa en la Argentina*. Buenos Aires: FLASCO/La Crujía, pp. 259–282.

Keane, W. 1997. *Signs of Recognition: Powers and Hazards of Representations in an Indonesian Society*. Berkeley: University of California Press.

Lambek, M. 2008. 'Value and Virtue', *Anthropological Theory* 8(2): 133–157.

———. 2013. 'The Value of (Performative) Acts', *HAU: Journal of Ethnographic Theory* 3(2): 141–160.

Langer, E. 2004. 'Indian Trade and Ethnic Economies in the Andes, 1780–1880', *Estudios Interdisciplinarios de América Latina y el Caribe* 15(1). http://eial.tau.ac.il/index.php/eial/article/view/825/904.

Larson, B. 1995. 'Andean Communities, Political Cultures, and Markets: The Changing Contours of a Field', in Larson et al. 1995, pp. 3–53.

Larson, B., O. Harris and E. Tandeter (eds). 1995. *Ethnicity, Markets, and Migration in the Andes*. Durham, NC: Duke University Press.

Latouche, S. 2000. 'Les stratégies alternatives des exclus face à la mondialisation: Les SEL et l'informel', *L'Homme et la Société* 136(2): 57–75.

Leach, J. W., and E. Leach (eds). 1983. *The Kula: New Perspective on Massim Exchange*. Cambridge: Cambridge University Press.

Lecoq, P. 1987. 'Caravanes de lamas, sel et échanges dans une communauté de Potosi, en Bolivie', *Bulletin de l'Institut Français des Etudes andines* 16(3–4): 85–96.

Lehmann, D. (ed.). (1982) 2007a. *Ecology and Exchange in the Andes*. Cambridge: Cambridge University Press.

Lehmann, D. (1982) 2007b. 'Introduction: Andean Societies and the Theory of Peasant Economy', in Lehmann (1982) 2007a, pp. 1–26.

Lévi-Strauss, C. 1943. 'Guerre et commerce chez les Indiens de l'Amérique du sud', *Renaissance* 1(1–2): 122–139.

———. (1947) 2002. Les structures élémentaires de la parenté. Berlin: De Gruyter.

Li, T. M. 2000. 'Articulating Indigenous Identity in Indonesia: Resource Politics and the Tribal Slot', *Journal of Comparative Study of Society and History* 42(1): 149–179.

Lorandi, A. M. 1992. 'El mestizaje interetnico en el noroeste argentino', *Senri Ethnological Studies* 33: 133–166.

Losonczy, A. M. 1997. 'Produire l'humain par la musique', in B. François et al. (eds), *Pom pom pom pom, musiques et caetera*. Neuchâtel, Switzerland: Musée d'ethnographie, pp. 253–274.

Madrazo, G. 1981. 'Comercio interétnico y trueque reciproco equilibrado intraétnico', *Desarrollo Económico* 21(82): 213–230.

———. 1982. *Hacienda y encomienda en los Andes: La puna argentina bajo el marquesado de Tojo, siglos XVII a XIX*. Buenos Aires: Fondo Editorial.

Malinowski, B. (1922) 2002. *Argonauts of the Western Pacific: An Account of Natives Entreprise and Adventure in the Archipelagoes of Melanesian New Guinea*. London: Routledge.

Marx, K. (1867) 2013. *Capital*. Ware, U.K.: Wordsworth Editions.

Maunier, R. (1927) 1998. *Recherche sur les échanges rituels en Afrique du Nord*. Paris: Editions Bouchène.

Masuda, S., I. Shimada and C. Morris (eds). 1985. *Andean Ecology and Civilization: An Interdisciplinary Perspective on Andean Ecological Complementarity*. Tokyo: University of Tokyo Press.

Mauss, M. (1925) 2002. *The Gift: Form and Reason for Exchange in Archaic Societies*. London: Routledge.

Mayer, E. 1982. 'Un carnero por un saco de papas: Aspectos del trueque en la zona de Chaupiwaranga, Pasco', *Nueva Antropología* 6(19): 81–96.

———. 2002. *The Articulated Peasant: Household Economies in the Andes*. Boulder, C.O.: Westview Press.

Miller, D. 1996. *A Theory of Shopping*. Ithaca, N.Y.: Cornell University Press.

Mintz, S. W., and E. R. Wolf. 1950. 'An Analysis of Ritual Co-Parenthood (Compadrazgo)', Southwestern Journal of Anthropology 6(4): 341–368.

Molinié, A. 1975. 'Contribution à l'étude des sociétés étagées des Andes: La vallée de Yucay (Pérou)', *Études Rurales* 57: 35–59.

Mombello, L. 2002. 'Evolución de la política indigenista en Argentina en la década de los noventa', draft for 'Self-Sustaining Community Development in Comparative Perspective' project, Center for Latin American Social Policy, University of Texas at Austin. http://lanic.utexas.edu/project/laoap/claspo/dt/0004.pdf.

Montero, R. 2004. *Caravaneros y trashumantes en los Andes meridionales: Población y familia indígena en la puna de Jujuy, 1770–1870*. Lima: Instituto de Estudios Peruanos.

Munn, N. 1986. *The Fame of Gawa: A Symbolic Study of Value Transformation in a Massim (Papua New Guinea) Society*. Cambridge: Cambridge University Press.

Murra, J. 1972a. 'El "control vertical" de un máximo de pisos ecológicos en la economía de las sociedades andinas', in Murra 1972b, pp. 427–476.

———. (ed.) 1972b. *Visita de la provincia de León Huánuco en 1562*. Huánuco, Perú: Universidad Nacional Hermilio Valdizan.

———. 1974. 'Débat sur la réciprocité', *Annales* 29(6): 1358–1380.

———. 1985. 'Limits and Limitations of the "Vertical Archipielago" in the Andes', in Masuda et al. 1985, pp. 15–20.

———. 1992. 'Quince anos después: balance de la noción de archipiélago', in P. Morlon (ed.), *Comprender la agricultura campesina en los Andes Centrales*. Lima: Institut Français d'Études Andines, pp. 130–36.

Myers, F. R. 2002. 'Introduction: The Empire of Things', in F. R. Myers (ed.), *The Empire of Things: Regimes of Value and Material Culture*. Santa Fe, N. M.: School of American Research Press, pp. 3–64.

Nora, P. 1989. 'Between Memory and History: Les Lieux de Mémoire', *Representations* 26: 7–24.

Núñez, L. 2007. 'Reflexiones sobre el trafico de caravanas y complementariedad circumpuneña', in V. I. Williams et al. (eds), *Sociedades precolombinas surandinas: Temporalidad, interacción y dinámica cultural del NOA en el ámbito de los Andes Centro-Sur*. Buenos Aires: Taller Internacional de Arqueología del NOA y Andes Centro Sur, pp. 33–58.

Ødegaard, C. 2010. *Mobility, Markets and Indigenous Socialities: Contemporary Migration in the Peruvian Andes*. Farnham: Ashgate Publishing.

———. 2011. 'Sources of Danger and Prosperity in the Peruvian Andes: Mobility in a Powerful Landscape', *Journal of the Royal Anthropological Institute* 17(2): 339–355.

Orlove, B. S. 1974. 'Reciprocidad, desigualdad y dominación', in Alberti and Mayer 1974, pp. 290–321.

———. 1986. 'Barter and Cash Sale on Lake Titicaca: A Test of Competing Approaches', *Current Anthropology* 27(2): 85–106.

Otto, T., and R. Willerslev. 2013. 'Introduction: "Values *as* Theory": Comparison, Cultural Critique, and Guerrilla Ethnographic Theory', *HAU: Journal of Ethnographic Theory* 3(1): 1–20.

Ould-Ahmed, P. 2010. 'Can a Community Currency Be Independent of the State Currency? A Case Study of the Credito in Argentina (1995–2008)', *Environment and Planning A* 42(6): 1346–1364.

Polanyi, K. (1944) 2001. *The Great Transformation: The Political and Economic Origins of Our Time*. Boston: Beacon Press.

Palomeque, S. 1994. 'Intercambios mercantiles y participación indígena en la puna de Jujuy a fines del periodo colonial', *Revista Andes* 6: 13–48.

Parry, J., and M. Bloch (eds). 1989a. *Money and the Morality of Exchange*. Cambridge: Cambridge University Press.

——— . 1989b. 'Introduction: Money and the Morality of Exchange', in Parry and Bloch 1989a, pp. 1–32.

Pearson, R. 2003. 'Argentina's Barter Network: New Currency for New Times?' *Bulletin of Latin American Research* 22(2): 214–230

Pickering, M., and E. Keightley. 2006. 'The Modalities of Nostalgia', *Current Sociology* 54(6): 919–941.

Platt, T. (1982) 2007. 'The Role of the Andean *Ayllu* in the Reproduction of the Petty Commodity Regime in Northern Potosi (Bolivia)', in Lehmann (1982) 2007a, pp. 27–69.

———. 1986. 'Mirrors and Maize: The Concept of *Yanantin* among the Macha of Bolivia', in J. Murra, N. Wachtel and J. Revel (eds), *Anthropological History of Andean Polities*. Cambridge: Cambridge University Press, pp. 228–259.

———. 1988. 'Pensamiento político aymará', in J. Albo (ed.), *Raíces de América: El mundo aymará*. Madrid: Alianza Editorial, pp. 365–450.

———. 1995. 'Ethnic Calendars and Market Interventions among the *Ayllus* of Lipes during the Nineteenth Century', in Larson et al. 1995, pp. 259–296.

Poole, D. 1982. 'Los santuarios religiosos en la economía regional andina (Cuzco)', *Allpanchis* 19(16): 79–116.

Radcliffe, S., and S. Westwood. 1996. *Remaking the Nation: Place, Identity and Politics in Latin America*. London: Routledge.

Rivera Andia, J. J. 2005. 'Killing What You Love. An Andean Cattle Branding Ritual and the Dilemmas of Modernity', *Journal of Anthropological Research* 61(2): 129–156.

Rivière, G. 1979. 'Évolution des formes d'échange entre altiplano et vallées: L'exemple de Sabaya, Bolivie', *Cahier des Amériques Latines* 20: 147–158.

———. 1991. 'Lik'ichiri y kharisiri . . . A propósito de las representaciones del "otro" en la sociedad aymara', *Bulletin de l'Institut Français des* Études *Andines* 20(1): 23–40.

———. 2007. 'De la chefferie à la communauté et retour? Les nouvelles organisations indigènes dans les hauts plateaux de la Bolivie', in D. Rolland and J. Chassin (eds), *Pour comprendre la Bolivie d'Evo Morales*. Paris: L'Harmattan, pp. 207–219.

Robbins, J. 2015. 'On Happiness, Values, and Time: The Long and the Short of It', *HAU: Journal of Ethnographic Theory* 5(3): 215–233.

Rostworowski, M. 1999. 'Los curacas costeños', *Historica* 23(2): 283–311.

Rutledge, I. 1987. *Cambio agrario e integración: El desarollo del capitalismo en Jujuy, 1550–1960*. Jujuy, Argentina: Centro de Invetsigaciones in Ciencies Sociales.

Saiag, H. 2013. 'Le trueque argentin ou la question du fédéralisme monétaire (1995–2002)', *Revue Française de Socio-économie* 12(2): 69–89.

Salhins, M. 1972. *Stone Age Economics*. Piscataway, N.J.: Aldine Transaction.

Sallnow, M. 1989. 'Precious Metal in the Andean Moral Economy', in Parry and Bloch 1989a, pp. 209–231.

Salomon, F. 1978. 'Systèmes politiques verticaux aux marches de l'empire inca', *Annales Histoire Sciences Sociales* 33(5): 967–989.

Schudson, M. 1995. 'Dynamics of Distortion of Collective Memory', in D. Schacter (ed.), *Memory Distortion: How Minds, Brains, and Societies Reconstruct the Past*. Cambridge, M.A.: Harvard University Press, pp. 346–364.

Seabright, P. 2000. *The Vanishing Rouble: Barter Networks and Non-monetary Transactions in Post-Soviet Societies*. Cambridge: Cambridge University Press.

Seligmann, L. 1993. 'Between Worlds of Exchange: Ethnicity among Peruvian Market Women', *Cultural Anthropology* 8(2): 187–213.

Servet, J.-M. 1994. 'La fable du troc', *Dix-huitième Siècle* 26: 103–115.

———. 1999. *Une économie sans argent: Les systèmes d'échange Local*. Paris: Seuil.

Sica, G. 2005. 'Maíz y trigo, molinos y conanas, mulas y llamas: Tierras, cambio agrario y participación mercantil indígena en los inicios del sistema colonial', in D. Santamaria (ed.), *Jujuy: Arqueología, historia, economía, sociedad*. Jujuy, Argentina: Ediciones Cuadernos del Duende, pp. 106–123.

Sieder, R. (ed). 2002. *Multiculturalism in Latin America: Indigenous Rights, Diversity, and Democracy*. New York: Palgrave Macmillan.

Sillar, B. 2012. 'Patrimoine vivant: Les illas et conopas dans les foyer andins', *Technique et Culture* 58: 66–81.

Simmel, G. (1900) 1990. *The Philosophy of Money*. London: Routledge.

Smith, A. (1776) 1991. *The Wealth of Nations*, 2 vols. London: Every Man's Library.

Smith, L. 2006. *Uses of Heritage*. New York: Routledge.

Strathern, A. 1971. *The Rope of Moka: Big Men and Ceremonial Exchange in Mount Hagen New Guinea*. Cambridge: Cambridge University Press.

Strathern, A., and P. Stewart. 2006. 'Ceremonial Exchange', in Carrier 2006, pp. 230–245.

Strathern, M. 1988. *The Gender of the Gift: Problems with Women and Problems with Society in Melanesia*. Berkeley: University of California Press.

———. 1992. 'Qualified Value: The Perspective of Gift Exchange', in Humphrey and Hugh-Jones 1992a, pp. 169–191.

Sturzenegger-Benoist, O. 2006. *L'Argentine*. Paris: Karthala.

Tassi, N. 2010. 'The "Postulate of Abundance": *Cholo*, Market and Religion in La Paz, Bolivia', *Social Anthropology* 18(2): 191–209.

Taussig, M. 1977. 'The Genesis of Capitalism amongst a South American Peasantry: Devil's Labour and the Baptism of Money', *Comparatives Studies in Society and History* 19(2): 130–155.

———. 1980. *The Devil and Commodity Fetishism in South America*. Chapel Hill: University of North Carolina Press.

Testart, A. 2001. 'Échange marchand, échange non marchand', *Revue Française de Sociologie* 42(4): 719–48.

Tolaba, M. 2010. *Tierra de sueños: Leyendas, cuentos y relatos quiaqueños*. Jujuy, Argentina: Self-Published.

Toren, C. 1989. 'Drinking Cash: The Purification of Money through Ceremonial Exchange in Fiji', in Parry and Bloch 1989a, pp. 142–165.

Turner, V. 1995. *The Ritual Process: Structure and Anti-Structure*. Piscataway, N.J.: Aldine Transaction.

van den Berghe, P. L. 2010. 'Compadrazgo', in A. Barnard and J. Spencer (eds), *The Routledge Encyclopedia of Social and Cultural Anthropology*. London: Routledge, pp. 145–146.

Wachtel, N. 1990. *Le retour des ancêtres*. Paris: Gallimard.

Weiner, A. 1992. *Inalienable Possessions: The Paradox of Keeping-while-Giving*. Berkeley: University of California Press.

Weismantel, M. 1995. 'Making Kin: Kinship Theory and Zumbagua Adoptions', *American Ethnologist* 22(4): 685–704.

———. 2001. *Cholas and Pishtacos: Stories of Race and Sex in the Andes*. Chicago: University of Chicago Press.

Wroblewski, M. 2014. 'Public Indigeneity, Language Revitalization, and Intercultural Planning in a Native Amazonian Beauty Pageant', *American Anthropologist* 116(1): 65–80.

Yan, Y. 2006. 'The Gift and Gift Economy', in Carrier 2006, pp. 246–261.

# Index